MISHEGAS: A Concrete Tale of Family Quicksand

Harley Dresner

Virginia

Some names and identifying details have been changed to protect the privacy of
individuals.

This story is told from the author's experience and perspective.

Published in the United States by WriteLife Publishing
(An imprint of Boutique of Quality Books Publishing Company)
www.writelife.com

Printed in the United States of America
978-1-60808-174-5 (p)
978-1-60808-175-2 (e)

Library of Congress Control Number: 2017932065

Book design by Robin Krauss, www.bookformatters.com
Cover design by Marla Thompson, www.edgeofwater.com

First editor: Pearlie Tan
Second editor: Michelle Booth

For Daphne and Zachary, who share my gene pool.
For Elyse, who shares my heart.

CONTENTS

PROLOGUE

mish·e·gas (n.) Insanity, madness, or craziness. Senseless activity or behavior.

Origin: Yiddish מישעגאַסoo (mishegoss), from עגושמ (meshuge), "crazy."

Let there be no confusion, here at the outset. Harboring a few quirks does not constitute *mishegas*. One of my fellow physicians chugs forty-eight ounces of Diet Mountain Dew most mornings for breakfast. A good friend wears his wife's socks and she doesn't know, doesn't care, or can't be bothered to expend what little energy she has left at the end of the day to break him of the habit. I have another pal who pulls an all-nighter once a year to carve a couple of pumpkins for his daughters before Halloween. To be sure, these are all examples of personal eccentricities, but they fall far short of qualifying for the *mishegas* standard set forth by my family.

Strictly speaking, *mishegas* has both serious and playful meanings. On the serious side, *mishegas* equates with insanity. It's madness, plain and simple. On the opposite end of the spectrum, it refers to clowning around and acting like a moron, whether intentionally or not. In between these extremes, there are wacky fixations, irrational beliefs, and absurd idiosyncrasies all embroiled within this single, powerful word. In common vernacular, *mishegas* is almost universally used in a lighthearted way to describe a state of affairs so ludicrous that it defies explanation.

As so often happens with Yiddish words, *mishegas* means far more than the sum of its literal parts: Craziness. Nonsensical activities. Inexplicable behaviors. Experiences that make you want to repeatedly bang your forehead onto the nearest wall or the steering wheel of your car until it's numb. When *mishegas* arises, a synergy inevitably follows. Two plus two equals eight when *mishegas* erupts onto the playing field. It's not an event; it's a phenomenon. *Mishegas* goes beyond words like glitch, nosh, schmooze, and shtick that have found their ways into the English language. For when *mishegas* is spoken of, it implies a broader cultural bond shared in the hearts and minds of Jews across the globe. It is like a secret handshake that unlocks a core element of the Jewish soul. A secular Jew like me practicing facial plastic surgery in Minnesota has a radically different life than an orthodox Jew studying Torah in Israel. Both of us work from sunrise to sunset—but that's where the similarities begin and end. Yet if the stars aligned and our lives randomly collided one day on the streets of Tel Aviv or Minneapolis, we could undoubtedly speak with ease of the *mishegas* in each of our lives. I could tell him all about the fifteenth rendition of a fifteen-minute story my mother repeated a few days ago, told under the auspices of keeping me current with the events in her life.

Every time Mom's friend orders a cheeseburger at a restaurant, she divides it in half to guarantee leftovers for lunch the next day. Mom can't figure out why her friend—an obviously overweight adult who has no intention of dieting—routinely refuses to finish more than one-half of a standard burger. I don't have the answer either.

Listening to this story, the Torah reader would stumble at "cheeseburger." There's nothing kosher about ordering a cheeseburger in a restaurant; it clearly violates several Jewish dietary laws. To right the ship, I would just say *"mishegas"* and he would instantly understand me as if we were brothers who had grown up under the same roof. There are ties that span time, generations, and geography. The Holocaust is the most obvious example. *Mishegas* is another, albeit in a logarithmically lighter tone. Those who have experienced Catholic guilt can relate.

To exhibit *mishegas* is to consistently display a caricature-like gross distortion of relating to the world. It is to display a state of existence on the fringes of reality, short of a diagnosable psychosis or other veritable form of mental illness. It implies a complete state of ludicrous existence, a farcical state of being on the outermost edges on the bell curve of human behavioral paradigms. If there's true *mishegas* in your life, you know it. You know it because *mishegas* wholly envelops you, becoming an intrinsic, inescapable part of your existence. Mix together a tablespoon of salt and a tablespoon of ground black pepper, then try to separate them grain by grain. You can't. If you dare to try, you'll be insane by the time you finish. So you realize that there's no point in even trying, just like you understand that *mishegas* will remain ingrained in your life.

The *mishegas* in my life lies with my family. I'm not referring to my beloved wife of sixteen years, Elyse. Nor am I speaking of my two fabulous children, Daphne and Zachary, currently eleven and eight years old, respectively. They, too, have their quirks, but they're basically normal people. Elyse likes to hide bags of gummy bears in the dishwasher and randomly present me with three-year-old sales receipts excavated from the bowels of her nightstand drawer. Daphne takes the processed-cheese centers of a few dozen Ritz Bits cheese cracker sandwiches, wads them up into a single nauseating ball, and eats it independently of the crackers. Zach has the bladder capacity of a dromedary and shops for clothing now as an eight-year-old with more fervor than the likes of a Coco Chanel in her prime. Again, these behaviors are certainly odd, but they do not represent *mishegas*.

My *mishegas* specifically pertains to my relationships with my parents, Sydelle and Gerry. It also includes my dealings with Sydelle's brother, my uncle Bern.

I was initially oblivious to the *mishegas*; I couldn't see it, even through the thick, five-and-a-half-diopter lenses required to correct my myopic vision. Elyse first detected it from her vantage point as a relative outsider, that is, as a non-blood relative. She was the one who realized that something wasn't kosher about my relationship with Sydelle and Gerry. She keyed me in on it, catching me asleep at the wheel while we were dating during medical school. There was no sudden epiphany. Howard Carter spent a couple of decades strategically exploring the Valley of the Kings before he famously stumbled upon the tomb of Tutankhamun in 1922. It was his life's quest that materialized in a flash. I, on the other hand, wasn't looking for anything at all. But with hindsight comes clarity, and upon reflection from my current vantage point tucked away in the Lowry Hill neighborhood of Minneapolis, I've gradually come around to the stark realization that my interactions with my parents live and breathe *mishegas*.

Now it's true that everyone thinks their parents have a certain constellation of oddities. At first, Elyse innocently questioned a few superficial chinks in my familial armor. Why does my mother microwave raw apples before biting into them? Why does she spend ten minutes urinating every couple of hours? How come my father startles worse than a cat hearing a sudden clap of thunder when you lightly tap his shoulder to catch his attention? Why does he stockpile ginger ale and ketchup in the basement like rare commodities disappearing from the earth in the face of an impending nuclear meltdown? Why does he speak so quickly that sometimes you're uncertain if he's conversing in Mandarin, English, or Swahili? Why does he always ask a third question before listening to the answer to the first two questions he has posed? And why on earth does he look forward to a colonoscopy the way a kid looks forward to unwrapping presents on Christmas morning? My wife's questions were all reasonable. I racked my brain and searched my soul for plausible answers, yet there were none. Zero. I tried in vain to convince Elyse that she just happened to observe a few innocent quirks. After all, everyone has a few peculiarities, don't they?

But over the years, it became plainly obvious that the spigot at the bottom of my industrial-sized urn of familial *mishegas* was locked in the wide-open position. Simply plugging the hole with a cork could not possibly stem the torrent. So instead of trying to keep it bottled up, I choose to embrace it and share it.

But be warned: even though many of the following scenes occur in Las Vegas, do not expect to be regaled with stories that could have been directly plucked from the screenplay of The Hangover movie trilogy. You will not find impromptu exchanges of drunken vows at the Little White Wedding Chapel in these pages. You won't find scenes of outrageous bachelor parties, drug-infused orgies, or brawls ending with time served in subterranean casino jails. You won't even find some of the more mundane stuff like losing next month's rent money at the craps tables while betting on eights the hard way until the sun comes up, stiletto-clad women dancing provocatively in skin-tight sequined minidresses in the city's most exclusive nightclubs, or good old-fashioned drinking until lying unconscious in a pool of your own drool. But have faith, faith in my personal *mishegas*.

This work is my attempt to own and thereby have some theoretical control over my *mishegas*. Over the years, this collection of my life stories has been told and retold in one form or another to dear friends and casual acquaintances alike. I never tire of telling these stories. For me they never get old. Compiling these tales has served to keep these cherished memories both vivid and timeless. Frankly, though, it has also been quite cathartic.

CHAPTER 1

LET'S ROLL THE DICE

It was 2012 and her seventieth year and eighth decade on the planet had been looming on the horizon for my mother, and it was not about to be ignored. Seventy called for a celebration, a family celebration. Translation: my father and Uncle Bern were welcome, but my physical presence as the only child within my nuclear family was essential. The customary Hallmark cards mailed from Minneapolis paired with good wishes for a happy and healthy year over the phone (typical of birthdays past) would simply not suffice. Two pink candles crammed into the middle of a chocolate cake with "Happy Birthday Sydelle!" scrawled in iced cursive would be rejected (even if Gerry ordered the cake from Flakowitz, the preferred purveyor of sweets among the Jews of South Florida). On the contrary, a destination trip was required to appropriately acknowledge this momentous occasion.

"You know, Harley, we're not getting any younger, after all. You're lucky—you're only in your mid-thirties. Who knows how much longer your father and I will be physically able to travel. We might as well go somewhere while we're still capable, thank God," my mother said with the subtlety of a bull in a china shop. The phrase "still capable" implied impending doom. I braced myself for our bi-weekly thirty-minute phone conversation.

Her thick, genuine New York accent had not softened one iota since retiring to South Florida more than a decade ago. She clings to it because it's part of her fundamental identity. Hell, it's part of my fundamental identity as well. Originally thick, harsh, and instantly recognizable, my New York accent has certainly softened since Elyse and I moved to Minneapolis in 2001. Yet I subconsciously cling to it and consciously refuse to shed it entirely because it's part of me. The green sea glass fragment your kid finds while collecting seashells along the beach originally belonged to a bottle of beer. The edges, initially sharp and jagged from the idiot that thoughtlessly tossed it into the ocean in the midst of a drunken stupor, have become smooth and tapered from the relentless force of the tides crashing into the shore. The same holds true for my accent; it's softened with time but it remains unmistakably present.

"Right, Mom," I replied.

"Having all the money in the world doesn't matter if you're not healthy enough to enjoy it."

"Right, Mom."

"You can't put a price on health, Harley."

"That's what they taught us in medical school, Mom. That lesson came right in between the anatomy of the pancreas and a survey of the parasites indigenous to sub-Saharan Africa."

Couching the sarcasm within a reference to my medical training allowed it to pass unnoticed. The medical degree was a foregone conclusion; my grandmother Anna allegedly declared that I would become a physician the moment she first laid eyes on me in the hospital nursery. Throughout my childhood, Uncle Bern reinforced the notion, declaring time and again that a surgeon's status was second only to that of God.

In Mom's mind, the letters MD after my name were a source of perpetual pride; fully spelled out, they stood for My Son the Doctor. Within Mom's circle of friends, a child with a medical degree elevated her social status. Anyone could brag about a child who made partner in some boutique law firm or was promoted to chief executive officer of Fill-in-the-Blank Corporation. Free estate planning and company discounts were nice, but neither trumped the value of free medical advice, the patience to listen to all that ails, and unlimited prescription medication refills conferred by My Son the Doctor, who was just one quick phone call away. To the extent that these fringe benefits made Mom happy, I was happy to oblige—most of the time.

This destination holiday also encompassed the celebration of Uncle Bern's eightieth birthday, which legitimized it even further. The fact that

Uncle Bern turned eighty years old eleven months before the projected departure date of said trip was immaterial. Sydelle was turning seventy and any other milestone paled in comparison. All of her cronies would have no choice but to acknowledge the grandiosity of the occasion, once they learned that the beloved son Harley was willing to cancel a few surgeries and board a plane for the affair.

Las Vegas was designated as the chosen city. On the surface, it made perfect sense: *mishegas* and Las Vegas seem tailor-made for each other. Where else in the continental United States can adults travel to year-round to completely let loose and take a temporary break from reality? "What happens in Philadelphia stays in Philadelphia" just doesn't measure up to the infamous slogan derived from the antics on the Strip.

I willfully overlooked the fact that my parents were about as comfortable in a Vegas nightclub as Hitler would have been at a bar mitzvah in Jerusalem. I tried to convince myself that a trip to Vegas was not necessarily all that absurd. Sydelle and Gerry played a mean penny slot machine together (they considered the stakes too high for them each to play side by side on separate machines). Uncle Bern still played poker routinely with his pals and taught me the basics of five-card draw and seven-card stud as a kid (in the 1980s, Texas Hold 'Em didn't have the global prestige it currently enjoys). Bern also taught me basic blackjack strategy while describing the highlights of his semi-regular weekend jaunts to Atlantic City with his buddies.

Buried underneath a mountain of self-imposed pressure to ace every exam and homework assignment handed out after the fourth grade, I envisioned joining him on these junkets once I reached legal gambling age. I saw the bachelor's life my uncle led. While by no means wealthy, he was single and financially independent. I saw him living his life on his own terms, coming and going as he so chose within the constraints of his job as a lithographer in Manhattan. None of my buddies had a close relative quite like Bern, a guy who made his nephew mini cups of coffee and slipped him furtive sips of beer. He was my cool Uncle Bern, revving his car's engine while I rode shotgun, tossing a football precariously close to our neighbor's brand-new Cadillac, and gambling his pocket change with me to demonstrate the nuances of poker. Unfortunately, the trips to Atlantic City never materialized during my twenties due to my steadily mounting medical school tuition loans and life as an otolaryngology resident, so the prospect of finally gambling alongside Uncle Bern in Vegas was enticing.

Vegas certainly offered enough to keep me entertained; Elyse and I typically spend a long weekend there every year or two. She tolerates the gambling, focusing like me on blackjack with an occasional stint at the craps tables. The dilemma for her is that she hates to lose more than she loves to win. Gambling aside, though, Vegas offers much of what we've both come to enjoy. A quick direct flight from Minneapolis lands us in the midst of a sea of lovely city-sized hotels replete with poolside lounging, luxury spas, world-class shopping, superlative dining, and Broadway-quality entertainment. The plethora of options adds to the allure. We don't stay in the high rollers suite at Caesars and we don't blow fifty grand on a shopping spree at the Chanel boutique. We don't rent out the poolside cabanas and we don't get daily tandem two-hour massages. We don't wash down caviar with the finest champagne and we don't sit in the front row waiting for Celine Dion to waltz out on stage. But we will stay in a standard room at the Venetian Hotel and purchase a few items to add to our wardrobes. We'll go for a dip in the pool and dry off while reading a novel. In the evenings, we may see a Cirque du Soleil show or a concert. And we always eat really, really well. Elyse and I have always appreciated great food. For us, it's not about the price or the name of the celebrity chef on the menu; a more expensive meal does not mean a more enjoyable meal. We both crave the experience of a great meal. That means starting off with a killer cocktail, eating flavor-packed yet reasonably healthy food, and enjoying the ambiance of an inviting room. So when a Vegas trip was up for discussion, no one had to worry about dragging me there kicking and screaming.

Sydelle and Gerry were also not Vegas neophytes; they'd been there a couple of times previously, though never with me. They went principally for the entertainment that abounds along the Strip. They filled their days catching the dancing water fountains at the Bellagio, the perfectly manicured floral gardens in the front lobby of the Wynn, and the gondoliers crooning in the canals of The Venetian. Nights were spent in the theatres, catching a musical or a variety show. In between, the people watching never ceased to disappoint.

As I thought more about the proposed trip, I pictured Bern playing the role of an essential accomplice. He was to be my wingman, insulating and buffering me from the parental *mishegas* that was certain to rear its ugly head. But Bern was so much more than an accessory; he was the most important male role model of my childhood. I looked up to him, I emulated him, and I strove to be like him from my first memories.

I was always a good kid through and through. I was a responsible kid in elementary school, a trustworthy kid in middle school, and a kid who never got into any real trouble or needed a curfew in high school. I could watch pretty much whatever I wanted on TV for as long as I wanted to watch it. It was hard to argue with my viewing patterns when the report cards I brought home from school were flawless. I was responsible for deciding to turn the TV off when I felt like I wasn't making sufficient progress on my homework or was having trouble concentrating.

As long as I left a note explaining my whereabouts, I was free to play sports or hang out with the guys after school. My decision to come home was mine and mine alone. I knew when dinner would be served and my weight proved that I didn't miss a meal. My bedtime was set at the point of equilibrium between the minimum sleep needed to ace the next exam and the maximum time spent studying for it. I respected my parents for granting me these freedoms that most kids didn't get to enjoy.

I owed my mother the trip to Las Vegas, but it was not because of the privileges I enjoyed as a child. I owed her the trip because I was her only child and I belonged there. I knew that my presence would make the trip special for her. I belonged on that trip, even though I knew parts of it were destined to be laden with *mishegas*.

There just couldn't be a trip to Vegas without Uncle Bern. Celebrating Syd's seventieth birthday on a destination trip while casting aside Bern's eightieth birthday made no sense. Bern was a perennial presence at all of our major family events, so we naturally assumed he would come along. It was a foregone conclusion that merited no formal conversation between my parents and me. We wanted him with us in Las Vegas and needed him in Las Vegas, albeit for different reasons. Although we all wished him to have a memorable milestone birthday, in practical terms Syd and Gerry recognized that his ability to travel was rapidly dwindling as the years piled up. I needed him there for balance; Bern was the most adept at calming my father down, reigning in his rants, and keeping him in line without offending him.

Bern and I remained close throughout my adult life, never missing a Sunday morning phone call unless I happened to be out of the country or occupied by some surgical emergency. We spoke on the phone every week beginning the day I left for my freshman year at Cornell in 1993. The topics didn't vary much, but that didn't matter to me. I never grew bored or tired of them, as some part of me subconsciously appreciated them as a tradition that would not last forever.

We always started with a reiteration of the same talking points: my week at work and his week at the poker table. We talked about Daphne and Zachary and his bottomless supply of coffee. We rehashed the events of his Saturday evenings out with his girlfriend at the Saravan Diner and his Sunday morning frustrations competing for an empty washing machine in his apartment building's laundry room. The progress of the New York Yankees and the New York Giants were always covered in due course, depending on the season of the year. He then inevitably worked a few anecdotes into the conversation, drawing from the lifelong influence that the US Army had on his philosophical approach to life on planet Earth. Despite the ability to complete his sentences, I laughed at the 831st rendition of any story just as hard as the thirty-first. As we prepared to hang up, Bern would always remind me to eat well, because "a Sunday without lox is like a day without sunshine." These phone calls were an immutable fixture of my Sunday mornings.

About a thousand conversations with Bern spanning twenty years of my life unfolded in this way, before we spoke one nondescript Sunday morning about the possibility of the Vegas trip. Uncle Bern didn't give a damn where we went to celebrate, as long as the four of us were all together. He reminded me that he came within a stone's throw of being shipped to the front lines of the infantry during the Korean War; at the last minute, he lied his way into a position as an army medic and was deployed to Germany instead. Never forgetting his good fortune, Bern contentedly kept his feet firmly planted on US soil since the day he received his discharge papers from the army. He saw no reason to get a passport now that his sister was about to turn seventy. Vegas was a perfectly fine destination. He only had one non-negotiable pre-requisite. Coffee.

Bern was a coffee- and liquor-guzzling Jewish Yankee fan from the brawling South Bronx whose lithography career fed the bottomless pit that was his stomach. To him, life was about coffee and food. Coffee and food were the vehicles through which Bern experienced life.

Consider religion, for example. In Bern's eyes, the significance of the Jewish religious holidays started and ended with the traditional foods and delicacies traditionally prepared for each special occasion. The holidays as an aggregate could be viewed as one huge meal consumed over the course of the year. In this scheme, the High Holidays of Rosh Hashanah and Yom Kippur represented the appetizers. Rosh Hashanah meant apples and honey. Yom Kippur equated to bagels, lox, tuna salad, chicken salad, and noodle kugel. Stepping out of order, the winter holidays meant dessert. Hanukkah and Purim were synonymous with chocolate gelt and fruit-filled Hamantaschen, respectively. The entrée course remained, and Passover boldly stepped in to satisfy the role. The two seder meals held during the first two nights of Passover together lasted a good six hours or so. By the end of the second seder, Bern would have put down enough food to tide his belly over through the summertime holiday lull. He spent the summer in a state of relative satiety. By the time the High Holidays rolled around again the following September, his stomach's equilibrium was sufficiently out of whack to start the feasting all over again.

Bern's caffeine addiction (and it was an addiction) began as an adolescent to compensate for the perceived mistreatment he suffered at the hands of his aunt Gertie. Apparently, my grandmother went into the hospital for a few days to give birth to my prematurely arriving mother. She left Bern in the care of responsible adults, who in this case took the forms of his aunt Gertie and uncle Julius.

Julius was severely crippled by polio at a young age, so he was of no help to Gertie in the kitchen. And it was the kitchen that proved to be Gertie's undoing; gastronomic monotony was Bern's official diagnosis. For three evenings, dinner consisted of nothing but a solitary matzo ball in chicken broth, a piece of rye bread, and a glass of cherry water. The big variable at dinnertime was whether the matzo ball would sink or float. As this culinary repertoire was presented on the third consecutive night, Bern stood up from the table, donned his coat, turned up the collar and walked home to an empty apartment in the South Bronx. Fiercely independent to a fault throughout his life, he willfully absconded at the age of eleven at night and in the middle of a winter storm.

As soon as he got home, he put a pot of coffee on the stove. It was the only hot beverage at his disposal, and desperate times called for desperate measures. A whole new world percolated through the filter in his mind when the first sips touched upon his lips. Tastes he didn't know existed exploded onto his palate. Ethiopia, the top coffee producing country in Africa, forever more served a legitimate purpose as a nation in Bern's mind. Outside his home, Bern wasn't particular about the brand of coffee he drank, so long as it was fully caffeinated. If a cup of decaf accidentally appeared, Bern would half-jokingly accuse the server of attempted murder.

"Are you trying to poison me with that damn decaf?" Bern would yell. He'd smile through the waiter's stammering apology before continuing. "A cup of napalm would be less toxic to my system. You think I'm afraid of a little caffeine? I was about to be shipped to the front lines of the infantry in Korea. That was something to worry about, not a few milligrams of caffeine." He even got a little jumpy if an orange-handled pot of decaf got within three feet of his cup. At home, though, it was Maxwell House all the way.

For such a devotee of coffee, you might think it surprising that Bern preferred instant coffee at home. His choice of Maxwell House above all other coffee brands was akin to a beer connoisseur preferring Bud Light to the hundreds of unique craft beers that fill liquor store refrigerators these days. But Bern was a fairly simple man with correspondingly simple tastes. Just because a product was fancier didn't automatically make it better. He knew what he liked, and he liked Maxwell House very, very much. Kraft

Foods should only know what a devoted customer Uncle Bern remained throughout his life. If they needed an eighty-year-old spokesperson with a bad temper and two false front teeth that looked like a pair of Chiclets, Bern would have happily obliged. I don't think he would have even charged Kraft Foods an appearance fee. He would have been happy enough just to promote his beloved Maxwell House, to give a little back to the company that had fed his caffeine cravings for so many decades.

Bern started boiling the water for his first cup of Maxwell House as soon as he rolled out of bed each morning. His last cup accompanied dessert in the evenings; in between, a new cup was served approximately every two hours. While I could not guarantee Maxwell House, I assured Bern that I could keep the coffee flowing throughout a weekend trip to Vegas.

Uncle Bern is a man who knows what he wants and when he wants it. Delayed gratification is not part of his persona. His life in New York is all about routine. Bern leaves little to chance. His local bagel shop has his everything bagel with cream cheese already wrapped in wax paper before he walks through the door every weekday morning. A fresh pot of coffee brewed especially for him finishes dripping into the urn just as Bern sidles up to the cash register. So it is especially these creatures of routine like Uncle Bern who need a little reassurance when found in unfamiliar territory. He tried his best to seem blasé, but his unease was obvious to my trained ear.

"You sure there will be a coffee pot in the Vegas hotel room, Harley?"

"Yeah, Bern. I'm sure."

"You're positive?"

"Quite."

"Okay, but how can you be so sure?"

"Because every hotel room I've entered in the United States of America in the twenty-first century has had a coffee pot in the room. Think all the way back to 2001. Remember my wedding in Santa Fe? Did your hotel room have a coffee pot?"

"Yeah, it did, Harl."

"Elyse didn't need to run out to Starbucks in her wedding dress for you, did she?"

"Nope." Bern laughed at the image of his veiled niece making a pit stop to order a large black coffee en route to our wedding ceremony.

"Santa Fe is in the desert, just like Vegas. Take some solace in the fact that you didn't go into the throes of caffeine withdrawal during my wedding. Use past precedent to your advantage."

"There will be coffee in the room, right? I don't need to throw a jar of Maxwell House into my suitcase? The coffee pot's no good without a good brew, Harl."

"Bern, we're talking about Las Vegas. These are major hotels big enough to have their own zip codes. They're designed and operated to satisfy your every whim and desire. If you're willing to pay for it, I bet the concierge will fly an employee to Colombia on a private jet and have him hike up into the mountains on a burro to handpick a pound of coffee beans directly off the trees. For an extra fee, the concierge may even be able to arrange same day service."

"Okay, okay, I get it, Harley. It's just that I can't afford to take any chances at my age. Remember, if I ever get hospitalized tell the nurse to shoot a cup of coffee directly into my IV line. That will be more powerful medicine than anything any doctor can prescribe."

"I'll have the nurse flush your line with coffee right after the morphine is pushed."

"That's good enough for me, Harley. Let's go."

So that was it. It was official. Las Vegas, Nevada was slated to host Sydelle's and Uncle Bern's birthday celebrations (mostly Sydelle's seventieth with a side of Bern's eightieth). All Bern required was a never-ending supply of coffee and pastries, a few beers, and the opportunity to grab a pair of hot dice and make a few points at the craps tables.

CHAPTER 2

ALEXANDER GRAHAM BELL WOULD HAVE HAD A CORONARY

The year 2012 started the same way that 2011 ended—in a whirlwind. The spring trip to Las Vegas was still months away, making it no more than a fleeting thought in my mind and a blip on my calendar's horizon. Life as Elyse and I knew it was semi-controlled chaos. We existed by rushing through our days. Time was perpetually short. My surgical practice was steadily growing. There was a semi-regular flow of extra patients needing urgent surgeries that ended well into the evenings. Make no mistake: a waiting room chock full of pacing patients was a good problem to have. No doctor wants his or her waiting room to double as an echo chamber. I carved out just enough time to drive the kids either to or from school twice a week, exercise three times a week, and throw weeknight dinners together as I sorted the mail. It took real concentration to avoid accidentally dousing the bills in vinaigrette intended for the salad and serving dinner with a letter opener rather than a knife. After a typical week, I didn't begin to feel even remotely relaxed until Sunday evenings rolled around.

Elyse's dermatology practice was equally if not more robust. She was pulling out her own hair navigating between the demands of her own overflowing clinical practice and her commitment to be fully invested in the kids' lives. She coordinated Zach and Daph's schedules, volunteered time she didn't have at their schools, and arranged our social calendars on the side.

Zachary was in preschool at our synagogue. He figured out how to pervert classic nursery rhymes by substituting words for disgusting biological functions, concentrated on honing his fine motor skills by coloring within the printed outlines of a medley of cartoon characters, and learned that it was never okay to bite another human. Daphne was mastering the major goals of first grade: learning how to read, keeping track of both of her mittens throughout the long winter, and remembering that it was never okay to bite another human.

I recognized early on in my career that the practice of medicine could be all consuming if I permitted it to be. There were the tangible leftovers at the remains of a twelve-hour day, regardless of how hard I worked. Partner meetings, practice-building events, charts to complete, surgical cases to dictate, patient telephone calls to return, emails to review, and urgent prescriptions to fill were but a few. These chores came with the territory. Elyse and I (and every other physician) unwittingly signed up for them when we were young and naïve, when our noble passions and idealism guided us to medical school in the hopes of curing disease, saving lives, easing suffering, and furthering the overall human condition. Some of these tasks could reasonably be postponed for a day or two. But procrastination never made them vanish. If postponed for too long, we would be quickly buried underneath an avalanche of falling medical bricks like the final moments of an unsalvageable game of Tetris.

Then there were the intangibles. These were the thoughts that stewed in the deep recesses of my mind and intermittently erupted like a geyser into conscious awareness without my permission. *That last rhinoplasty went fairly well, but how could it have been better still? Would the patient ultimately be pleased with the results? In what precise sequence should I perform tomorrow's cheek reconstruction? Would the results of the biopsy I took earlier in the week be finalized before the weekend? Can I finish tomorrow's office appointments in time to relieve the nanny as planned?* The list of questions could be endless, if allowed. Thankfully, I was always pretty good at separating my work life from my home life.

Our basic approach to parenting and to our lives in general was to divide and conquer. I'd pour Elyse a cocktail while she changed Zach's diaper. The next evening, the roles reversed. Most of the time it worked out pretty well, provided that our paths didn't cross and the lime wedge destined for the martini glass wasn't placed into the Diaper Genie instead. Nonetheless, between the attention we devoted to our careers, kids, and each other, there was little free time left over. Simple luxuries like leisurely chatting up friends on the phone were relegated to fantasyland. Our phone use was radically different from that of Mom and Dad.

~

Syd and Gerry shared one cellular telephone in 2012. This extraordinary electronic device came fully equipped with the technology to make and receive telephone calls. It had no text messaging or photographic capabilities. Apps were items ordered in restaurants prior to the entrée course; they were not to be found on this vintage flip phone. The term "Bluetooth" referred to a dental emergency, not a method of hands-free communication. Music played on the FM band of their car radios, not their phone. This phone was turned off when not in use; the battery had to be conserved and preserved. It was powered on twice a year when Syd urgently needed to make a call. It was also powered on when Syd expected to receive a call, an event that occurred with similar frequency. Otherwise, the phone was only left on in dire circumstances, like the threat of an impending global thermonuclear war. My parents thought that leaving the phone on indiscriminately was irresponsible, if not highly negligent.

The phone took up permanent residence in the deep recesses of my mother's purse. There were approximately thirty-seven different compartments in this purse, each secured with a zipper, latch, magnet, snap, or some other closure mechanism. Thus, even when the stars aligned sufficiently for the phone to be on during an actual incoming call, the chances of Syd answering it prior to going to voice mail were somewhere between zero and nonexistent. I found Syd's cell phone habits shocking, considering that she used her home landline phone so often that it could be viewed as an extension of her hand.

My father, on the other hand, completely disavowed himself of all things telephonic. At least he did so at home. I can't recall a single instance when he picked up the phone to voluntarily initiate a social call to anyone besides Uncle Bern. As a career insurance salesman, my father spent a fair amount of time at work on the phone with clients. How he managed to use the phone well enough to commandeer a paycheck ranks up there with the great mysteries of the world. Why? The man spoke so quickly, and in such a pressure-packed manner, you were lucky to understand two words in ten. He always asked you second and third questions before allowing you to answer the first. His mind raced so quickly that he often didn't listen to a word you said.

Given this background, communicating with my father was always difficult. Once I left home for college in the mid 1990s, however, the telephone posed another barrier when Dad answered the phone.

"Hello?"

"Hi, Dad."

"Hello? (Pause.) Hello?"

"Dad. Hi, Dad. It's me."

"Who is this?"

Even at this early point in the conversation, I recognized an all-too-familiar pattern unfolding.

"Who the hell do you think this is?"

"Oh, Harley. It's you. Why didn't you say so?"

"The last time I checked, I'm an only child. There's no one else on the planet that calls you Dad. Who the hell did you think was on the other end of the line?"

"Right. You're right, Harley."

"No shit I'm right! Unless there's some love child out there you'd like to divulge."

"Hold on a minute. I'll put your mother on the phone."

"Good talk, Dad."

That was about the extent of our phone conversations while I was away at college. Gerry was never one for making small talk on the phone. The arrangement worked well for me, consumed as I was with my undergraduate pre-med courses in biology and organic chemistry.

Throughout my childhood, Mom arrived home from work in the elementary school trenches of Queens, New York at about 3:45 p.m. Her daily game of Phone-A-Friend started shortly thereafter. If my mother was on the phone, she was on the phone. Her vast network of like-minded lifelong friends enabled her with an equal desire to yak away on the phone, unlimited by any time constraints.

The rotary dial landline phone we had was replaced with a newfangled push-button model (complete with mute and redial buttons) in the late 1980s. Call waiting was still a radical, cutting-edge concept in those days. No one had heard of a cell phone; the closest gadgets at the time were the walkie-talkie and the CB radio. The push-button phone was tricked out with an extra-long cord and a rubber shoulder rest that eased neck strain. These features allowed Sydelle to converse for hours at a time without exacerbating the TMJ syndrome she suffered from ever since her crooked pediatric dentist filled about eighteen cavities she never actually had. Even so, her neck gradually developed a permanent slight cant to the left (like the Leaning Tower of Pisa) from the thousands of hours cumulatively spent cradling the phone receiver between her left ear and left shoulder. The extra-long extension cord allowed her to prepare dinner as she meandered throughout the four corners of the kitchen, from the table to the appliances to the cupboards, without having to set the phone down.

~

In Long Island in the 1980s, I was a kid in my prime. I was in that sweet spot between the ages of ten and fifteen, only peripherally aware of the fact that there was a serious world somewhere out there. I played pickup games of football and basketball after school with the guys in the local park, did my homework, ate dinner, and then did some more homework while watching the Yankees on TV. As an only child, my friends were vitally important to me. I had a large gaggle of close pals distributed radially about the neighborhood like the spokes on the wheels of the ten-speed bike I relied upon to navigate the not-so-mean streets. We all went to the same public school, Hebrew school, and summer day camp. So I fully acknowledge the importance of Mom's friends in her own life. To do otherwise would be hypocritical.

But with Sydelle on the phone from roughly 4:00 p.m. until dinnertime at 6:45 p.m., it was quite difficult to commandeer her attention. So I kept myself entertained, creating diversions and interludes in place of real conversation. Sometimes, I used the extra-long phone cord as a jump rope. When retracted, the cord functioned as a giant slingshot. Held taut, it served as a quasi-horizontal bar with which I practiced my burgeoning limbo dance skills (I attended two or three bar and bat mitzvah parties per month in 1988, after all).

Over time, Dad created nicknames for Mom's innermost circle of telephone cronies. There was the elementary school crew, headed up by "Blackie" and "The Flying Nun." Blackie was nothing more than an abbreviated surname, while The Flying Nun described a particularly pious woman who enjoyed world travel and gladly tithed about 85 percent of her annual salary to the New York Archdiocese. Then there were my friends' mothers, led by "Stache." This moniker referred to a woman with an abundance of darkly pigmented upper lip hair. Syd would have four to five conversations with Stache weekly, each of which Dad referred to as "reporting in." A dump truck hurtling through the side of the house to drop a load of concrete cinderblocks onto the middle of the kitchen floor couldn't derail a Stache report.

No stone was left unturned, given the amount of time Sydelle and Stache devoted to the reports each week. Email was a good ten to fifteen years away from common use. Blogs, text messages, instant messages, and chat rooms were about twenty-five years from becoming mainstream. Yet somehow, the speed with which the gossip mill radiated outward from the Sydelle-Stache core trumped all of these modern technologies. No detail was irrelevant until proven otherwise. They thoroughly chewed the information cud before packaging it and disseminating it for further use. Gossip trickled in from disparate sources, and was broadcast to strategically targeted audiences. Together, they were a powerful duo. Through over thirty years of friendship, I don't think they've ever had a single argument. As Vesuvius smothered Pompeii with a blanket of volcanic ash, Sydelle and Stache maintained a stranglehold on the minutia of life in my Long Island hometown.

Syd and Stache have physically slowed over the years, but Phone-A-Friend continues full-throttle. To her credit, Mom maintains an email account, but the landline still reigns supreme as a means to stay connected with her friends and family. Her cell phone remains steadfastly by her side, a loyal extra appendage. She talks to her old friends still entrenched on Long Island. She chats up other friends who have migrated to South Florida from Long Island. She converses with new compatriots in her South Florida neighborhood without any New York connections. If it wasn't for the unlimited local and long distance calling plan, she'd be flat broke. Her network has been cultivated and expanded with the attention to detail of a Japanese bonsai tree master.

~

It was thus that I came to set limits with Mom on the phone. She knows to expect a routine call from me on my drive home from work on Wednesday evenings and while I am out for a coffee run on Sunday mornings. We spend about thirty to forty-five minutes on the phone and then I'm done. My familial obligation and my conscience are fulfilled. As Popeye used to say, "That's all I can stand, I can't stands no more." I repaid the debt I, an only child, owed my parents for twenty-five years worth of food, clothing, and shelter (I had been a financial burden with a negative cash flow until medical school graduation). The food, clothing, and shelter were each problematic at times but undeniably good overall. I held a grudge against Mom for making me wear stiff brown dress shoes to elementary school when all of the other boys wore Nike tennis shoes. She also forced me to wear long pants to a pal's summer swimming party when it was ninety-two degrees outside. Yet she made sure I had at least a couple of the trendy items the popular kids sported each season. Like most kids, I ate plenty of burgers and pizza. But I couldn't overcome the revulsion generated when Mom doled out the gefilte fish suspended in a jar of murky gelatinous goo every Passover. As a teenager, I almost popped a brain aneurysm when Mom crept into my bedroom at three o'clock in the morning and hovered within an inch of my face to verify that I was still breathing. Yet I had my own bedroom and Mom and Dad were open-minded enough to let me decorate it from floor to ceiling with New York Yankees posters.

I was fundamentally grateful for the trendy clothes, the burgers and pizza, and the bedroom full of New York Yankees posters. Not to mention the unconditional love, paid college education, first car, and probably a thousand other privileges Syd and Gerry gave me and of which I was at best cursorily aware.

It's nice to be grateful; it's undeniably a nice quality to possess. It's humbling to remember where you came from and how you got to be where you are. But the static gratefulness taking up permanent residence in my heart is subservient to the reality of time dynamically and unrelentingly marching along on my wristwatch. Time is my most important commodity. Between the demands of my surgical career and my intent to be fully engaged in the lives of Elyse, Daph, and Zach, free time is in exceedingly short supply. Within this context, leisurely phone conversations are just not a practical part of my life. Yet I prioritize these biweekly calls home to Mom and Dad because I'm their only child and I live halfway across the country with their only grandchildren. They cherish the opportunity to keep current with the events in my life, no matter how monotonous or mundane. I remind myself that I have only one set of parents and neither should be taken for granted. Just hearing my voice is vitally important to them. So if Syd wants to chat about why I was delayed in the operating room until 6:13 p.m. yesterday or Dad wants to discuss the last time the oil level in Elyse's brand-new car was checked, I do my best to oblige while maintaining a semblance of patience.

Syd is welcome to call at any other time during the week, should she have a quick question about the efficacy of some new prescription sinus rinse that her fourth ENT doctor recommended to bail her capsizing nose out from a biblical flood of mucous, or should she need to share some vitally important information like the details of a flight reservation to Minneapolis she made three months in advance of the departure date. At these other times, I'll pick up the phone and address the pressing matter at hand, but that's it.

My rationale for the scheduled biweekly chats was fairly simple. I thought that limiting the frequency of the phone calls would improve the quality of our conversations. We would concentrate the quality rather than dilute it. In the process, I would maintain my sanity. As a father, Gerry was physically present but emotionally absent. After he retired, Dad kept himself busy puttering about the house. The house invariably looked the same at sunset as it did at sunrise. The only difference was a new set of multicolored Post-It notes scrawled in chicken scratch and layered on the side of the kitchen counter. By the time 8:00 p.m. rolled around, he was snoring soundly on the den couch. There was no opportunity for me to start probing his political views or the items on his bucket list.

Syd, by contrast, could be physically and emotionally smothering. Deadly afraid that I would catch a cold, she dressed me in long pants en route to swimming pool birthday parties at the height of a ninety-five degree August afternoon. She was afraid that my legs would get exposed to a brutal eighty-six degree wind chill after jumping out of the pool. Mom dragged me into the pediatrician's office every time I used more than three tissues or coughed more than twice in a twenty-four hour period. During my first semester of college, I had the audacity to casually date a girl who wasn't Jewish. The relationship lasted all of two or three months. Yet with every phone call home, Mom grilled me about the proposed religious persuasion(s) of our nonexistent offspring. Home for the summer in between my junior and senior years of college, I was once again startled awake at 3:00 a.m. to find Mom hovering an inch and a half over my face, verifying that I was still breathing.

So how wrong was I about the quality versus quantity trade-off with Mom and Dad over the phone? One of our more recent calls went something like this:

"Hi, Mom."

"Oh hi, Harley. Just a second, let me get off the other line." Naturally she was gossiping with one of her chums about something important—human rights violations in North Korea, the current state of Israeli-Palestinian relations, or the shiny new Cadillac that just rolled into her neighbor's driveway—when my call triggered her call waiting signal.

Gerry started hollering in the background about whether the London broil was ready to go onto the grill and who it was on the phone. In general, it's rare for me to have a separate conversation with Dad. Usually, I speak directly with Mom and indirectly with Dad, simultaneously. Not content to let Mom have an uninterrupted conversation, Dad lurks in the background, injecting his two cents over my mother's voice. Sometimes he'll offer up unsolicited comments about whatever he hears us talking about (or what he thinks he hears us talking about). Other times, he'll bark out topics for Mom to discuss with me. Most often, though, he'll echo and reiterate whatever he hears Mom say, like a deranged version of Dolby surround sound. Any way you slice it, the interruptions are at best irritating and more often infuriating. I lose my train of thought; the conversation fragments. It has to be rehashed as the pieces are retrieved and cobbled back into some semblance of cohesiveness.

"Wait a minute, Gerry! What's the rush? Don't put the meat on the barbeque yet. Wait until I'm off the phone with Harley," came Mom's irritated reply. I can't blame her. Trying to focus on multiple phone conversations simultaneously is exasperating, especially when one of the participants isn't even on the phone.

But Dad didn't want to wait. He was anxious, just because he's always anxious and rarely content to live in the moment. He was never able to cloak his nervousness, make a spontaneous decision, or simply have faith that most things in life tend to work themselves out. I understood these aspects of his personality because I see them all in myself to some degree. I don't like them so I try to mitigate them, with variable success. Sometimes I wish I was one of those carefree spirits that worked just enough odd jobs to support the most basic of human necessities, spending the remainder of my time surfing the Hawaiian waves. That's not ever going to happen, so instead I make smaller concessions. I leave my pager at home when I'm not on call for my practice on weekend evenings. I don't worry about an ordinary Sunday night dinner the preceding Tuesday. I pay attention to Daphne's violin recitals and Zachary's hockey games rather than hide behind a camera lens or read text messages notifying me that my frequent patronage at the local coffee shop has earned me a complimentary small beverage with the purchase of a breakfast sandwich anytime in the next five days. The memories of the moments are better than the photos stored in my computer. And I truly do believe that most things in life tend to work out at the end of the day. Spontaneity remains a pretty big struggle, but I'm working on it.

Gerry was still hollering, only now it was about depleting the grill's propane tank (forgetting the fact that he has a dozen spare propane tanks stockpiled in the garage. There's enough gas in the garage to blow his neighborhood a square mile in all directions, should the South Florida heat cause them to spontaneously combust.) Sydelle shooed him away while reiterating that she was speaking with me on the phone. I imagined her brandishing some cooking utensil in Dad's general direction, in the style of an uncoordinated fencer with no formal training.

"Oh, it's Harley. Why didn't you say so?" Gerry replied. He trudged off to find some other less-than-essential task to bide his time. He was probably making his evening rounds around the house, holding his outstretched palm over each of the air conditioning vents to make sure they were all putting out the appropriate amount of air to keep the house temperature a steady seventy-eight degrees.

"How are you, Harley?"

"I'm fine, Mom. Everyone's fine. Elyse is fine. Daphne is fine and Zach is fine." I tried to cover all of my bases at once. It didn't work.

"So Elyse is okay, then?"

"Yes."

"And the children? They're okay too?"

"Yes. Didn't I just say that everyone's fine?" I had intentionally reported that everyone was fine at the beginning of the conversation to avoid this redundant line of questioning, but to no avail.

"You did, but I'm just asking."

"Well, I'm hereby confirming everyone's fineness."

"That's good to hear. Elyse is all better from her awful cold?"

"She had a cold three weeks ago. Maybe longer. Who the hell besides you can remember? She's probably due to get another one in a few days. The kids' classrooms are giant petri dishes."

"Don't say that, Harley. You'll give her *kneina hura*." Kneina hura is an old Yiddish phrase meaning an evil eye capable of bringing harm to a person.

I wholeheartedly endorsed her infusion of Yiddish into any conversation. Yiddish is such an expressive language; it conveys in one simple phrase the equivalent of a full page in English. Mom's use of Yiddish provided a direct link to my past. My grandmother spoke the language fluently. Mom understood it but could not speak it very well. I'm lucky to retain a few key phrases. The language itself is a veritable dinosaur; it's dying before my eyes, so I find myself clinging to what vestiges I can grasp and conscientiously passing them on to Daph and Zach.

"I saw on TV this evening that it's only going to be a high of two degrees tomorrow in Minneapolis." Apparently, foreshadowing an episode of the common cold translated into the actual passage of a cold front through the Minnesota skies.

"I wouldn't know, Mom. I don't pay attention to the weather forecast."

"Don't you look at the weather forecast?"

"No. The weather is irrelevant. The garage is four steps from the side door of the house and the operating rooms at my hospital are all individually temperature controlled."

As soon as I mentioned temperature controls, I felt like I had stuffed my foot in my mouth. Mom suffers from a blood circulation disorder called Raynaud's Disease. Those afflicted have an intolerance to all things cold, and Syd is no exception. She's always cold. Always. Cold even in her home county of Palm Beach, Florida in the middle of August. For Syd, staying warm is a constant struggle and efforts to do so feature prominently in her daily life. For example, it means wearing a winter parka into a grocery store on a ninety-degree August afternoon just because she needs to pick up a package of frozen vegetables from the freezer section of the store. The woman microwaves refrigerated fruit before biting into it. Orange juice coming out of the refrigerator succumbs to the same fate. You can't help but feel badly for her. Sydelle doesn't stoke the national political fire on controversial issues like abortion rights or police brutality. But I'd hazard an educated guess that she staunchly supports global warming rather than efforts to quell it via carbon footprint reductions. I think she actually would relish the earth heating up a few degrees.

"You can control the temperature in the operating room? What temperature do you set it at?"

"I don't set it at all."

"But, Harley, you just said that you control the temperature."

"I said that the temperature *can* be controlled," I explained. "But I don't personally walk over to the thermostat and fiddle with the settings."

"Why not?" Mom wasn't going to let this one slide. Temperature was one of Syd's most prized topics of conversation. I expect Warren Buffett to discuss the trends on the stock exchange, Bob Costas to cover the Olympics, and Syd to talk about internal and external climate control.

"Because other people in the OR take care of that stuff. The anesthesia team makes sure that the OR temperature is high enough to keep the patient warm. It makes no difference to me. I'm gowned, gloved, and baking under the overhead spotlights like an overstuffed box of french fries at McDonald's. The temperature just doesn't matter to me, Mom."

"I don't know how you do it, Harley. I have to check the forecast before I leave the house each morning."

I can't be too critical of my mother here. I can't leave my own house without checking the score of the prior evening's Yankees game. It's evolved into part of my daily routine. Surgeons are generally creatures of routine. We're also control freaks. There's no point devoting physical time and mental energy to things over which we have no control. The weather is a prime example. Weather forecasts in Minneapolis are about as useful to me as the outlook for next year's potato crop in Russia. When I watch the news on TV, I want to learn about real news, not some meteorologist named Storm with a fake smile plastered across his face predicting the dew point and barometric pressure next Thursday. I freeze my ass off every day from November through April, regardless of whether the temperature is twenty below or twenty above zero. The fewer things I need to track and check every day, the better.

The conversation with Syd was rapidly deteriorating. I launched a counter-attack to try to get things back onto a more meaningful track before I got too aggravated.

"I don't know why you can't have one lousy conversation with me that doesn't involve the temperature in Minneapolis. Every time I speak to you, I beg you not to talk about the weather. I've yelled, I've pleaded, and I've forbid you to discuss the weather. I'd wager a fair amount of money that you and Dad are the only people in South Florida who regularly watch the weather channel to learn about the weather in Minneapolis. Can't you just let it go?"

"I'm your one and only mother, Harley. I can't let it go."

Syd counterattacked with a sortie of guilt, nailing me in the solar plexus.

"Is it so terrible for me to be interested with what's going on in my only son's life? Is that so bad?"

"No, I guess not, Mom," was all I could sheepishly muster in response.

She didn't stop there.

"I feel badly for you, suffering through those brutal winter conditions in Minnesota, especially when it's so beautiful here in Florida. It was just gorgeous outside today. The sun was shining. There wasn't a cloud in the sky. And the temperature—the temperature was a perfect eighty-two degrees. I took a long walk after lunch this afternoon. I think I may have overdone it. I'm tired, my leg muscles are aching, and I'm producing more phlegm."

"You're still talking about the damn weather, Mom." I quickly regained my composure as the pangs of guilt dispersed.

"Well then, tell me what's going on with you and the rest of the family."

"Nothing new to report. Elyse and I go to work and the kids go to school."

"What are you and Elyse doing this weekend?"

"I have no idea. Elyse is in charge of the social arrangements. I imagine we'll have dinner and drinks with friends on Friday night and Saturday night. Maybe take Daphne and Zach for skiing lessons during the day. Throw in a birthday party or two for the kids' friends and that will pretty much take care of the weekend."

"Well, let me tell you what's going on over here. Tomorrow, I'm going to meet Blanche and Linda for a luncheon after my annual gynecologist appointment in the morning. You know how much I love going to the gynecologist, but I'm due for a Pap smear."

She was oblivious to the fact that no son is remotely comfortable discussing his mother's gynecological health. Male gynecologists don't even want to talk to their mothers about it. I wanted to stick my fingers in my ears and yell, "I can't hear you, I can't hear you, I can't hear you" until she stopped. She mercilessly continued.

"I just can't stand the gynecologist's office, Harley. I shudder just thinking about it. That paper gown they put you in always makes me so cold; it takes so long for me to warm up again. But I'm looking forward to the luncheon. We're going to a very nice Italian restaurant in Boca—we've all been there before. I'm sure I won't be hungry for dinner, but I suppose I'll have a light bite because your father will have to eat. Then on Friday, I'm going to a free lecture sponsored by Brandeis University about a half-Nepalese, half-Austrian woman with twelve toes who survived the Holocaust, went on to make custom necklaces with dried rigatoni noodles, and now travels the country recounting her memoirs to the tune of a pan flute."

"Sounds riveting, Mom."

"Are you on call this weekend?"

"No. I'm not on call on a weekend again for about another six weeks or so."

"Thank God. Who needs to work on the weekends, when you work so hard during the week?"

I didn't reply, preferring to sidestep questions that have no answer.

"Maybe we can Skype with the kids one day this weekend?"

"Maybe, Mom. We'll see."

"It would be nice if you could set aside some time to Skype on Saturday or Sunday morning, so that your father and I can bond with the children." New pangs of guilt reverberated and ricocheted inside my chest walls.

"I'll try. You know it's not the easiest thing to arrange. Daphne has her group violin lesson every Saturday morning and Hebrew school every Sunday morning. You and Dad are usually out gallivanting at the clubhouse pool in the afternoons. And I'm trying to catch up on all the crap around the house that I don't have time to do during the week."

"Okay, okay. Just try, because you know how much pleasure it gives to me to see those darling little faces and hear those sweet little voices." Syd layered in another slab of guilt. "It gives me so much happiness whenever we Skype, it makes me happy for the rest of the day."

"We'll try."

"So, what else can you tell me, Harley?"

"I've got nothing."

"What are you making for dinner tonight?"

"Lemon chicken with roasted cauliflower."

"Oh, God! Harley, I don't know how you do it. To work all day as hard as you work, then come home and have the energy to cook such a fancy meal. You are incredible!"

"It's really not so hard. The nanny does most of the prep work for me."

"Still and all, you have to put everything together, cook the meal, and then clean up. I couldn't prepare meals like that when I was working. And I don't have the desire to do it now in retirement, either."

"I don't know what to tell you, Mom. Elyse hates to cook and I enjoy it. We both need to eat, and we both like to eat well. There's not much more to say."

"I could never do it."

"Good thing you don't have to. Look, I'm almost home from work. Is there anything else hanging in the balance that needs to be urgently discussed?"

Here's where I learned how divergent my mother's definition of urgent was from my own.

"No, not really. I spoke with my good friend Eileen on Tuesday. She's not doing well. Her sarcoma recurred in the right shoulder. She's recovering from surgery—they maimed her. The poor thing is never going to have normal use of her arm again."

"They maimed her? What the hell is that supposed to mean?"

"Her doctors had to cut out so much of her shoulder; she'll never regain full arm function. She's handicapped."

"Christ, Mom! That surgeon probably did his damnedest to save the woman's life. That's not maiming. That's called a heroic effort. I call it radical extirpative surgery performed with the intent to cure."

All physicians feel an emotional bond with one another, however weak it may be at times. It's the result of the calling to help those in need mixed with the painstaking training process and the hassles of the current national medical climate. Sensing this connection, I rose to the defense of Eileen's surgeon, whoever he or she was.

"What the hell do you expect a surgeon to do when faced with a recurrent sarcoma? Give it a kiss and slap a Band-Aid on it? Maybe add a little ibuprofen for discomfort? You make it sound like a blindfolded hack high on crack cocaine deliberately took a rusty machete to the woman's shoulder."

"I just feel so bad for Eileen. She's such a nice person."

"Nice people get bad cancer, Mom. It's sad but true. At any rate, I'm pulling into the garage, so I'm going to say good night." For the record, I wasn't actually in the garage at this point in the conversation. I was still on the highway, coming through downtown Minneapolis about five minutes from home. I typically initiate the good-bye sequence as the Minneapolis downtown skyline comes into view from the road. Saying good-bye is a process, and that process is not speedy.

"Oh, you're almost home?"

"No. I've just been sitting in the car with the engine off outside my office, soaking in the luxurious view of the parking lot."

Syd ignored my sarcasm, knowing that no ill will was intended.

"Do you have a busy day tomorrow?"

"Typically busy but nothing out of the ordinary. I do have to get going, though. I'd like to spend a few minutes with the kids before bedtime."

"Okay, then. Go ahead. Your father and I are going to sit down to dinner ourselves. I have to call Sheila after dinner. If there's time after that, I owe Roberta and Marty a call. Their daughter Rachel just gave birth to another granddaughter. They named her Sophia—that's a pretty name, don't you think?"

Syd didn't give me the opportunity to respond to this rhetorical question.

"The baby's healthy, thank God. Marty and Roberta certainly deserve a break, what with all of the horrible chemotherapy their other grandson needed to treat his cancer."

Still on a mission to defend my fellow physicians and now actually rolling into my garage, I moved to wind up the call.

"It goes without saying that everyone on the planet with a shred of compassion and decency knows how awful it is to put an innocent child through chemotherapy to treat a cancer that he or she certainly does not deserve. Be that as it may, it doesn't change the fact that I need to hang up the phone right now, Mom. So good-bye."

"Go ahead, go ahead. Other than that, nothing much is going on here."

"Have a good night."

Having pulled into my garage, I gently knocked my forehead against the top of the steering wheel and inhaled and exhaled deeply five times. I shook my head from side to side, collected my things, and walked into the house, hoping that the phone didn't ring any more that evening. It's no wonder I have a hard time chatting on the phone with anyone for more than ten or fifteen minutes.

~

Mom commandeered the Las Vegas airline arrangements from her home base in South Florida. This made some sense, as Bern didn't own a cell phone, personal computer, or even an email address. She always coordinated Uncle Bern's airline itineraries. Mom's phone company could have optimized its operating efficiency if it had erected a cell tower amid the alligators lurking in her backyard swamp. The medley of phone conversations required in her travel concierge role included:

- Calling the airline to verify flight prices and times for Bern to travel from his home in New York to Vegas. She didn't trust the airline's website.

- Calling the airline to verify flight prices and times for herself and Gerry to travel from Florida to Vegas.

- Calling Bern to make sure the price of the flight was agreeable to him.

- Calling the airline to book Bern's ticket.

- Calling me to make sure I did everything in my power to arrive from Minneapolis relatively close to the times her flight and Bern's flight arrived in Vegas.

- Calling me to advise the purchase of travel insurance.

- Calling me several weeks after my airfare reservation was confirmed to again recommend travel insurance.

- Calling me the week before the trip to suggest purchasing travel insurance one final time. (My patience was wearing thin at this stage. Was my mother on the take? Did she stand to earn a commission if I took the damn travel insurance? We were going to Vegas, and I was willing to let my confidence in the airline industry ride, so to speak.)

- Calling Bern to give him the flight itinerary for herself and Gerry.

- Calling Bern to give him my flight itinerary.

- Calling the airline the day prior to departure to request a seating change.

- Calling the airline on the day of departure to confirm that our flights still existed.

These were the known phone calls. Who knows what went on below my radar? Twelve phone calls about flights were a drop in the proverbial bucket for Sydelle. I'd personally rather yank twelve clumps of hair out of my head or shove twelve shards of bamboo under my fingernails. Both would be about as painful and require a whole lot less time. Nonetheless, Syd dutifully informed me that Uncle Bern was scheduled to land first in Las Vegas McCarran Airport at precisely 12:47 p.m. on a Thursday. I was slated to land shortly thereafter at 1:20 p.m. Mom and Dad were to arrive last, at approximately 3:30 p.m.

Aside from the air travel, the weeks and months preceding our departure for the Vegas trip were fraught with other logistical issues. Sydelle had to overdose on extra vitamin C tablets to ward off any looming rhinoviruses. The common cold petrifies my mother; it's a real phobia. For Mom, catching a cold is akin to releasing the hounds, so to speak. It sets off a Rube Goldberg-like chain reaction of ailments that derails her life for the next month. The rhinovirus threat was omnipresent in her world, easily overlooked by the casual observer but just as easily spotted with her discriminating eye. Retail store merchandise tainted by a guy who made a quick finger swipe of his nostrils to satisfy an itch. Concert hall silence momentarily disrupted by a cough from the mouth of the patron seated directly behind her. Shaking a friend's hand that may have been withdrawn from a pocket housing a handkerchief. Mom subconsciously played a microbial game of Where's Waldo. I think she crushed up a few dozen tablets and slipped them sporadically into Dad's food as well.

Years ago, I told Mom that the human body can only absorb a finite amount of vitamin C, with any extra excreted in the urine. I laughed to myself at the dichotomy that clearly existed in Mom's mind. On the one hand, she acknowledged this statement of fact. Nonetheless, her actions proved that she clearly didn't believe me enough to alter her ways. I conjured an image of my medical school professors in a bar sharing a pitcher of beer, laughing as they reminisced about the time they fooled their medical students about vitamin C metabolism. Mom became preoccupied with satellite weather forecast checks twice daily, calls to the pharmacy for medication refills, and purchasing just enough food to satiate Gerry while still leaving the refrigerator nearly empty by the morning of departure. Syd also had to think about packing for the trip before she could actually pack for the trip.

Dad had his own problems to solve. He needed to install the storm shutters on the exterior windows of his house, just in case the first hurricane of the season decided to strike four months prematurely. He also needed to have the neighbors sign a notarized contract agreeing to pick up his mail during his three days away. This decision didn't come easy, by the way. Dad spent a fair amount of time debating whether to have the mail formally held by the US Postal Service before ultimately saddling his neighbor with the responsibility.

Uncle Bern and I did nothing outside of our daily routines.

CHAPTER 3

WASTING AWAY IN GERIATRICVILLE

Once the air travel arrangements to Las Vegas were set in nonrefundable stone (at least from my standpoint, having cast off travel insurance), Mom and Dad took a brief hiatus from further organizing the trip and returned to their day-to-day life in what I privately call Geriatricville. The long weekend was still about six months away, and they took some time to let their excitement and anticipation mount. They had only been to Vegas once since retiring to South Florida in 2003, and they were eager to return to the place where they briefly considered spending their golden years.

My mother transitioned beautifully into retirement, never manifesting a single ounce of regret. My last day of medical school coincided with Sydelle's last day of teaching New York City's impressionable youth; she and Gerry prepared to retire as we removed our caps and gowns. After spending thirty years making sure her students didn't lick too much lead paint off the walls, she was done. Her cronies at Public School 107 threw her a luncheon retirement party at a restaurant located not too far from the school. It was Syd's moment to bask in the glory of her occupational twilight, soaking up the adulation and jealousy of her colleagues.

Having hung up the chalk, Mom slept as late as she wished, lunched and noshed with the ladies, caught up on her needlepoint, kept the phone company's earnings reports ahead of projections, and started auditing classes at some of the local colleges. Dad continued to work selling insurance. He needed to keep himself occupied during the day, as the man never had any hobbies besides clipping coupons, filing miscellaneous paperwork, and finding new uses for duct tape.

Elyse and I were occupied in our own ways. Upon graduating from the Albert Einstein College of Medicine in 2001, we immediately left New York to start our residencies and newlywed lives together in Minneapolis. We left Bern to watch over his beloved New York Yankees along with an assurance that we would never, ever embrace the Minnesota Twins. I spent five years as a resident in otolaryngology—head and neck surgery (also known as ear, nose, and throat surgery), which led to a postgraduate yearlong fellowship in facial plastic surgery. Elyse devoted four years of her life to a residency in dermatology. Fortune prevailed, permitting us both to simultaneously train throughout these long years at the University of Minnesota. Destiny led us both to remain in Minnesota to establish our respective medical practices.

My parents' grand plan, though, was to spend their retirement in a warm climate where Mom's Raynaud's Disease could be perennially kept at bay. Shortly after Mom walked away from 107 in Queens, she and Dad began to explore possible options. The list was quickly whittled down to three warm-weather finalists—Las Vegas, Arizona, and Florida. Florida was always the leading candidate, but they exercised due diligence in throwing the other two locations temporarily into the mix.

Las Vegas was first excluded from contention due to constraints imposed by the United Federation of Teachers, the union that manages Sydelle's health care plan. It had something to do with either the network of physicians available in Vegas or the logistical impediments of arranging referrals to specialist physicians. To be fair to my parents, the quality of healthcare was a legitimate factor to consider in choosing a place to retire, just as new parents look at the quality of school districts when selecting a new home to purchase. If Syd sneezes the wrong way, she wants an otolaryngologist to examine her to ensure she doesn't have a bacterial sinus infection requiring a double course of the strongest oral antibiotics available, a neurosurgeon to evaluate her for potentially complicating pneumocephalus (air around the brain generated when a violent sneeze breaches the sinus walls), and a gynecologist to make sure that the pressure generated from the same sneeze hasn't exacerbated her uterine prolapse and her associated urinary frequency. She doesn't want her health insurance card burning a hole in her pocket like a surprise windfall wad of cash.

In the event of a stubbed toe, Mom basically wants the option to simultaneously consult with a podiatrist, dermatologist, orthopedic surgeon, and physical therapist. As a trained medical professional, I'd like to see a shaman summon the supernatural to convince her of the body's natural ability to heal. At any rate, Vegas quickly became untenable from the healthcare delivery standpoint. In retrospect, given the number of doctor visits my parents make per week, they made the right choice.

Arizona was next up on the chopping block. I forget which part of Arizona they were specifically considering; the Scottsdale area rings a bell. The thought of retiring to the Southwest initially seemed enchanting. The one hundred twenty degree summer days called out to Mom with the force of an industrial electromagnet. Images of being surrounded by an invisible, omnipresent electric blanket danced in her head. Icarus didn't stand a chance, but Sydelle would have thrived in that kind of heat.

Scottsdale bore no resemblance to any place either Mom or Dad had ever previously resided. It was for this reason that the Arizona plan collapsed. The Southwest was just too far away from everything comfortable and familiar. The time zone was different (Dad still occasionally asks me what time it is in Minnesota). The cuisine was different. The local accents were different (in that there were no accents). The names of the gas stations, banks, and grocery stores were all different. The flights back to the East Coast were inconvenient and long, and there weren't many direct flights to Minneapolis. The Arizona desert was just too much of a figurative sea of change (pun intended). It was all too foreign, too far outside of their East Coast comfort zone.

The Sunshine State was designated the Promised Land of retirement. In retrospect, the other options didn't really stand much of a chance. Florida had everything going for it, short of the inescapable fact that it was not New York. The weather was nearly perfect, hurricane season notwithstanding. There were plenty of like-minded east coast snowbirds that shared common upbringings and had the same New York accents. A plethora of direct flights from Fort Lauderdale and West Palm Beach provided crucial links back to Long Island and over to Minneapolis. Restaurants with wait staff crying out the multitude of daily early bird specials were as plentiful as the patrons' hearing aids struggling to amplify their voices.

If they had to leave New York for good, Florida was, in my view, an excellent choice for my parents' retirement. I was genuinely happy for them and the choice they made. But I was also pleased for my own reasons. I selfishly didn't want obligatory parental visits to interfere with the revelry Elyse and I enjoyed on our trips to Vegas. But more than that, I saw Florida, with all its palm trees, swimming pools, and beach resorts as offering a welcome respite from the hectic lives Elyse and I created in Minneapolis—especially in February. I supported their decision and urged them to move forward at whatever pace felt comfortable.

So Sydelle and Gerry set their myopic and presbyopic visions on the communities of Palm Beach County in South Florida. I'm referring to Delray Beach, Pompano Beach, West Palm Beach, Boynton Beach, and Boca Raton. A small horde of their friends had already purchased homes in these areas, and the reports back to Long Island were radiant. My parents would have been more likely to move to downtown Jakarta than to relocate to the panhandle or west coast of Florida.

Before deciding, they planned to spend a few weeks each winter in a different Palm Beach County community. That way they could determine the perfect pill-popping palace of pre-death that best-suited their fancy before taking the plunge. Basically, Syd and Gerry sought the Floridian equivalent of the Long Island ghetto in which I was raised. Now by "ghetto" I do not at all intend to convey the idea that I grew up in some impoverished, segregated, downtrodden community of an urban metropolis. I simply mean that I was raised in a community where there was a whole lot of uniformity and not a whole lot of diversity. It seemed entirely normal that nearly all of my childhood friends were Jewish. This was illustrated succinctly by the soft orange glow of electric menorahs in living room bay windows during Hanukkah. You had to look far and wide before coming across the occasional Christmas tree. Nearly everyone lived in modest two-story split-level homes with dark wooden paneling in the family room, kitchens decorated in yellow-orange-brown color schemes held over from the 1970s, and three bedrooms upstairs.

Nearly everyone had two parents who worked standard middle class jobs—mostly in primary school education and sales. My parents fit this mold perfectly: Sydelle taught elementary school, mostly kindergarten and second grade. Gerry sold insurance, initially for Prudential and later on for Allstate. We all wore the same types of clothes, which, in the 1980s involved lots of Champion brand sweatshirts and whitewashed jeans. Everyone listened to the same classic big hair rock bands: Motley Crue, Def Leppard, Guns N' Roses, and Poison. Country music was a myth on Long Island; no one was really sure if it truly existed.

The first winter my parents Lewis and Clarked their way into West Palm Beach occurred in 2003. Elyse and I were entrenched within our respective residency training programs. Mom and Dad found themselves smack in the middle of a full-on senior living community gold rush, a residential arthritic and osteoporotic equivalent of the running of the bulls in Pamplona. Brand-new housing developments were springing up everywhere they cast their gaze. Swamplands were converted into twenty-first century equivalents of medieval fiefdoms almost overnight. In the blink of an eye, whole towns sprang up, consisting of walled-off communities of a thousand-plus homes separated by strip malls. Each new community was more monstrous than the last, and residence in each came with a correspondingly steeper price tag than the last. Syd and Gerry were enveloped into this funnel cloud of boomtown hysteria; there was no escape. They caught the fever and purchased a brand-new cookie-cutter home that had yet to be built. It was the first, impulsive, spontaneous decision they ever made. Within twelve months, the house I grew up in on Long Island was sold. My parents became permanently entrenched in Geriatricville, moving into their new home with all of their belongings except a sieve with which one could pan for gold. They didn't need a sieve; they could find plenty of gold by accidentally stepping on lost jewelry at the bottom of their clubhouse pool.

Only my Uncle Bern remained to represent the family in New York. Eleven years older than his sister, Sydelle, Bern had been around the block enough to be quite comfortable in his own skin. Sure he was sad to see us fan out across the country as we went our separate ways. But he prized his independence and wished the same for Syd and Gerry.

In the decade or so since their relocation to Geriatricville, Elyse and I have visited often enough to appreciate the basic lay of the land. Each community comes emblazoned with a transporting name such as Valencia Shores, Versailles, and Isles at Wellington. Once you get past the names written in elaborate cursive on the facades, all of these communities distinctly resemble one another. Electric gates operated by key cards and supervised by "security guards" permit entry in the style of a medieval moat and drawbridge. As a car inches up to the guardhouse, residents and visitors alike are welcomed by perfectly manicured grounds and elaborate European-style fountains spouting gently arcing streams of bacteria-laden swamp water. Guests are obliged to stop at the gatehouse, where the semi-comatose security guard verifies their presence. While pleasant enough, these bastions of quasi law enforcement cannot help but be jaded by the utter monotony of their jobs. It would be far more stimulating to operate a toll both on the Jersey Turnpike in February, even without the bridge scandal in which Governor Chris Christie was recently embroiled.

Once cleared for entry, the electric gate ascends about as fast as those electric, motor-powered beige chairs that transport the infirm up and down home staircases. (Why are those chairs always beige? Just once, I'd love to see one in neon green or a zebra pattern.) Having crossed the threshold, you are progressively immersed into the warped Geriatricville subculture, just as Dante described the descent through the successive levels of hell. Behind the apparent serenity lurks pathology. While the community may technically boast fourteen different home floor plan variations, they may only differ in whether the attached garage is located to the left or to the right of the front door. A ceramic frog partially hidden within the shrubbery of the front lawn may be painted lime green with mustard yellow accents or mustard yellow with lime green accents. In practice, all of the houses on a block look the same, all blocks on a street look identical and all streets are geometrically positioned with respect to the main clubhouse. The street names even sound the same: Shores Avenue, Shores Way, Shoreview

Place, Coastal Road, Coastal Road East, North Central Coastal Road, etc. As long as the lone fixed point of reference that is the clubhouse remains in your line of sight, you have a fighting chance of getting to your destination. Otherwise, you're screwed until nightfall, when Polaris can guide your course. GPS devices don't function within these Bermuda triangles. My theory is that the hearing aid frequencies and pacemaker circuitries together scramble the satellite brains of the GPS systems. I'd love to see how long it would take Ferdinand Magellan to circumnavigate any one of these communities in broad daylight.

Some of the most highly coveted plots of real estate come complete with "lake views." Apparently, in the minds of the community developers, a lake is defined as a shallow, man-made stagnant swamp into which an unsuspecting alligator is thrown against his will to live out the rest of his existence looking for frogs and salamanders to munch. Boating, fly-fishing, swimming, and water skiing are all inconceivable activities in these lakes. But if gazing out of your living room window to the sight of a hose-filled mud tub gives you pleasure, go ahead and fork over the extra tens of thousands of dollars for this option.

The clubhouse is the lifeblood of Geriatricville culture. It's the glue holding the social fabric of the community together. The golf course and tennis courts are managed through the clubhouse, as are the schedules of the poker room, crochet club, oil painting club, and homeowner's association board. All nighttime and weekend entertainment is performed on the clubhouse stages.

If the clubhouse is the social core, then the outdoor swimming pool is the nucleus of the core. Uncle Bern always criticized the swimming pool at Geriatricville due to its lack of a diving board. I suspect that this was a conscious omission on the part of the architects and developers, given the limited pulmonary reserves of the homeowners combined with a 30 percent risk of popping a cerebral aneurysm or dislocating a hip with each attempted dive.

Once in a great while, some man or woman can actually be seen swimming in the pool. Most of the time, the pool scene uncannily resembles a high school hallway lined with rows of wall lockers adorned with those multicolored Master combination locks. Cliques of men, cliques of women, and cliques of couples wade together in clusters about the pool. An aerial shot would make them appear like a bunch of matzo balls floating in a vat of low sodium chicken broth. The neon-colored Aqua Noodles keeping afloat those in the deeper parts of the pool and the simmering water temperature bolster the soup imagery.

The gossip-laden discourse in the pool centers around death and destruction: updates on old diagnoses, newly rendered diagnoses, recent deaths, impending deaths, doctors visited within the past week, doctor visits scheduled in the upcoming week, and afflictions which modern medicine cannot yet identify. No eavesdropping is needed to overhear these conversations; hearing aids aren't waterproof.

"Every day at about 3:15 p.m., I get this throbbing pain in my left bunion that shoots directly into the right side of my pancreas. At the same time, both of my lower eyelids twitch. I went to see my internist last month about it. He told me that all of my blood work came back normal and that I have the heart of an eighty-year-old. But this just doesn't seem right to me. I'm considering going for a second opinion. What do you think?"

"Did you hear about what happened to Estelle this past Thursday? What a terrible thing to happen to such a gem of a woman. A debilitating stroke three years ago, and now another one three days ago? Such a pity. The first stroke left her weak and feeble on her left side. She never recovered full strength in her left arm and leg. Can you imagine what might happen if this new stroke cripples the right side permanently? The poor thing might become an invalid. I heard she may be discharged from the hospital tomorrow, but they don't know whether she'll be able to come directly home or spend a few weeks recovering her strength at one of those awful transitional care facilities."

"We're going to miss the meeting of our knitting club this week, so that we can pay our respects at Saul's funeral. He was only seventy-seven years old! He passed far too soon and far before his time. And the way he died? My God! One minute, you're just sitting on the toilet, taking care of your business. The next minute, your head hits the hard tile floor during a fainting spell and that's it. Dead, from a brain hemorrhage brought on by a bout of constipation. What a way to go. Norma is devastated, just devastated. I hope she decides to stay here in Florida, because the rest of her family is in New Jersey. Now she's all alone here, so who knows?"

"Did you schedule your TURP yet? Well, don't worry about it too much. What does it stand for? Trans-something prostate removal, I think. At any rate, I had mine done about five years ago. It wasn't too bad. There was some searing, burning pain that makes you think your core is going to split in two. And of course there was some bleeding initially. All of that goes away after a week or so. The pain wasn't there all the time, but every time you try to urinate during those first few days, it feels like someone is twisting a hot switchblade through your rectum."

"Where should we go for an early bird special tonight?"

~

By the grace of God, none of the women at the pool wear two-piece bathing suits. Horizontally striped suits are similarly scarce. It would take a stack of *Penthouse* magazines and biannual visits to Amsterdam and Bangkok to counteract the visual apocalypse silk-screened onto my retinas, should these women decide to wear string bikinis while partaking in a rigorous aqua aerobics session. I oftentimes wish, though, that the homeowners' association board would require the men to wear two-piece bathing suits. I'd vote for the maximum fabric to cover up the sagging man boobs, billowing chest hair, bear-like carpet of back hair, and faded blue-green military tattoos of entwined reptiles and scantily clad women draped over ship anchors. Pent up intestinal gas left over from lunches of hot dogs and baked beans maintains their buoyancy against the weight of their solid gold necklaces and bracelets.

The homeowners' association board is a legislative body that comes straight out of a 1990s television sitcom. Larry David could not have scripted his characters' condominium association board any better. While Seinfeld pre-dated the construction of Geriatricville, a "chicken or egg" scenario comes to mind when observing the Geriatricville homeowners' association. Similar to the way the Freemasons govern, outsiders like me are not privy to the inner workings of this well-oiled machine. Nevertheless,

I can bear witness to the swift hand of its operational machine. If the US Congress functioned like this board, Obamacare would have been pared down into a twenty-page bill that passed through both the House and the Senate in about four days flat.

I took Daphne down to visit Sydelle and Gerry when she was about four years old. Zach stayed back in Minneapolis with Elyse, having just celebrated his first birthday a few months prior. After playing in the pool with Daphne for a couple of hours, we decided to take a quick dip in the hot tub for a few minutes before heading back to Mom and Dad's house. Daph loves hot tubs. She bounded over to the edge of the circular whirlpool with the typical exuberance of a four-year-old girl. After she waited for me to catch up, we stepped gingerly into the hot tub and sat down. An elderly man was already inside. We were polite; there was no yelling, splashing, whining, or crying. Daphne just sat on my lap, playing with the bubbles and white foam percolating circumferentially around her. Yet from the moment we sat down, I felt the uncomfortable glare of this other guy in the hot tub. I never learned his name, but let's just call him Morrie. At first, I thought that perhaps my daughter reminded him of one of his own grandchildren. Then I wondered if Morrie was trying to connect us with any of his Geriatricville acquaintances. I was wrong on both accounts. About two minutes into our hot tub soak, he wagged an arthritic finger at a sign posted a few feet away. The sign stipulated that minors using the hot tub were required to be accompanied by an adult. A perfectly reasonable rule, I thought. It then forewarned that prolonged use of the hot tub could potentially prove hazardous to the health of small children.

"Thanks. I got it," I said looking back to Morrie.

"You know, your daughter really shouldn't be in here," Morrie replied.

Attempting to be friendly and polite, I replied, "She just loves hot tubs. We're in the midst of a severe winter back home in Minneapolis. We'll only be a few minutes longer."

Morrie was clearly not satisfied. "You're risking the health and welfare of your child by keeping her in the hot tub," he said while judgmentally cocking his head to the side.

Let's be fair and consider exactly where ol' Morrie was coming from.

With prolonged immersion in a hot tub, the body's core temperature rises. In a compensatory attempt to dissipate the excess heat, peripheral blood vessels in the arms and legs dilate. This places proportionately more blood in the extremities and less blood in the carotid arteries feeding the brain. The relative drop in blood pressure can, in turn, predispose a healthy person to a sense of lightheadedness or, at worst, a fainting spell upon rapidly rising to exit the hot tub. I suppose there is a theoretical risk of an unstable arrhythmia or heart attack in an elderly person with a history of any combination of open-heart surgery, pacemaker placement, arrhythmia requiring blood thinners, and refractory high blood pressure requiring a medley of medications to control. Prudence is in order if these ticking time bombs continue to stuff their coronary arteries full of eggs Benedict and cannoli. The last time I checked, Daphne's pediatrician did not feel as though she needed an angiogram or cardiac catheterization procedure, so I decided to silence Morrie.

"While I appreciate your concern, I am a responsible father who is perfectly capable of deciding the appropriate amount of time my daughter can stay in a hot tub. Furthermore, as a licensed physician with a double board certification, I'm guessing that I know a little more about the physiology of the human heart than you. Are you a retired chief of cardiology or cardiothoracic surgery, by chance?"

Morrie didn't say a word. He just frowned disapprovingly, the contempt in his eyes growing with each jet of bubbles floating by.

Five minutes later, Daphne and I strode confidently out of the hot tub. I told her to splash about a bit on the way out. But she sensed it wasn't proper etiquette and took the moral high ground. Stopping for a moment along the tiled outer edge of the pool, I looked Morrie directly in the eye and said, "No need to use the poolside emergency cardiac defibrillator today. Shall we say same time, same place tomorrow?" While these words were admittedly petty, they made me feel a little better.

I may have won the battle, but Morrie won the war. He had the last laugh. The situation was promptly weighed and measured by the homeowners' association board. The board deliberated, voted, and acted. By the time I returned to the pool two years later (this time with both Daphne and

Zachary in tow), a new sign had been impaled into the ground beside the hot tub. In large capital letters, the sign forbade anyone under the age of fifteen from setting foot in the hot tub. As I feared that Mom and Dad would be ostracized from the pool scene if they incurred the wrath of the board, I chose not to test the overheated waters.

~

Elyse and I would never, ever consider retiring to a place like Geriatricville. It's just not our style. We dream about returning to a modest apartment in Manhattan, from which we can explore the world. But Mom and Dad are happy in Florida, and that makes me really happy. Throughout their working lives in New York, they envisioned exactly this type of retirement, and to see it come to fruition is a wonderful thing for me to behold. They fit seamlessly into the Geriatricville scene, like they truly belong there. As long as they both continue to thoroughly enjoy their retirement, that's good enough for me. I'm happy to visit, the kids are happy to visit, and we take pleasure in knowing how very much Mom and Dad love and appreciate our visits. In this context, the culture shock of Geriatricville is really no price for me to pay at all. Plus, every now and then we get to visit on neutral territory, in a place like Las Vegas.

CHAPTER 4

HOUDINI, HOFFA, AND . . . UNCLE BERN?

Upon arriving at the Minneapolis-St. Paul International Airport for the Vegas trip, I was immediately greeted with the news that my flight was delayed. I reacted ambivalently; I couldn't decide if this news was good or bad. On the one hand, the four of us only had a few days together in Vegas and I wasn't willing to cede the first day to the airline industry. On the other hand, the prospect of having a couple of extra hours alone with no agenda was highly appealing. Unencumbered free time was an exceedingly rare commodity for me, between the incessant demands of my surgical practice and my wish to be a complete husband to Elyse and father to Daphne and Zach.

I sauntered into the nearest bar and ordered a draft of whatever was on tap. Before immersing myself in a novel, I dutifully left a voice mail message on Mom and Dad's cell phone, having learned that the one-hour delay was due to a mechanical issue with the plane's on-board plumbing system. Since global thermonuclear war was not impending, Syd's phone was naturally powered off, rendering voicemail the only option.

An hour and a half later, my plane casually taxied to the runway before returning to the gate, this time due to an undisclosed electrical problem. Back inside the terminal yet again, my quick check of CNN revealed no new global instability. So I recorded a second voicemail on my parents' shared flip phone apprising them of the now painfully stagnating situation in Minnesota.

I finally landed in Las Vegas at about 4:00 p.m., a mere two hours and forty minutes late. Uncle Bern landed on time at 12:45 p.m. Syd and Gerry landed on time at 3:30 p.m. I thought it plausible that my parents were still somewhere in McCarran International Airport. After all, Syd conservatively requires eleven minutes just to urinate in unfamiliar surroundings. However, I couldn't find either of them in the baggage claim area. Bern was nowhere to be found, his flight having landed over three hours earlier. My parents' damn flip phone was still off and I was pissed off. Their phone should have been turned off en route to Vegas. The phone should have been fully charged, powered on, and accessible enough to be answered while their plane was taxiing to the gate. "Screw it," I said to myself as I grabbed my luggage and walked outside.

There were at least a thousand people ahead of me in the ninety-five degree heat at the taxi stand outside the airport. Snaking through the switchbacks, one couldn't help but pick up snippets of conversations about fortunes waiting to be amassed at the craps tables, last-minute bachelor party plans, reunions with colleagues at upcoming trade conventions, general drunkenness, the latest designer drugs, and other forms of debauchery. About twenty-five minutes after wading into this sea of humanity, I finally got the call; Syd and Gerry had decided to check in with me. As the phone rang, I felt like an elite college football player anxiously awaiting a call from an NFL team during the waning moments of the last round of the NFL draft. I thought about letting the call go directly to voicemail out of pure spite. But I knew that even though they kept their phone off, they truly didn't intend to make life difficult for me. I answered. Mom and Dad were in their rental car on the way to the hotel. I must have missed them by five lousy minutes.

After explaining that I was still at the airport, we realized that none of us knew the whereabouts of almost eighty-one-year-old Uncle Bern. Remember that Bern had no cell phone. We weren't even certain that Bern knew which hotel we were staying at, since I was supposed to meet him at the airport. I begrudgingly left the taxi stand line and went back inside the airport. I performed one last cursory sweep of the baggage claim area without locating Uncle Bern. I went so far as to have him paged in the airport terminal—twice. It should come as no surprise to learn that both of these attempts failed miserably. There was a greater chance of finding Jimmy Hoffa than my uncle at this point. Recalling Bern's generally combative nature, I feared he might have been arrested.

I returned to the exponentially expanding taxi stand line. The ambient temperature still exceeded ninety degrees. I was overdressed, having arrived from the Minneapolis March wearing multiple layers of wool-based clothing. Combined with my mounting annoyance, the sweat started pouring off my brow. I found myself sandwiched between a woman dressed in chest-to-toe skintight pink leopard print who was hollering a steady stream of profanity into her cell phone and a guy wearing a vintage ET T-shirt that was similarly skintight. Thirty minutes later, as I melted into the pleasantly air-conditioned confines of a cab, Syd called back with an update. She and Gerry had located Uncle Bern. He was safe and sound, having a grand old time watching sports highlights in the hotel bar with a tall glass of beer. Exhaling in relief and willfully ignoring the fact that the cab's backseat was inexplicably sticky, I leaned back against the coffee-stained upholstery and let my sweat evaporate in the air-conditioning.

As I decompressed in the taxi, I figured that Mom and Dad had arrived at the Paris Las Vegas hotel and immediately started their search for Uncle Bern. I was right; later that evening, Bern described all that happened during the time it took me to get from the airport to the hotel. He spared no details.

Apparently, Mom and Dad logically searched for Bern in the most likely places he would be: the hotel bar and the coffee shop. Sure enough, they found him contentedly sipping a beer in the lobby bar. Upon sighting his brother-in-law, Gerry hollered out from clear across the lobby, acting like Bern was a five year-old about to step into the path of oncoming highway traffic.

"Bernard! Stay there, Bernard! Don't move! Stay there! We're coming over! Coming over!"

From his tone, it was clear Dad feared that Bern had been sold into slave labor aboard some dilapidated fishing boat in the South China Sea.

"Why the hell are you so worked up, Gerry?" Bern asked as Dad sprinted across the lobby. Sydelle lagged behind, having last sprinted in a former life.

"Planes got all screwed up! Harley was stranded in Minnesota! Damn airlines! Mechanical problems! Delayed in Minneapolis twice! Plane malfunctioned! We didn't know if you could get to the hotel by yourself!"

"I'm a grown man, aren't I, Gerry?"

"Yeah, sure. But—"

Bern cut off his brother-in-law.

"Settle down, Gerry! At ease, soldier! I survived basic training, didn't I? I was prepared to serve in the infantry in Korea, wasn't I?"

"Yeah, yeah, Bernard. But Harley was supposed to meet you at the airport."

"I know that, Gerry. Sydelle only reminded me about sixteen times last week. The United States Army told me that my IQ was high enough to qualify for Officer Candidate School, remember? But Harley wasn't there and I needed a cold brew. What should I have done, curl up into the fetal position and cry for my mommy?"

"We're just relieved to see that you're safe and sound, Bern," Sydelle finally chimed in as she sauntered up to the bar.

"I'm a grown man! I can handle myself! Now why don't you both sit down, calm down, and order a couple of stiff drinks? You won't believe what happened on my way to LaGuardia."

Uncle Bern traveled according to his own rules, and those rules were not necessarily commensurate with the regulations established by the Federal Aviation Administration. For example, in Bern's brain, the jetway doors can't close unless he has sixteen ounces of coffee in his hand and a submarine sandwich filled with at least two kinds of meat secured in the crook of his elbow. But his difficulties with airports started long before he boarded any plane. Bern and airports never got along. I think he associated air travel with the Korean War; the first time he boarded a plane was to travel to Hawaii for basic training. He never truly felt comfortable in airports, much preferring the feel of tires on asphalt.

"I ran into a little trouble with an unsuspecting taxicab driver in the parking lot of LaGuardia this morning," Bern said with a smile.

"Trouble? What kind of trouble? I didn't hear about any trouble at the airports today."

"Damn, it Gerry! If you shut your mouth for a minute, I'll tell you exactly what kind of trouble! At ease, soldier! At ease!"

"Let him talk, Gerry," Sydelle said. "Let the man talk."

"Okay, okay, Bernard. Sorry."

Bern glared at his brother-in-law without blinking, silently warning Gerry to cede the floor. Taking the hint, Dad caught the bartender's attention and ordered himself a draft of beer as well and a cup of tea for my mother.

"I drove to the airport but was feeling a little edgy, because I was overdue for a cup of coffee and a snack. I got even more annoyed when I couldn't find a spot in the airport parking lot. After methodically circling up and down the rows of parked cars, I finally saw someone tossing luggage into a trunk. I rolled to a stop but left enough room for the car to comfortably pull out. Following the rules of parking lot etiquette, I staked my claim to the spot by turning on my blinker."

Bern paused momentarily, shooting another steely look at Dad to keep him quiet.

"Out of nowhere, a taxi approaching from the opposite direction turned into the empty spot, ignoring my blinker. I couldn't believe it! At first, I gave the taxi driver the benefit of the doubt. Since the spot was located near the end of the row, I figured that the cabbie saw it just as he turned the corner. I figured it was an honest mistake; it could have happened to anyone. So as the driver got out of his cab I rolled down my window and told him that he had mistakenly stolen my spot."

Sydelle detected a mischievous spark in Bern's eye and a smile forming in the corner of his mouth. Knowing her brother, she thought it was probable that Bern may not have come across in the kindest, most genteel manner in the eyes of this stranger.

Bern continued. "So I said, 'Hey, what do you think you're doing? You just stole my spot! I was waiting for this spot. My signal was on.'"

"Maybe he was in a rush." Mom gave the cabbie the benefit of the doubt.

"Never mind that. My time is just as important, Sydelle! The cabbie nonchalantly shrugged me off, turned his back, and started to walk toward the terminal. He even tucked the newspaper under his arm. I wasn't willing to let it go."

"What's the big deal, Bernard?" Mom was non-confrontational by nature.

"It's the principle, Sydelle! It's a big deal to me! So I asked that bastard, I said to him, 'Hey, are you deaf? Where the hell do you think you're going? I just told you that you took my parking space!' Now get this. You know what he said to me, Gerry? He said, 'What are you going to do about it, you old Jew?' Can you believe that?"

Gerry gasped. Syd's mouth silently gaped open as she rolled her eyes.

"In that dank parking lot, don't ask me how the cabbie had the wherewithal to glance at me and instantly figure out my heritage while the ownership of the parking spot was being hotly contested. I could have more easily understood it if the driver called me an 'old man' or an 'old fart.' It only takes a quick glimpse to determine a person's relative age. But don't you think it takes considerably more insight to determine the ancestry of a Caucasian man with whom you're arguing in a dark parking lot? To be fair, that cabbie was probably Arabic, but I saw no reason to bring up *his* heritage."

Bern shifted his weight to lean against the bar with his elbow. He took a big swig from his glass as he settled into the meat of the story. Gerry helped himself to a bowl of pretzels on the bar.

"The point of no return came and went once the word 'Jew' spilled out of the cabbie's mouth. You both know that I'm a proud Jew. It doesn't matter that the only times in my life I set foot in a synagogue were for my bris, my bar mitzvah, and Harley's bar mitzvah. That doesn't matter. Being Jewish is part of my makeup, part of my constitution. I'll tell you the same thing while eating either a BLT sandwich or a salami and cheese on rye. It doesn't matter."

Bern didn't need to make this last statement. Aside from the gastronomic function that Judaism played in his life, Sydelle and Gerry saw only one other outward manifestation of the role of religion in Bern's life—a race card of sorts—and they both knew it implicitly. He didn't actually practice Judaism, but he resolutely defended his inalienable right to practice it.

Bern's unique version of faith was not open to judgment or interpretation by anyone, let alone a random taxicab driver who clearly subscribed to an entirely different religion.

"'You come over here and I'll show you exactly what I'm going to do about it!' I shot back to that lousy cabbie."

Dad stopped drinking his beer mid-sip. Syd stopped blowing on her hot tea, which she had been encouraging to cool up until this point. The better part of a decade probably passed since the last time a patron of the Paris Hotel lobby bar ordered hot herbal tea during cocktail hour on a Thursday when it was still well over ninety degrees outside.

"'I dare you!' he said. The cabbie challenged me! Can you believe that? He dropped the newspaper he was carrying and walked toward my car. I knew I could protect myself. When I finished basic training in the army, Colonel White told me I'd be good until at least eighty.'"

"You didn't, Bernard. Please tell me you didn't get yourself into another fistfight." Syd didn't need her brother's confirmation. She already knew the answer.

"You're goddamn right I did, Sydelle! That bastard! I got out of my car and mixed it up with the cabbie—he was only about half my age. I was a gentleman; I let him throw the first punch. It barely grazed the side of my jaw before landing harmlessly on my shoulder. I threw the rest of the punches—all of them. I landed jabs to his cheekbones and body blows to his midsection before finishing him off with an uppercut to the jaw. The cabbie didn't know what hit him; the fight was over in seconds. At the end of the affair, the cabbie was a bloodied heap lying on the asphalt. He went down for the count, Gerry!"

Bern knew he held Syd and Gerry spellbound. He shadowboxed the specific combination of punches he threw so as to give his audience a visual replay of the fight.

"A narrow stream of blood trickled down the side of his face from a gash near his right eyebrow. Black eyes were spreading across his rapidly swelling eyelids. The bridge across his upper teeth was also knocked loose. While still cowering on the floor with me towering over him, the cabbie dialed nine-one-one on his cell phone. I stood there motionless in a white-knuckled boxing pose for the two or three minutes it took the NYPD to arrive."

Pretzel crumbs began to spew out of Dad's mouth. "The cops came? You could have been arrested, Bernard! What would you have done then? This isn't some playground in the Bronx in 1941. You can't behave like that in airports these days! You could get locked up!"

"I was willing to chance it, Gerry! That racist bastard had it coming to him! Anyway, two squad cars arrived within thirty seconds of one another, sirens blaring, and lights flashing. One pair of cops escorted me back to my car, while the other pair tended to the wounded cabbie. I told the cops that I was a medic in the Korean War, but they told me that my services weren't necessary. We each gave the cops our own version of the altercation. After huddling up for a couple of minutes, the cops were surprised to learn that our reports were nearly identical."

With her brother sipping a beer directly in front of her, Mom realized that Bern didn't get himself arrested. She felt comfortable enough to start sipping her tea.

"When the police brought the two of us back together, the cabbie said that he wanted to press charges. Can you imagine that, Sydelle?"

"How can you blame him, Bernard? You physically assaulted the man." Sydelle had a habit of restating the obvious.

"The cops were quick to remind the cabbie that he admitted calling me an old Jew. They also pointed out that I was about double his age. The cabbie persisted, though. I give him credit for that. He hollered back to the cops that I assaulted him and that I knocked his teeth out."

"He can sue you for damages, Bernard! You need a lawyer! Or an attorney! Maybe a litigator!" Gerry exclaimed. My father had a penchant for assuming the worst theoretical outcome was already a foregone reality.

"He can sue me if he wants, Gerry. I don't have much worth taking. Listen though! Just be quiet and let me finish. The cops frankly told the cabbie that he got exactly what he deserved. They told him he was lucky I didn't knock him out cold and into the middle of next week."

"They did not, Bernard." Syd clearly thought that the response from the NYPD was a bit far-fetched.

"So help me, Sydelle, that's exactly what they said! I don't lie, Sydelle. But listen, it gets better still. The cabbie asked the cops who was going to pay his medical bills to fix his top teeth, and the cops told him to sign up for a few extra shifts behind the wheel next month. He got no empathy from the police."

Bern laughed from ear to ear as he drained the last drops from the bottom of his beer glass. "The taxi driver reluctantly got back into his cab and drove away. He didn't seem too happy with the outcome. The cops clapped me on the back, told me to keep out of trouble, and left the scene. My blinker was still flashing, so I promptly rolled my car right into the vacated parking space and walked into the terminal."

~

I walked into the lobby of the Paris Hotel as Bern finished his story. My family was positioned in the absolute center of the bar. It was easy to spot Syd, as she was the only person decked out in a knee-length wool coat zipped up to the neck. Smiles and hugs abounded. I reluctantly permitted Mom to smear some of her recently applied, too-red lipstick onto my cheek as she greeted me. Only half an hour ago, I had been mentally preparing the missing persons report I would have to file with the Vegas police to locate Bern. Now we were all together at the hotel, safe and sound, ready to properly celebrate Mom's seventieth and Bern's eightieth-and-eleven-months birthdays.

Wasting no time, Bern repeated his story of pummeling of the cab driver for my benefit. It was vintage Bern, and I thoroughly relished every moment of the story. That day in the parking lot, one random cab driver learned the hard way how proud my uncle was of his Jewish heritage. It's become one of my favorite Uncle Bern stories to tell. People get a kick out of hearing how a guy in his eighties kicked the tar out of another guy in the prime of his life. They like the David versus Goliath scenario, Bern's feistiness, and the way the cops meted out justice. For me, though, the story's significance goes beyond age disparity, religious pride, and the loss of a few teeth. While I'm equally proud of my Jewish heritage, I've fortunately never experienced the brash anti-Semitism Uncle Bern dealt with at LaGuardia airport. I'm non-confrontational by nature, probably to a fault. I almost always take what I consider to be the moral high ground to avoid a fight. Perceived insults roll off my back; the people who say them tend to be either ignorant or oblivious to the fact that they insulted me. Maybe they simply lack the social graces to keep their mouths shut. Plus, fistfights and surgeons go together about as well as ice skates and a sandy beach. But stories like Bern's are important for me to keep fresh in my mind because there's a difference between ignoring some ignorant schmuck and letting someone walk all over you. Bern's actions remind me that pride must not always be swallowed. It's okay to stand up for yourself, your honor, and your beliefs.

CHAPTER 5

OF COURSE THERE'S SUCH A THING AS A FREE LUNCH

Since Mom coordinated the air travel, I had volunteered to spearhead the hotel, dinner, and entertainment reservations for the Vegas fete. This arrangement proved mutually beneficial. At that point in my life, having spent a decade in training after college and another half-decade building my medical practice, Mom and Dad knew that I stayed in fairly nice hotels and dined in similarly nice restaurants when out of town. Neither Elyse nor I routinely travelled for work, and we both worked hard enough to treat ourselves during the few trips we did take. We don't seek out the most expensive hotels and restaurants simply to say that we've stayed and dined at the best. Oftentimes, we don't particularly care for these types of establishments and avoid them intentionally. At the same time, we're neither ashamed nor embarrassed to like what we like, and we have no trouble paying extra to maximize our enjoyment while on vacation.

Sydelle and Gerry, on the other hand, vacation on a more modest budget that matches their own comfort level. Bern was still just happy to be along for the ride. That's part of what made Bern such a terrific uncle. Always up for a good time, he lived in the moment and for the moment, cherishing the memories that followed. He'd rather spend an extra twenty-five dollars buying another round of beers for his buddies than expend the time and effort needed to save the same amount on a hotel room.

I ultimately selected the Paris Las Vegas hotel for its central location on Las Vegas Boulevard. I knew that it would fall comfortably within everyone's budget. Syd was quite pleased, as she enjoys just about anything with a European theme. Gerry was also content once I broadcast that I capitalized upon an Internet-only 20 percent discount on our rooms. A 20 percent savings translated into 40 percent more enjoyment in Dad's mind. As per their entrenched preferences with all hotels, I secured quiet, non-smoking rooms on a high floor as far away as possible from the elevator and as far away as possible from the ice machine. The staff at the Paris graciously agreed to accommodate the myriad requests. I emailed the room costs and specifications to Mom and Dad within forty-eight hours of receiving confirmation from the hotel. This didn't stop them from calling the hotel to guarantee that these specifications did not irretrievably disappear into the digital abyss of the hotel's computer system.

~

Sydelle and Gerry tend to stay at the same hotels when they routinely travel to places like Minneapolis and New York. This is only partially because they are creatures of habit. To some extent, we all find some comfort in our routines. To have a routine is to be a normal human. To be unable to waver from a routine under any circumstance is another matter. Throughout his adult working life, Dad packed a sliced turkey breast sandwich for lunch every Monday, Wednesday, and Friday, complemented by a Muenster cheese sandwich every Tuesday and Thursday. This regimen never varied. Ever. I never saw a roast beef, chicken salad, or salami sandwich thrown into his brown paper lunch bag. Ever. If NASA landed me in the middle of my childhood kitchen following a two-month stint on the International Space Station, I could have told you beyond a shadow of a doubt what day of the week it was simply by watching Dad pack his lunch.

Sydelle is equally predictable. Lipstick goes on following an evening meal out, even if she's going directly home and straight to bed. Raw fruit taken out of the refrigerator crisper drawer gets nuked in the microwave before it gets eaten. Their idiosyncrasies can be listed off ad infinitum, like the laundry list of side effects printed on the paper insert that accompanies virtually any prescription medication.

So other than familiarity, why stay in the same hotel over and over again when visiting a city like Minneapolis? Convenience? Nope. The proximity to my house? Incorrect. The location in the bustling downtown area? Irrelevant. The fantastic personal service? Not a chance. Bed linens with high thread counts? Doubtful.

Free rooms. That's the answer. Who says there's no such thing as a free lunch? You can debate the existence of the Ark of the Covenant and the Holy Grail until you are blue in the face. But the free hotel room exists on this earth, should you be able to muster the mettle to seek it out and grasp it by the keycard-entry doorknob. Elyse and I have stayed at nice hotels under a "stay four nights, get a fifth night free" promotional special. But the terms under which Sydelle and Gerry stay free are neither advertised nor special. They're not comped like the high rollers in Vegas. They're not cashing in credit card reward points or hotel chain reward points. And the traditional baker's dozen does not apply to the hotel industry; paying for twelve nights does not get you an automatic complimentary thirteenth. Mom and Dad earn free nights the old fashioned way—through a solid day's worth of hard work complaining to management. An unjustified sense of entitlement whisked into a cast iron pot of unrealistic expectations doesn't hurt the effort either. Complaints issued long enough, vociferously enough, and often enough usually result in a free room. As a duo, they average about one free night for every 4.6 nights registered as guests of a particular hotel. A list of slights that will deliver a night's stay gratis according to my parents has never before been formally tabulated. These wrongdoings exist as a loose collection of theoretical possibilities in the recesses of their minds, ready to be brought into the public domain should any actually occur. They appear in print now for the first time:

- Too much noise in the hallway after 10:00 p.m.

- Too much noise in the adjacent room after 10:00 p.m.

- Too much noise in the hallway before 7:00 a.m.

- Too much noise in the adjacent room before 7:00 a.m.

- Failure of management to promptly stifle excess hallway noise, once formally alerted to its presence.

- Room located too close to the ice machine, when a room far away from the ice machine was requested.

- Room located too close to the elevators, when a room far away from the elevators was requested.

- Room located on a floor too close to ground level, when a room close to the clouds was requested.

- Room overlooking a major street/intersection, when a room overlooking a quieter side street was requested.

- Room temperature did not rise to eighty-four degrees within fifteen minutes of turning off the air conditioner and cranking the thermostat up to the maximum heat level.

- Extra towels were not delivered to the room within fifteen minutes of placing the request with the housekeeping department.

- Extra blankets were not delivered to the room.

- Extra pillows were not delivered to the room within fifteen minutes of placing the request with the housekeeping department.

- Delivered extra pillows were stuffed with feather down, rather than the requested hypoallergenic alternative.

- Original pillows were stuffed with feather down, rather than the requested hypoallergenic alternative.

- Bathroom sink faucet leaked at a rate exceeding one extra drop per ten minutes.

- The hot water tap on the bathroom sink did not get hot enough.

- The hot water tap on the bathroom sink did not stay hot long enough.

- The cold water tap on the bathroom sink was too cold.

Within this smorgasbord of complaints, the ice machine deserves special mention. According to Sydelle, the ice machine is an evil contraption; it is a manifestation of the devil incarnate. The bubonic plague mercilessly terrorizing the European landscape in the Middle Ages is but a gentle summer evening's breeze off the Nantucket coast compared with the horrors of the ice machine. No good can possibly be associated with the ice machine. If you asked Sydelle to conjure an image of hell on earth, it would include imprisonment in an ice-machine factory. Afflicted by Raynaud's Disease, there's no place for ice in Sydelle's life. She gets cold just watching the figure skating competition during the Winter Olympics. Theoretically, hotel ice machines invite additional traffic in the hallways about their immediate vicinities. Ice scooping generates noise that can interfere with one's sleep cycle. Lastly, who can forget that the handle of the ice machine will undoubtedly harbor teeming quantities of the rhinoviruses that trigger Mom's self-professed phobia of the common cold.

Like a Vegas slot machine that yields an elusive million-dollar jackpot just often enough to comply with the bare minimums set forth by the Nevada Gaming Commission, a hotel stay will rarely be marred by an unforeseen, unpleasant event that truly justifies a free night. Elyse and I scored a free night once in Puerto Rico upon discovering that we were sharing our room with an infestation of ants. Mom and Dad have scored a free night legitimately as well. The trouble comes with wading through all the preposterous grievances until the real mishap comes to light.

~

Back in the lobby bar of the Paris hotel in Las Vegas, Gerry was raring to go like a racehorse corralled in the starting gate. He was a bundle of nerves, the thoughts of his nearly lost brother-in-law still ricocheting around in his brain. The story of Bern's morning fistfight had sent a vicarious adrenaline rush surging through his veins. We left Bern to settle up at the bar and walked toward the reception area. The myriad sound effects from the slot machines disrupted Dad's focus. He stopped dead in his tracks.

"Sydelle! What's that noise, Sydelle?"

"It came from one of the slot machines, Gerry."

"Slot machines? Which slot machines? How do you know it came from a slot machine?"

You would think the man had heard something truly extraordinary, like a braying donkey or a howling pack of wolves in the middle of the casino.

"I don't know which slot machine, Gerry. There are quite a few here, in case you haven't noticed."

"It's the Wheel of Fortune slot machine, Dad." I had no idea which slot machine specifically distracted my father, but that was of no importance. As long as I came up with some plausible explanation, it would satisfy him. "This isn't your first time in a casino. Let's just keep moving. I promise you'll have plenty of time to get acclimated after you set up shop in the penny slots area."

"Penny slots? Where do you see the penny slots? How do you know where the penny slots are, Harley?"

I should have kept my mouth shut. Mentioning the penny slots was a mistake.

"I don't specifically see the penny slots, Dad. This is a big casino. Ninety percent of the casino floor is covered with slot machines. Don't worry. I'm sure they have penny slots here. Don't worry. We'll find them. Let's just stay focused and get ourselves checked into the hotel, okay?"

Gerry resumed walking. I silently prayed that his hotel room met with his expectations. The reservations at the Paris were all made in my name; I wondered what it would take for the Paris to blacklist me from a future stay. Then I recalled that the Caesars Entertainment Corporation owned the Paris, in addition to Bally's, Caesars Palace, Harrah's, and the Rio. Plus it was a well-known fact that the Vegas hotels and casinos routinely shared mutually beneficial information with each other. I felt my face flush as I pictured myself barred from vast sections of the Strip. What would happen if Dad found some feather down pillows atop his bed?

CHAPTER 6

EVEN LEONA HELMSLEY WOULD HAVE APOLOGIZED

Even though the Paris hotel reservations were listed under my name, Dad felt compelled to accompany me as I strolled up to the check-in counters. Mom went off to urinate and Bern kept himself installed in the lobby bar, finishing his second beer while settling the tab and catching up on some more sports highlights. Unlike my father, Bern thought that a thirty-six year-old man with a medical degree would be capable of getting us checked into the hotel unassisted. I wasn't The Godfather and I didn't need a consigliere to check into a hotel.

However, whenever money changes hands, Gerry likes to feel in control of the situation. As I devote some more thought to it, my father likes to feel in control of most situations. So do I; I've yet to encounter another surgeon who callously throws caution to the wind and lets the chips fall where they may. That's not necessarily a bad thing. It's just the way it is. Zachary will not take after me in this regard, but I'm not so sure about Daphne. Regardless, I try to let both kids do as much for themselves as possible without triple checking every move they make.

A warm greeting and the customary exchange of pleasantries from the suited woman behind the marble counter began the customary registration process. As printed on her name badge, her name was Jasmine. She seamlessly confirmed the dates of our arrival and departure, as well as the room types, room numbers, room locations, checkout time, and elevator locations. The contents of the minibar were reviewed and she even cited our request to be stationed at least four zip codes away from the dreaded ice machine. Everything was fine until she mentioned the room rates.

Having reviewed my email confirmation from the hotel prior to arrival, I knew perfectly well that the rates Jasmine quoted were correct. But Gerry perceived an injustice. He thought the hotel was charging an unanticipated extra $50 per night. When Gerry thinks he is on the receiving end of a financial injustice, however slight, a single snowflake evolves into a full-scale Himalayan avalanche in the blink of an eye. Trying to stop the process before it plays out is futile. It would be easier to scoop back all of the molten lava into a recently erupted Vesuvius using a single plastic teaspoon.

I watched as Dad scowled and a unibrow formed on his forehead. I felt his systolic blood pressure increase by about forty points as he reviewed his handwritten notes of the hotel reservation I had verbally communicated over the phone months ago. (His handwriting resembles an amalgamation of Egyptian hieroglyphics, ancient Sanskrit, and Mandarin). For the record, he refused my offer to send him an email copy of the reservation booking.

"What do you mean?" said Gerry to Jasmine. "Two twenty-nine a night? That's wrong!"

"Excuse me, sir?" Jasmine replied.

"It's wrong! Wrong, wrong, wrong."

"Sir, is there a problem with the room rate?" Jasmine kept up her professional demeanor.

"What are you people trying to do to me?"

"Sir, I don't quite understand. Can you please explain the nature of the problem?"

A punctuation-free tirade spewed forth from Dad's mouth. I empathized with Jasmine's plight, as I've been on the receiving end of similar tirades countless times before.

"Manager. Get me the manager! Where's the manager? I want to talk to the manager. Who's in charge here? What are you people trying to pull around here?"

Jasmine became as stone-faced as the marble counter her palms were resting upon. She didn't say anything further. Her training and experience in hotel reception had clearly not prepared her for the unforeseen contingency that was Gerry. It was neither the fault of the hotel nor of the employee. There are simply no scripted algorithms for managing my father. By this time, I began to notice the obvious glares of the other guests checking in at the counters adjacent to us. As my cheeks began to flush with embarrassment, I attempted to place a stranglehold on the situation.

"Dad!"

He ignored me.

"Dad! Dad! Dad!"

Four "Dad's" were required to disrupt his tirade and divert his attention. I spoke in as calm and as even a tone as I could muster.

"Relax. Please just relax for a moment. Just give me a moment."

"They've got their figures wrong, Harley," he persevered.

"I and everyone else within a twelve-foot radius heard you. Just please be quiet for a minute and let me speak," I begged.

I made eye contact with Jasmine. She pointed her index finger toward the tip of Dad's nose. Shaking this finger at him, she shed her reserved and composed demeanor and exclaimed, "This man is rude! He is obnoxious and he is impossible to deal with! He will not let me answer!"

This was a fairly jaw-dropping utterance to emerge from the mouth of a young professional woman behind the solid marble front desk of a prominent hotel on the Las Vegas Strip. Common knowledge holds that these hotels want your future business; they are not merely content with your present patronage. I was quite impressed and amused.

I took a moment to collect my thoughts. A quick mental check of the scorecard showed that the fault continued to lie exclusively with my father. I had no choice but to abandon my familial ties as I addressed Jasmine.

"Ma'am, I am this man's only son. I, too, find him rude. I, too, find him to be obnoxious and impossible to deal with. And he will not let me answer questions that he asks of me." With this reply, Jasmine's tightly pursed lips gradually eased into a grin. She recognized an ally when she saw one.

With Gerry reluctantly listening, his brows still furrowed, Jasmine and I reviewed the nightly room rates, taxes and other applicable fees for each day throughout the duration of the trip. There was no yelling. There were no insults levied. Amazingly enough, the owner of the hotel conglomerate and his entire legal team did not have to intercede.

After we finished, I turned back to Dad and said, "The rates that were quoted are correct to the penny. There's no discrepancy. It's all correct, plain and simple." So why was there all of this confusion? As it turned out, Jasmine quoted the average nightly rate, and Gerry's below average ability to listen resulted in his declaration of impropriety.

"Ma'am, my father clearly owes you an apology. Unfortunately, he's gotten himself so worked up that he's unable to offer one. So I'm apologizing on his behalf. Please accept my apology. It's not the first time I've had to apologize for my father's behavior and all experiences to date suggest that it won't be my last." I even offered to buy Jasmine a drink at the end of her workday (I would have put the tab on my father's room bill). As expected, Jasmine politely declined. Instead, she smiled warmly, thanked me profusely for coming to her aid, shook my hand heartily, and wished us a pleasant and lucky stay.

I had no choice but to assume that we were all blacklisted from future stays at the Paris. Bad as Dad's behavior was, a similar performance in a place like The New York Helmsley Hotel could have resulted in a far worse outcome. Leona Helmsley, the Queen of Mean, would have risen from her grave and pelted Gerry with verbal obscenities as her henchmen threw him off the premises by his shirt collar. Infamous for firing any employee who committed even the slightest mistake under her watch, Leona would have rewarded a competent receptionist like Jasmine with open access to the legendary shoe collection of her friend Imelda Marcos.

~

Like a blackjack dealer waving empty palms to the casino security cameras before leaving the table, Dad turned his back to Jasmine and walked away from the reception area. He saw no need to look back and spoke of no remorse. Falsely and rudely accusing Jasmine of taking him for a financial ride was the cost of doing business, Gerry style.

Where was Sydelle during this fiasco? Why didn't she attempt to corral Gerry's verbal stampede? Why did the burden of responsibility rest solely upon my shoulders? Sydelle was in the bathroom, for a change. She was still urinating. She missed the whole thing. Born without a sense of direction, she got lost in the maze of slot machines on the casino floor. By the time she escaped from this labyrinth and returned to the lobby, the smoke had cleared and she had to urinate again.

When Sydelle returned, we retrieved Bern from the bar and then meandered through the aisles of the casino until we found the guest elevators. Bern enjoyed the skimpy outfits of the cocktail waitresses. I enjoyed the relative silence and calm that came with the walk down the long corridors en route to our adjoining corner rooms. On the way, I made it a point to note the specific coordinates of the cursed ice machine. We were obviously staying at a classy establishment, as the ice machine was located behind a closed door. Sydelle was unmistakably pleased. Ripping the 'Ice Machine' sign off the wall, super gluing the door shut, or severing the power supply cord with a pair of garden shears would have been ideal, but this was a satisfactory alternative.

It was 6:05 p.m. when we walked into our rooms. I tossed my bags aside, flopped face down on the bed, and closed my eyes. Our dinner reservations were at 7:00 p.m. so there wasn't much time for relaxation. It was Thursday evening on the Las Vegas Strip, the crowds were beginning to increase in anticipation of the upcoming weekend, and the restaurant I had booked was located about halfway down the Strip in the MGM Grand Hotel. Sydelle needed her exercise, so before we went to our respective rooms, she'd decided that we should walk to dinner. After all, we had been cooped up in airports and on planes most of the day. I acquiesced, allowing for her admittedly broad definition of the term "exercise." Giving myself fifteen minutes to gather my thoughts, I may have even fallen asleep before rising to begin the weekend-long celebration of Mom's seventieth and Uncle Bern's almost eighty-first birthdays.

CHAPTER 7

MUCOUS AND PHLEGM

After freshening up, I walked next door to Syd and Gerry's room. I thought about raiding their minibar to get Dad all riled up with extra room charges, but his demeanor showed that this was not a wise course of action. He stood in the middle of the bedroom area with his hands on his hips and a disapproving frown on his face. He then went hard to work on the phones. Housekeeping was informed of the washcloth, hand towel, and bath towel deficiencies. In-room dining was notified that a half-consumed tray was lying on the floor outside of a room twenty-four doors down from ours. A request was made to the front desk to have a hotel employee demonstrate the nuances of the room's thermostat. The last call went to the bellmen, since the luggage had not arrived in the four minutes since Dad officially took occupancy of the room.

With my father preoccupied on the phone, Sydelle escaped into the bathroom. A full forty-five minutes had passed since she last urinated. Upon emerging with a temporarily empty bladder, Mom settled into the hotel in her own uniquely typical way. She waged chemical warfare upon all of the doorknobs, faucets, and drawer handles in her hotel room with a medley of premium antibacterial wipes and disinfectant aerosols. Deathly fearful of the omnipresent threat of upper respiratory tract infection, she seems to overlook the fact that most upper respiratory tract infections are viral rather than bacterial in nature. She finds comfort merely in taking a proactive stance, given the perils at hand.

Most people with a competent immune system contract a few upper respiratory tract infections a year. While wholly unpleasant, the rhinovirus bug is an accepted part of the natural human experience on planet Earth. There's complete nasal congestion complimented by fountains of thick snot requiring a box of tissues each day to sop up. Fits of sneezing exacerbate the already pounding temporal headaches. For good measure, throw in some low-grade fevers, a sore throat that feels worse than swallowing shards of glass, swollen walnut-sized neck glands buried underneath the skin, and a solid wet cough. With a box of artificially sweetened cherry cough drops, a small handful of ibuprofen tablets, a few cups of hot lemon tea, and a bowl of chicken soup, most people just suck up the rhinovirus and trudge through their lives while it runs its course.

Not Sydelle. She has devoted a good portion of her life trying to outsmart and evade the rhinovirus the way most people avoid an IRS audit, landmines, and black mambas. During the thirty years she taught elementary school, she surveyed the health of her students each morning as they filtered into the classroom. (If human-size filters existed that could have been mounted on door thresholds, she would have purchased them in lieu of blackboard chalk). Any sneezing, sniffling, or coughing infractions were treated with a two-pronged approach. First, any symptomatic child's seat was relocated as far away as possible from her own desk while still technically remaining within the boundaries of the classroom. If it had been an option, she would have either quarantined the kid at home for forty days or transferred the kid into another teacher's class. Second, any afflicted child that came within about five feet of her desk was enveloped in an aerosolized cloud of Lysol—either original or lemon scented. (I never had the heart to tell her that the droplet dispersal of the human sneeze can reach ten to fifteen feet). She literally spray-sterilized each child who came within firing range. The woman can't toss a golf ball through a hula hoop-sized opening from an arm's length away, but no child escaped the Lysol nozzle without sustaining a direct hit.

Now well into retirement, her fear of the rhinovirus hasn't diminished. Instead, it has evolved. She's replaced her original World War I-style trench warfare tactics with updated ground and aerial-based strategies commonplace in World War II. But the essence of her fear remains unchanged. Completing a phone call with Syd without a discussion of health is next to impossible, even when everyone in the family is well. Should anyone actually be sick, it is next to impossible to discuss anything besides health. So I disclose only about one-third of the minor illnesses we contract, mentioning them at those times when I have relatively more patience in reserve to deal with the drama that inevitably follows.

What I have no control over, however, is Mom's insistence on broaching every nuance of her health and my father's health, then beating the topics to a pulp until my brain needs a run through the National Hockey League's concussion protocol. Like Syd, I, too, have a phobia. My phobia, though, is suffering through Mom's description of a cold without warning.

~

I called my mother on one nondescript Wednesday evening a few years ago. We were in the dead of winter—prime rhinovirus season. Half the families in Minneapolis with kids sitting in those petri dishes called elementary school classrooms had someone with a cold. In South Florida, public venues like restaurants and retail stores weren't much different.

"Hi, Mom."

"Harley! I'm so glad you called. Hi, how are you?"

My guard instinctively rose. For a random January evening, she seemed a little too excited to hear my voice.

"Just fine, Mom. Haven't spoken to you in a few days. What's going on down there in South Florida?"

"Oh, Harley. We're not doing so well. We're having a tough week." She sounded despondent. Then, pausing for dramatic effect, she exclaimed, "Your father has a cold!"

I instantly knew where this conversation was headed. Rolling my eyes, I silently wondered when the New York Times and the Associated Press would be running with the story as she began the tale of woe.

"We called our internist to inform her all about it," she said. Apparently, the perceived severity of my father's symptoms required a group conference call. The term "group" was loosely applied in this instance. Mom consulted with the doctor while Dad meandered about the garage, cursorily aware that his wife was on the phone.

"Actually it was one of her partners, a male partner. He seemed like a nice doctor. He spent about ten minutes on the phone with us, recommending some Tylenol and Afrin spray as needed. He said a prescription wasn't necessary. Our internist wasn't in the office. She must have taken the day off. I don't know why—her partner didn't say. I suppose she's allowed to take a day off, right? Even doctors get sick occasionally. Even a doctor is entitled to a day off every now and then, right?"

"Uh-huh. I suppose." I uttered just enough to indicate that I was keeping track of the conversation. It was already laborious to stay focused. The specific reason my father's internist needed a day off was not exactly going to keep me awake that night.

"How come you never take a day off when you get sick, Harley?"

"Because fortunately, I'm never too sick to work and the ramifications of canceling a day at the last minute bring more punishment than the time off is worth. If I cancel my surgical cases on a Monday, I'll have to reschedule them such that I'll be operating into the night the remainder of the week. It's just not worth it, Mom. Not by a long shot. I'd much rather suck it up and work through a cold."

"At any rate, your father went for a checkup yesterday, when his doctor was back in the office. As it turns out, I was right; he has a cold! You see, Harley? I made the right diagnosis without even going to medical school. I could have been a doctor too! Aren't you impressed? At any rate, she didn't seem overly concerned about your father's condition."

I wanted to ask my mother if this internist was preparing an original manuscript of my father's case for publication in the New England Journal of Medicine. Instead I said, "That's probably because it took all of four milliseconds for the doctor to figure out that Dad has a cold. It's a cold, plain and simple. There's no diagnostic quandary and there's nothing to do apart from allowing the virus to run its course." I thought about sarcastically suggesting a formal follow-up appointment with their internist to confirm the rhinovirus diagnosis. Instead, I chose to keep my mouth shut because Mom would have surely called my bluff.

"Well, what should we do, Harley? I'm sure it will clear up in a few days, right? You're a doctor, Harley. What should we do in the interim?" There was actual worry in her voice. It was as if the woman had never encountered the rhinovirus before, as in the era of the inexplicable opportunistic infections arising in those afflicted with undiagnosed HIV/AIDS before these terms became household names in the mid 1980s.

There was nothing that needed to be done. I knew it and my mother knew it too.

"Summoning all of my medical experience, you have two options as I see it, Mom. Option one is to let Dad's ordinary cold run its ordinary course over the next few days. Watch the runny nose, stuffy nose, sore throat, swollen neck glands, and cough gradually dissipate. Option two, which is the choice I officially recommend with the powerful backing of all of my years of training at the Albert Einstein College of Medicine, is to buy Dad the biggest carton of unfiltered smokes you can find. That way, the cough provoked by the cigarettes will overpower the cough from his cold."

"Enough already, Harley."

"Enough with the melodrama, Mom! Let's just change the topic."

Of course I didn't want my father to be sick. But at the end of the day, it was just a lousy cold. I would have been much more empathetic if, for example, his pancreas fell out while he was walking down the street.

As bad as a cold is, there remains one common malady that's even worse in Mom's mind: the sinus infection. Over the years, Syd has racked up a constellation of ailments that all relate back to her sinuses. Diagnoses of allergic rhinitis, chronic non-allergic rhinitis, Eustachian tube dysfunction, acute sinusitis, sub-acute sinusitis, chronic sinusitis, and atypical facial pain are brandished as badges of courage, just as a high-ranking military officer sports rows of award ribbons and bars on his or her dress uniform. As you may imagine, there's a fair amount of symptom overlap among these diagnoses. And even after Sydelle has spent thirty minutes elaborating upon the nuances of the symptom spectrum du jour, I'm never any closer to figuring out which of these diagnoses is actually in play. Devoting an hour of time to debate the differences between the colors teal, turquoise, and aquamarine would be more rewarding. After explaining the symptoms in the greatest of detail, she'll spend some time juggling the merits of visiting with the allergist, internist, otolaryngologist, and neurologist before deciding to see the first specialist who will grant her an audience and prescribe an antibiotic.

As I watched my mother tear open a fresh pack of sanitary wipes in her futile attempt to sterilize her hotel room, I recalled with painstaking clarity the details of her most recent infection she shared during one of our bi-weekly chats.

"Oh, the mucous, Harley! The mucous is god-awful! You should see the mucous, Harley!"

Original works by Vincent Van Gogh and Claude Monet, the Taj Mahal, and the summit of Mount Kilimanjaro are all things I would never tire of seeing. I could not place my mother's nasal emissions in this same category.

"It kept me up all night, Harley. The mucous, I mean."

She didn't need to clarify. Her Geriatricville neighbors weren't known to host rave parties that end at dawn.

"It's so thick! And it's so green! Sometimes, it's yellow-green but most of the time it's green. Thick and green. When I'm well, it's normally clear or white. Sometimes, it's off-white or even light yellow. Today it's green! And thick! When I'm healthy, it's never green. So I know I'm infected. And I know exactly when it happened: last weekend, when that inconsiderate yenta coughed all over me at the movie theatre. I changed my seat to get away from her, but it was too late. The damage was done."

I said nothing but observed that she took a page from her classroom germ warfare tactics and transferred it to the movie theatre audience.

"The mucous is just pouring out of my nose like Niagara Falls—both sides, mind you. I think the left side is worse than the right, but it's definitely coming out of both sides. The left side is probably worse because the throbbing, aching pain in my face is worse in my left cheek than in my right."

Mom was gathering momentum; there was no foreseeable halt in her diatribe. She would have never sensed my absence if I had walked away from the phone for a few minutes to sort through the mail and pay a few bills.

"I blow all day and all night. I just blow and blow. I should buy stock in Kleenex. My nostrils have been rubbed red and raw from all the blowing. I'm lubricating my nose with Vaseline three times a day, but it doesn't help much because the Vaseline gets wiped off with all of the subsequent blowing. I wish all the blowing would unclog my ears, but it hasn't. So I started myself on Afrin spray. I ran out to pick up a new bottle yesterday. Otherwise, I would have stayed in the house to recuperate. I didn't know what else to do. What else could I do? I couldn't take it anymore. That's okay, right, Harley?"

This was a rhetorical question. I still couldn't inject a word into her monologue.

"The instructions say that you shouldn't use the spray for more than three days in a row. But today is day number four for me. I don't want to become addicted to Afrin. I should be fine, right?"

Another rhetorical question. Most in-patient rehab facilities treat patients with addictions to alcohol, cocaine, heroin, and narcotics. They don't have the patient volumes or profit margins to support wings devoted to nasal spray chemical dependencies.

"The Afrin helps me, Harley; it cuts down my voluminous mucous production. But of course it doesn't get rid of it entirely. I'm also using the fluticasone nasal spray—the Flonase—for my allergies. My allergies won't magically disappear just because I picked up a sinus infection."

"Of course." I proved that I was still listening.

"Between the two of them, the Afrin and the Flonase, my nose is so dry on the inside. How can that be? How can I be drowning in a tidal wave of mucous and yet feel so dry on the inside? So I started to irrigate my nose. I'm using Ayr gel on top of the sinus rinse machine my ENT doctor recommended. I use it about six times a day. I'd like to use it more. I'd like to take a bath in it. I wouldn't mind submerging my whole head in it. It feels good to use the Ayr gel but it doesn't last that long. That's the problem—it's only temporary. I wish it would last all day and all night. You know what does last all day?"

This was a third rhetorical question.

"The damn relentless mucous! All day and every day, the mucous torments me. It taunts me. And now it's not just coming out the front. The mucous is also dripping down the back. I feel that thick, copious mucous constantly draining into the back of my throat. That damn postnasal drip is driving me crazy! I try to swallow it, but more just accumulates in my throat. So I'm constantly clearing my throat, constantly trying to bring the mucous back up so that I can expectorate it. Your father is so annoyed with me—he can't stand the sound of me clearing my throat."

This I understood. Babbling brooks, ocean breezes, and rustling leaves can lull a person to sleep at night—not the sounds of Sydelle hocking up loogies. I'd rather doze off to the sound of fingernails scraping against a blackboard.

"But what else can I do, Harley? I'm already taking the maximum dose of Mucinex. I can't take any more; I don't want to overdose on Mucinex."

I laughed silently, imagining an absurd scenario where hospital emergency rooms are teeming with patients OD'ing on Mucinex, the newest designer drug fad for rebellious teenagers and out-of-work Hollywood celebrities.

"I wish the Mucinex would settle my cough. According to the label on the bottle, it's supposed to act as a cough suppressant. I feel the phlegm inducing my cough throughout my whole chest. So naturally, I try to cough it up—the phlegm, that is."

Thankfully, Syd clarified this last point. Otherwise, I would have assumed she coughed up a furball.

"I don't know where the postnasal drip ends and the phlegm begins—it's all just pooling there in my throat. If I were forced to make a distinction, I would have to say that the phlegm has a more frothy consistency than the mucous; if you look carefully, you can see little air bubbles in the phlegm. My phlegm is also more of a dark yellow color, rather than the fluorescent green that more closely characterizes my mucous. At any rate, I'm so frustrated that I don't know what to do with myself anymore."

As the conversation ended, I thought the Jews wandering through the desert for forty years following the Exodus from Egypt probably felt equally exasperated. However much money Sydelle's doctor was reimbursed from her health insurance company for the office visit spent evaluating and treating the mucous and phlegm flood, it wasn't nearly enough. As a physician, listening to a patient drone on and on with minor complaints that cannot be concretely diagnosed nor effectively treated is an exercise in true patience, especially when I'm running behind schedule. Nonetheless, the act of listening is a vitally important part of the doctor-patient relationship. Patients usually consider themselves well cared for if they leave my office with the feeling that I listened to them, even if I couldn't cure their presenting symptoms. In Mom's case, I knew with absolute certainty that nothing was seriously wrong—or even moderately wrong. So I gathered my patience and just listened to her. I admit that there's also no cure for the sarcasm that pervades my thoughts at these times.

By the look of content I saw on Mom's face and the heaping pile of antibacterial wipes overflowing the wastebasket in the bathroom at the Paris, Syd and Gerry's hotel room was now satisfactorily decontaminated. The room was declared sanitary. Should the need have arisen, I could have performed surgery in their room without preparing and draping the patient under standard sterile conditions. It was now time for dinner.

CHAPTER 8

CHINESE CHEMICAL WARFARE: MONOSODIUM GLUTAMATE VERSUS CALCIUM

Mom made the expected comments about the pleasantries of the "dry heat" during our walk to dinner at the MGM Grand. Gerry set the pace, as we were running late; he was leading by about six lengths. Syd and Bern had no desire to keep up. They walked with the urgency of cattle being led to the old Chicago slaughterhouse. Relegated to the middle of the pack, I kept tabs on them among the sea of humanity crowding the streets of the Strip. "It's wonderful. Just wonderful. There's not even a breeze," remarked Sydelle as we passed the Planet Hollywood Hotel and Casino.

"It's too hot," Gerry shot back from his lead position without turning his head around to make eye contact with us.

"Oh, not for me. I love it. It's just wonderful. I'll take this weather three hundred sixty-five days a year, year after year."

Uncle Bern chimed in. "Not for me. It's stifling. I don't begin to feel alive until the temperature dips below thirty degrees. I'd like to hibernate until Thanksgiving." He cited the good fortune that landed him in the German hinterlands rather than Korea during the Korean War.

"You're crazy, Bernard. I don't know how anyone can feel that way," replied the Raynaud's Disease-stricken Sydelle.

We were still running late, but the sheer mass of the crowd on the sidewalks slowed our forward progress. Plus, a fast walk for Syd is slightly slower than a one-armed person attempting to walk upside down. I called the restaurant to notify them that we were running a bit late.

We were promptly seated upon arriving at the Pearl restaurant in the MGM Grand Hotel. I ordered an ice-cold martini before the menus were presented. Uncle Bern ordered a whiskey and soda on the rocks. I could tell that Mom and Dad were really in the mood to party, as they each ordered a glass of white wine. As it turned out, the drinks complemented the Chinese food quite nicely. I would have been happy drinking motor oil, glad as I was to have not lost the reservation.

Dinner actually progressed nicely, the usual dysfunctional comments notwithstanding, until the entrées arrived. Piping hot platters of beef and chicken accompanied by mountainous heaps of white rice were presented to the table. But the rice was not the only accompaniment. In the movies, gangsters and hit men whip out concealed sawed-off shotguns from within the folds of their trench coats. Well, here in the Chinese restaurant, Mom and Dad extracted their pillboxes with similar speed. I have no idea how they each comfortably transported these pillboxes; they looked almost as long as a pair of yardsticks. Mom's pillbox appeared too long to fit inside her handbag. Dad's was too long to fit inside the pockets of his slacks. I suppose he could have strapped it to his thigh with some sort of custom-made Velcro band or brace, but I didn't see him groping underneath the tablecloth before his pillbox emerged.

The dinner plates were nudged toward the center of the table to make room for the pillboxes. The opening ceremonies followed. This did not merely involve the uncapping of a couple of plastic lids. These were precisely choreographed maneuvers. Again referencing the movies, think of the two highest-ranking military commanders who each have to simultaneously insert and turn their unique keys into the control panel slot to launch the nuclear missile. Gold medal-winning synchronized swimmers and Irish line-dancing ensembles strive to achieve my parents' level of coordination. The finest Swiss watchmakers periodically send out scouts to Geriatricville to uncover their secrets and incorporate their technological savvy into the next generation of high-end timepieces.

I unsuccessfully tried to ignore this pill popping performance. I was a thirty-six-year-old self-respecting male who cared about how I presented myself in society. Admittedly, I've never felt comfortable in places like Vegas nightclubs. But popping cholesterol-lowering medication in a nice restaurant on the Las Vegas Strip on a Thursday night is not at all commensurate with the personal image I sought to impart. Doing lines of cocaine with rolled Benjamins in the bathroom would have come considerably closer.

Gerry popped his medley of pills and started to attack his entrée with the ferocity of a rabid wolf pack. Syd, however, was struggling.

"My calcium pill got stuck in my throat on the way down." She started to clear her throat as if she was in the throes of a full-blown rhinovirus. In her defense, this calcium pill was about the size of her pinky finger.

"Drink some water, Mom," I advised.

"I did," she replied in a raspy voice.

"Drink some wine, then."

"Don't be sarcastic, Harley. I swallowed the wrong way," she said as she cleared her throat even more forcefully.

"I know, I know. Drink some more water." I took a sip of my own water to prove that I practiced what I preached.

She took several more sips of water, swallowing deliberately after each gulp as her Adam's apple bobbed up and down.

"It's still lodged. It won't go down." Her voice was getting audibly more hoarse. Since she was able to talk and swallow and breathe comfortably, I knew there was nothing seriously wrong. I encouraged her to take some slow, deep breaths and drink some more water.

Instead, she cleared her throat with steadily increasing fervor, interrupted only by the onset of a vigorous hacking cough. Together with the slurp-slurp of Dad inhaling Mongolian beef, a symphony of biological sounds erupted at the table. Even as she continued to cough, Mom somehow managed to not only eat her dinner but also proclaim "the wine just hit me" near the end of her meal. (It usually takes about one-third of a standard glass of wine for Mom to appreciate the effects of alcohol.) Without seeming insensitive to her plight, I focused on the ambiance set by the piano concerto playing in the background. I also concentrated on finishing the bottle of wine we ordered. The throat clearing and coughing continued throughout dessert and the ensuing walk back to the Paris, neither worsening nor abating. The relentless sound of a woodpecker going to task immediately outside my bedroom window at six o'clock in the morning would have been more soothing.

We arrived back at the Paris exactly at 10:53 p.m. Since I was still on Minnesota time, it felt every bit like 1:00 a.m. to me. By 11:00 p.m., the lights were out and I was ensconced within the cool cotton sheets and covers of the king size bed in my room. Sleep and alcohol were both essential to optimally prepare for the next day's antics. I had had enough of the latter and couldn't wait to catch up on the former.

It was not meant to be. Exactly eight minutes later, Dad violently pounded his fist on the door of my room. I reluctantly dragged myself out of bed as his repeated calls of "Harley! Harley!" dispelled the hope that any other hotel guest besides my father was demanding my attention.

"Harley, come quick! You've got to come quick! Your mother's not doing well!"

"What's the problem?"

"She's still coughing. She can't stop coughing."

I walked through the hallway in my T-shirt and boxers to my parents' room next door. In contrast to the scene at the Chinese restaurant a short while ago, I couldn't care less about how I presented myself to society at that particular moment in time.

"I know she's still coughing, Dad. She's been coughing for the past two and a half hours."

"She can't go to sleep coughing like this, Harley. You've got to do something!" he implored.

I found Syd hovering over the bathroom sink, her hands braced on the faux marble vanity. To the baseline mix of throat clearing and coughing, she added some guttural expectoration of saliva mixed with gastric juices that did not quite meet the criteria for actual puke. She was breathing normally, without any signs of wheezing or shortness of breath. I confirmed that she was still physically able to swallow and thus wasn't too concerned about any impending health catastrophe.

"What exactly would you like me to do about this situation, Dad?"

"I don't know. You're the doctor. Do something! Help your mother!"

"I've got nothing new for you, Dad."

"Well, something's got to be done! She can't go to sleep like this. Look at her coughing. Can't you prescribe something?"

"What on earth would you like me to prescribe for a pill particle that got temporarily wedged in Mom's throat?"

"We're going to have to go to the emergency room, in that case."

"What?"

"You heard me! I'm going to have to take your mother to the emergency room. She can't sleep in this condition."

"Let me get this straight, Dad. You want to take Mom to the ER in Las Vegas in the middle of a weekend night for a coughing spell? Do you realize what the scene will be like in triage? People with acute alcohol intoxication will be seated to your left. Those with accidental or intentional drug overdoses will be on your right. Musculoskeletal injuries and cognitive deficits resulting from alcohol and drug poisonings will be in front and behind you. Hangnails, hiccups, earwax accumulations, and similar afflictions are generally put off until the next morning. If any of these ailments is particularly troublesome at night here in Vegas, the first line of treatment involves either alcohol or drug ingestion, not a trip to the ER."

"What other choice do we have?"

"The other choice is to have some patience and allow Mom's sore throat and cough that obviously resulted from the calcium horse pill to run its course. What do you think they'll do for her in the ER? Start an IV? That should help. Run a pregnancy test? How about an MRI scan? All sound like sure-fire ways to cure a cough to me. They can't even rush her into surgery, since she has a full stomach."

Gerry remained silent. I continued.

"Go ahead. Take her to the ER. Let me know how it works out for you. I'm going back to bed. You're welcome to wake me up if her cough worsens or if she has any new symptoms. Otherwise, fill me in on the details of your visit to the Las Vegas ER in the morning."

CHAPTER 9

DOCTORING FOR SPORT

Dad's knee-jerk reflex to drag my coughing mother to the Vegas ER and her willingness to even consider the proposition exemplify their intimate relationship with the US medical establishment. Medicine and all things medicinal have kept Syd and Gerry occupied during their retirements. It's a sport, a hobby, a pursuit, a calling. Many days of the week are orchestrated around visits to their doctors' offices, with an average of three appointments every week. Between the two of them, they have consulted with every type of physician except a pediatrician, nephrologist, and endocrinologist in the two years leading up to the Vegas trip. In alphabetical order, this included the fields of allergy and immunology, cardiology, cardiothoracic surgery, colorectal surgery, dermatology, gastroenterology, internal medicine, interventional radiology, neurology, neurosurgery, obstetrics/gynecology, hematology/oncology, ophthalmology, orthopedic surgery, otolaryngology, pathology, podiatry, psychiatry, pulmonary medicine, rheumatology, and urology. Who needs shuffleboard when you can juggle this cornucopia of medical disciplines?

To be fair, Mom and Dad carry some legitimate diagnoses that merit periodic medical evaluations. Dad's glaucoma, high blood pressure, and colon polyps, for example, all need to be monitored by qualified specialists. Preventive health care offered by primary care physicians is certainly valuable as well. But you would not find me alongside Sydelle in an orthopedic surgeon's waiting room every time I had a minor pain in my hip that lasted more than a day and a half. I also would not be running into an allergist's office every time the color of my snot changed from clear to opaque to pale yellow to chartreuse before reverting back to clear. And only in the case of a true emergency would you find me in an emergency room in Las Vegas.

When I'm not working, I consciously avoid thinking about practicing medicine. I'm like most surgeons in that I find the full-time practice of medicine rewarding and intellectually stimulating yet at times all-consuming and physically and emotionally exhausting. Yet as I drifted off to sleep at the end of our first night in Vegas, my thoughts involuntarily reverted to my parents' preoccupation with medicine and their health.

I thought of all of the doctor visits Mom and Dad described to me over the phone each week. Reviewing the intricate details of each office visit with me is comforting for them, even though I am usually unqualified to weigh in on the judgment of their small army of treating physicians. The first rule of medicine is to do no harm. As a facial plastic surgeon, I can only do harm by commenting on the care my mother's gynecologist provides from my home halfway across the country. But it makes them happy for me to verbally sign off on the care they receive, so I oblige—most of the time. The exceptions occur when they dislike a doctor or some aspect of the care they receive. If I look at their grievances objectively at these times, I am much more apt to defend than criticize the doctor.

As my thoughts percolated some more, I remembered that mainstream doctoring sometimes isn't satisfactory for Mom and Dad. That's when Gerry sprinkles in his own unique brand of alternative medicine. He injects a little variety, a little spice into the mix to keep life fresh and exciting. That's when I started to worry just a little about my mother coughing in the hotel room next door, wondering what intervention my father was potentially concocting.

By "alternative medicine," I'm not talking acupuncturists, gurus, nutritionists, or herbalists. Forget about chia seeds, ginkgo biloba, St. John's Wort, and fish oil. Instead, I'm going to take you off the Vegas Strip. Picture yourself on a Caribbean cruise. You're enjoying the island breezes, the amenities of the luxury liner, the solitude, the vastness of the ocean, the sunsets over the cloudless horizon, and the little pink umbrellas in your fruity tropical drinks. You have a full week without a care in the world, awaiting exotic ports of call such as St. Barts, Nevis, St. Kitts, and Montego Bay. You have no idea how your investment portfolio is performing, nor do you care. Hell, you're not even certain if it's Tuesday or Friday. Serene, isn't it?

Bam! A harsh dose of reality hits home as you unwittingly squirt liquid styptic solution in your eyeball, rather than the prescription eye drops intended for your borderline glaucoma. I've never read the instructions on a bottle of liquid styptic, but I'd wager a fair sum that the phrase "for external use only" appears somewhere in the not-so-fine print. What do you do after the initial shock passes? What's your next play after the water you splash into the affected eye fails to neutralize the searing pain? What course of action do you take when the white part of your eye has been replaced by a uniform shade of fire engine red?

I'll tell you exactly what you do. Alternative medicine, Gerry style. This incident actually happened; in the middle of an ocean cruise with no port of call on the horizon, my father accidentally squirted himself directly in the eyeball with the stuff that helps your blood clot after you cut your face shaving. So what did he do? He threw on some clothes and navigated through the bowels of the cruise ship until he arrived at the door of the shipboard physician. The doctor on board may have been perfectly competent and up to the task at hand. Then again, he could have flunked out of medical school in Guadalajara and drained a bottle of rum ten minutes before Dad landed on his doorstep. Nonetheless, he welcomed my father into his office. The doctor was probably pleased to be treating an ailment other than an epidemic of norovirus or some similar diarrheal pestilence plaguing the cruise ships of the world in recent years. Wading through Gerry's moans and pleas for help, the doc performed a cursory exam and formulated his assessment: Gerry's eye looked like hell. The plan? Throw the bottle of styptic overboard. Use lubricating artificial tears if you can find any lying around, flush the eye with warm water periodically, apply warm compresses regularly, and tape the eye shut. Out of sight, out of mind, I guess. Gerry was rather pleased with the experience, though, as he received free medical care from a new doctor courtesy of Celebrity Cruises. Dad's binocular vision was fully restored the next morning. His shave went smoothly, without even a single nick. The bottle of styptic solution was stowed away in the bottom of Dad's toiletry bag, out of harm's way.

~

Under normal circumstances, when my parents need to see a new physician they use a set of criteria finely honed over the years by their sheer volume of doctoring. The factors at play are tossed into their subconscious melting pot, where they are whipped around for a while with a mental eggbeater. Similar to a hot dog, the product that emerges bears no resemblance to the raw ingredients. Some of the criteria are quite logical; not so for some of the others:

- *Reputation*: Just like the search for a good early bird dinner special, a forthright, unqualified endorsement from one of Mom and Dad's fellow Geriatricville cronies goes a long way.

- *Credentials*: Board certification is a must. I wholeheartedly agree. No arguments here.

- *Proximity*: A trip to the Mayo Clinic in Jacksonville, Florida is in order if you can no longer slide your pants up your left leg because the festering tumor exploding out of your thigh is sprouting hair, teeth, and a few extra fingers. For a routine blood pressure check, on the other hand, keep it local.

- *Bedside Manner and Physical Appearance*: A little charisma goes a long way for Syd and Gerry. I agree that it makes for a more pleasant doctor-patient relationship. But if you need your chest cracked open to remove the part of your lung harboring a potentially lethal cancer, I advise lying down under the knife of the most qualified thoracic surgeon. The tumor doesn't care if the first surgeon's necktie perfectly matches his shirt.

- *Office Hours*: Any medical practice in South Florida worth its weight in salt and pepper closes down for a two-hour lunch break. A red flag will automatically trigger if Mom and Dad are offered a 12:15 p.m. appointment.

- *Ability to Get a Prompt Appointment*: This is a tricky one; a double-edged sword is at play here. A same day or next day appointment may seem great at first. On the other hand, maybe the doctor who can see you the very day you request an appointment has an echo chamber for a waiting room because he or she is a lousy practitioner.

- *Waiting Room Essentials*: A current selection of the most popular periodicals should be available for perusal. The waiting room chairs should be spaced far enough apart to avoid cough- and sneeze-related droplet dispersals of contagious microorganisms from the other patients. Receptionists at the front desk should engage in small talk. The availability of free coffee (decaf) and herbal tea doesn't hurt either.

- *Time*: The treating physician should ideally block out an unlimited amount of time for a new-patient appointment. If an entire morning or afternoon needs to be reserved for Syd or Gerry, then so be it. For routine follow-up appointments, they expect a solid hour. The time spent with the doctor should allow Sydelle to touch upon all sorts of topics that are at best tangentially related to her symptoms. Time spent should also allow for a thorough discussion of the patient's social history. Most doctors usually elicit a cursory social history when they first sit down with a new patient. This typically consists of figuring out if a patient smokes, drinks alcohol, and works. But Syd and Gerry consider the social history and the social visit to be interchangeable terms. There should be ample time to catch up on events that may have transpired in their lives or the doctor's life since the last visit. *Mishegas* never exists in isolation. Whether conscious of it or oblivious to it, *mishegas* ensnares those around you. It may take a village to raise a child. The same village is needed to properly vet the *mishegas* when people like Syd and Gerry sit down for a chat.

- *Religious Persuasion*: When deciding among two or more equally qualified physicians, always pick the Jew. It's good karma to keep the faith.

- **Satisfaction**: The ultimate criterion. If, by the end of the office visit, the above factors do not cultivate the warm, fuzzy feeling of a piping hot cup of cocoa settling in your stomach, it's back to the drawing board for Syd and Gerry. But satisfaction only sometimes pertains to results that either maintain or improve your actual health. Most people would be thrilled to learn that the scaly lesion on their scalp is a benign seborrheic keratosis that needs just a two-second application of liquid nitrogen spray for definitive treatment. Alternatively, a biopsy could be recommended for a similar lesion. In the unlikely event that the lesion proves to be cancerous, the biopsy results parlay into a solid three-month wait to see a Mohs' surgeon, followed by a visit to a plastic surgeon to sew up the crater created from tumor removal. Throw in a few post-op visits to check that the scars are healing properly and make sure the tumor hasn't recurred, and you have about a half dozen visits spread out over the better part of a year. That's six visits for the price of one lesion. What a deal! For the nominal price of six co-pays, they receive six face-to-face visits with the doctor, each of which has the potential to generate an additional set of visits to perpetuate the cycle.

~

The beds at the Paris Hotel were surprisingly comfortable but I woke up in the night. I found my semi-conscious self still trained on my parents' approach to all things medicinal as I tossed and turned into a new position of comfort. No doors opened or closed in the hall outside my room. That either meant the ER visit was postponed or that my father was arranging for a physician house call with the hotel concierge. I pictured the hotel elevator filled with half-naked paid escorts sporting condom-filled, sequined purses and one doctor clutching his trusty black leather medical bag. I thought about some of the more interesting (and unpleasant) aspects of my parents' gynecological, gastrointestinal, and ophthalmologic health histories.

~

"You know, I was the product of a dry birth."

I choked on my wine as I heard Syd strike up a conversation with one of our closest friends in the middle of the reception we hosted in honor of Daphne's Hebrew baby-naming ceremony in the winter of 2006. Despite the noisy conversation of the fifty or so friends and family members gathered for the occasion, this "dry birth" comment also caught Elyse's attention from clear across the other side of the crowded room. For the record, there were no other even remotely related topics being discussed at the time. There had been no talk of pregnancy, labor, delivery, hospitals, infant care, or postpartum issues. Syd just decided that our friend would be interested to learn all about her dry birth.

Now you may ask, what in the name of everything sacred and holy is a "dry birth"? Elyse and I completed our medical school rotations in obstetrics and gynecology, yet neither one of us had ever heard of this term. Elyse's curiosity was piqued enough to allow Sydelle to recount uninterrupted the tale of her dry birth. Our friend meanwhile, looked utterly bewildered. I could tell that she was paying attention to Syd, though, because one of her eyebrows ascended to the level of her mid-forehead while the other remained in the neutral position.

"You see, my mother's water broke, but she didn't realize it at the time."

Our friend remained catatonic. Unless you're in a swimming pool or bubble bath, a sudden outpouring of uterine fluid soaking through your underwear and streaming down your leg has to be hard to miss. Elyse continued to look on, camouflaging her expression behind her wine glass.

"I was finally born a week later—vaginally. It was a very difficult labor for my mother. Very difficult. Even still, I came out premature. I was about four weeks early. My mother hired a wet nurse to help out initially. Other than that, I was okay."

Our friend wisely took advantage of Syd's momentary pause to excuse herself and refill her wine glass.

In the days after the baby-naming ceremony, I researched the subject of "dry birth." As it turns out, the term actually exists—in mythology. Bear with me; I'm not going to get too technical here. "Dry birth" relates to an actual medical term called "premature rupture of membranes (PROM)."

When the amniotic sac breaks or ruptures at least one hour before the onset of contractions, PROM has occurred. The myth of the "dry birth" holds that once the amniotic sac ruptures, the subsequent labor will be more arduous due to the absence of lubricating amniotic fluids as the baby passes through the birth canal. However, leakage of amniotic fluid is a natural aspect of labor. Combined with fetal urination, maternal blood, and maternal mucous, there is nothing remotely "dry" about the birthing process.

~

Elyse remains convinced that the "dry birth" is directly and exclusively responsible for Sydelle's wandering left eye. Together with Mom's nearsightedness and farsightedness, her eyeglass prescriptions have always been extremely complicated (in Syd's opinion, I would add). According to my mother, there was only one ophthalmologist in the entire New York metropolitan area capable of deciphering the mysteries of her vision. Only Dr. Stanley Chin could pin down her wandering eye long enough to determine the precise fractions of diopters needed for her prescription eyeglasses and matching prescription sunglasses. No other board-certified ophthalmologist was up to the task. She wouldn't even think about using an optometrist, other than as a source of frames to house the hallowed Chin-prescribed lenses.

Chin practiced off Mott Street in the heart of Chinatown in lower Manhattan. I think he established his office there just as Galen decided to hang up his sandals and call it a career in ancient Greece. Other than rent and electricity, there were virtually no other operating costs for Chin's practice. His wife served as receptionist, scheduler, biller, office-rooming assistant, and nurse. She granted little if any mercy for patients arriving late. An unmistakable icy stare met any child who made more than a few peeps or squirmed in the wooden waiting room chairs. This woman was a strict, punctual, efficient, no-nonsense entrepreneur. She would have thrived as headmistress in a convent, a bouncer in the city's hottest nightclub, or a military drill sergeant in the middle of an international war.

Chin was warm, kindhearted and competent. Combined with his clinical acumen, he was Mom's ophthalmologist for several dozen years. The folks in Stockholm have not yet granted him a posthumous Nobel Prize in Medicine, though. I was admittedly less than pleased when he told me that I needed to start wearing eyeglasses at the age of seven. I shot right back at him, saying, "I may need glasses, but you need braces to straighten out your bucked front teeth!" He graciously laughed heartily at that wisecrack; Mom was justifiably mortified.

After leaving Dr. Chin's office, we routinely headed straight for a traditional Chinese lunch nearby in Chinatown. Our pupils remained fully dilated for an hour or two, so we followed the enticing scents as we fought off the sun's glare with every step. The food was reliably fantastic. It had to be fantastic, considering that the restaurant was housed in some OSHA code-violating, Department of Health-mocking walk-up hovel. It was one of those dives where the menu was printed only in Chinese. You ordered by pointing to the picture of the dish you wished to devour. We never once got mugged on the walk over to the place—I think it was called Wo Hop—but we probably should have been. I wouldn't have been surprised if the other entrepreneurs on the block were involved in opium distribution, human trafficking for overseas prostitution rings, or cock fighting. The gut-busting, MSG-laden plates of chicken and beef made the visit to Chin's office almost worthwhile.

~

Distant memories of Wo-Hop turned into the fresh memory of Pearl's Mongolian beef snaking its way through my gastrointestinal tract. Indigestion has never been a problem for me; I inherited my cast-iron stomach from my father. Gerry generally disavowed Chinese food, for reasons he never convincingly explained. He never requested it, never craved it, and made a disgusted face at the suggestion of it. Yet he never refused to eat his share whenever Mom made occasional dinner plans with friends who wanted it. His dislike was surprising for the traditional New York Jew he considered himself to be. Christmas Day for Jews in New York customarily meant two things: movies and Chinese food. His dislike also wasn't for fear of disrupting the fragile interplay of chronic constipation, internal hemorrhoids, and external hemorrhoids that raged in his colon and the region immediately beyond.

I was a teenager when I first realized that an industrial sized canister of orange flavored Metamucil does not traditionally accompany a saltshaker and pepper mill on the American tabletop. As it turned out, the Metamucil canister was also not a great conversation piece when your high school buddies came over to hang out. Mornings in my house were not characterized by the aromas of freshly brewed coffee and blueberry buttermilk pancakes but rather by the sound of a spoon stirring up a highball glass full of neon orange Metamucil. He preferred it neat, not on the rocks. For a rare treat, Gerry would occasionally switch up the orange flavor for the neon green citrus blend.

Daph and Zach will have their own childhood breakfast memories one day. They can make fun of me all they want for my weekday caveman breakfast of a couple of handfuls of raw almonds and blueberries, plus plenty of coffee—dark roast with just a touch of cream. I don't think I'm traumatizing them. My breakfast is quick, filling, high in protein, and high in fiber. But most important for me are the natural colors and the avoidance of flashbacks.

The Metamucil, as I came to learn, stood sentry in the vital role of protecting my father from a hemorrhoid flare up. The threat of a hemorrhoid flare always lurked in the background, and the bastion of defense that was the Metamucil acted like a veteran offensive lineman reliably providing the crucial block for his running back coming out of the backfield. The offensive lineman was never the star of the game; when was the last time a lineman on either side of the ball was named league MVP or awarded the Heisman Trophy? Standing alone in the spotlight at center stage, the real star of the show responsible for maintaining Gerry's intestinal health was the colonoscopy.

Most people view a colonoscopy somewhere between a necessary evil and a recurring nightmare that begins at the age of fifty and plagues you every five to ten years thereafter. Having multiple teeth yanked out with rusty pliers without novocaine may be preferable to some people. Not so with Gerry. The colonoscopy is a marquee event on his calendar.

"October? No good, Harley. Can't come to Minneapolis for a visit in October. I have a colonoscopy coming up in October."

He broadcasts the auspicious date of the procedure to his close friends weeks in advance, not by way of an unavoidable explanation but rather as a matter of pride:

"Sorry, Bob. Sydelle and I would have loved to go to dinner and a movie with you and Agnes next Friday night. Unfortunately, we'll need to take a rain check. I'm scheduled for a minor medical procedure that same morning, so I'll need to take it easy for the remainder of the day. Can we please reschedule?" would be a perfectly polite excuse, but would never play out in reality.

In reality, the conversation would go something like this, instead:

"Dinner and a movie next Friday night? You and Agnes are out of luck, Bob. Out of luck. I have a colonoscopy scheduled! I scheduled it about two months ago. I'll tell you all about it after it's all done. I go in first thing on Friday morning; they wheel me in at seven in the morning on the dot! They want me there at six thirty to check-in. Should be out by nine thirty or ten or so. The follow-up appointment with my Ass Man is not until the following Thursday. I'll get the results then." It went without saying that "Ass Man" was Gerry's colloquialism for his gastroenterologist.

Protocol dictates that the gallon size jug of translucent clear fluid called Golytely must be consumed in its entirety on the evening prior to a colonoscopy. This "bowel prep" enables the gastroenterologist to accurately examine the intestinal walls with the colonoscope. For the patient, though, the bowel prep is experienced on an entirely different level: after forcing yourself to guzzle down this gallon of revolting liquid, you spend the rest of the evening married to the toilet, uncontrollably crapping your brains out with no "end" in sight.

This torturous session somehow equates with medical bliss in Dad's eyes. About forty-eight hours before the prep is scheduled to start, the jug of Golytely takes up a position of prominence on the kitchen countertop. A couple of highball glasses flank the jug on either side. There's also a tablespoon, a timer, and a terrycloth towel in the vicinity. An overhead spotlight illuminating the jug is the only thing missing. While the purpose of the spoon is obvious enough, I've always been afraid to ask Dad about the rationale for the towel. As a kid, I made it a point to stay upstairs if the bowel prep was going on downstairs and vice versa if the upstairs toilet was getting a workout. These days, I try to avoid all mention of the bowel prep, with varying success.

Fortunately, I've never accompanied Dad to the actual colonoscopy procedure. Living halfway across the country and suffering through the Minnesota winters has its advantages. From what my mother tells me, he arrives at the outpatient gastroenterology suite early and engages the staff in friendly banter until the moment the intravenous anesthetic usurps his senses. He'll pick up the small talk in the recovery room upon awakening from scope dreamland. The car ride home is a compare-and-contrast session.

"Let's see, Sydelle. They wheeled me in at seven thirty-three this morning. Last time it was seven thirty sharp. What time did they wheel me out?"

"I don't know, Gerry. I wasn't invited into the recovery room the moment your procedure ended."

"Well what time did you get in there?"

"I don't know exactly. I wasn't paying attention to my watch, Gerry."

"Oh come on Sydelle! What time is it now?"

"Nine forty-three."

"How long have we been in the car?"

"About four minutes."

"Backtracking, that puts us at nine thirty-nine. Figure about forty-five minutes in the recovery room and ten minutes to get dressed and walk to the car . . . That means they were finished with my ass at eight forty-four. So the colonoscopy took an hour and sixteen minutes. They went snaking around in there for an hour and a quarter last time, so it was almost exactly the same today. Boy, that's some factory they're running in there. The Ass Man told me he does about eight of these scope jobs a day."

"Well sure, Gerry. They're specialists. That's what they're equipped to do."

"They gave me a few crackers and some watered down apple juice to drink in the recovery room. Last time it was graham crackers and ginger ale."

"It's good to get a little something in your stomach after a procedure."

"Speed it up, will you? My ass isn't doing well. I feel like I have to go to the bathroom."

"We'll be home soon, Gerry. I don't want to get a speeding ticket."

"What's for lunch?"

~

Three weeks after any colonoscopy, Dad would still be fondly recollecting the nuances of his sunrise scope, sharing all kinds of unsolicited nuggets about the procedure with his cronies over chicken salad sandwiches at the Geriatricville poolside café.

"They found more polyps—nothing cancerous, thank God. Took five biopsies. Boy, that prep stuff is powerful; I was on the toilet for a solid eight hours, plus some more bathrooming on and off throughout the night before the procedure. I was famished by the time I got home the next morning. Famished!"

He paused just long enough to cram half the chicken salad sandwich into his pie hole and take a few swigs of decaf coffee before continuing.

"Took about two to three days before my ass fully recovered and I was back to normal. So I started back up on my Metamucil the following Monday. Pass the salt, will you?"

As much as I'd like to throw caution to the wind, I know that I'll go for a colonoscopy when I turn fifty. This milestone is fortunately about a decade away. Even still, I will be sure to schedule it no sooner than the week before I turn fifty-one.

Uncle Bern didn't criticize his sister and brother-in-law for spending much of their time doctoring for sport. He simply chose to pursue a radically different approach to safeguard his own health. A physical exam meant one exam performed by one physician on one occasion—per lifetime. According to Bern, the military doctor declared that he was the very picture of health when he reported for active duty at the start of the Korean War. About sixty years later, Bern still claimed to feel as physically strong as the day he started basic training. At the age of eighty, he complained of no ailments, carried no medical diagnoses, took no prescription medication, and was not under the routine care of a single physician. He practiced his own brand of medicine, a brand that required no formal training and had no stipulations for licensure. Treatment for the common cold meant adding a little whiskey or brandy to a cup of hot black tea. The colonoscopy was indeed a great screening test for colon cancer for men over fifty who were not named Uncle Bern. Blood pressure control meant calming down with a cold beer if the closer for the Yankees blew a save. He practiced ophthalmology by trial and error. Whenever he found a pair of eyeglasses accidentally left behind by some stranger on a subway seat or park bench, he tried them on. If his vision improved, he pocketed the glasses.

The less I knew about Mom's dry birth and Dad's colonic health, the better off I would have been. From time to time, though, I enjoyed challenging Bern about his use of the medical establishment. My uncle had no trouble taking the bait whenever I dangled it over the phone lines during our weekly Sunday morning talks:

"Look at me, Harley. I'm over eighty years old and I'm on no medication."

"You're on no medication simply because you refuse to go to the doctor, Bern."

"What the hell do I need to go to a doctor for? I feel great. Besides, doctors and I don't get along so well."

"That's because you provoke a hostile, contentious relationship with your treating physicians."

"None of those incidents was my fault. Those doctors were all crooks and morons."

"So you say." For the moment, I sidestepped the derogatory comments about these doctors whom I'd never met. Normally defensive of my fellow physicians, I gave Bern the benefit of the doubt, like a trial judge allowing an attorney to pursue a questionable subject with a witness on the condition that a legitimate point would soon be made.

"Well, how am I supposed to react when that schmuck Doctor Shankman told me fifty-five years ago that I had six weeks to live? I was in perfect health. He waltzed into the examination room and told me I had a maximum of six weeks to put my affairs in order. Should I have given him a hug and a kiss on the cheek and congratulated him for showering me with a death sentence? Should I have asked him for a recommendation on a wood finish for my coffin?"

"I don't know, Bern. How about asking Shankman for an explanation?"

"Shankman had no time for an explanation. He had a big salami and cheese sandwich waiting for him on his desk for lunch."

"Okay, Bern. Perhaps you could chalk up the whole Shankman conversation to one big miscommunication. But that was hardly an isolated incident. What about the doctor who ordered a routine screening chest x-ray for you that one time?"

"That was Doctor Krinicke. He said that because I made my career as a lithographer, I was at a substantially higher risk for contracting mesothelioma of the lung."

There was some truth in that statement, and I told Bern as much.

"Yeah, yeah. Be that as it may. The point was that I felt fine at the time. I could see getting an x-ray if I walked into his office gasping for air and coughing up a bucket of blood. But I had no symptoms at all, Harley!"

"Still and all, Bern. The guy was simply trying to get you to take a quick, simple, cheap screening test to detect a potentially life-threatening cancer. You turned around and insulted the man." Having heard this story about once every three months since the day it occurred, I knew full well the path we were headed down.

"Insulted him? I merely suggested that I would go for the chest x-ray right after Krinicke got himself tested for endometriosis."

"You knew perfectly well that it's anatomically impossible for men to acquire endometriosis," I laughed, unable to suppress the reaction that this outrageous statement of Bern's always elicited. The thought of Uncle Bern having the audacity to tell a male physician to submit to a gynecological exam for a uterine problem always made me laugh out loud. Needless to say, Dr. Krinicke told Uncle Bern that there was no need to schedule a follow-up appointment.

"Give me the name of the last physician you got along with, Bern."

Silence.

"What about the last internist Mom made you establish primary care with?"

"You mean the Indian guy with the schmatta on his head?"

"Yeah. And you know perfectly well that the garment you're calling a schmatta is called a turban. Can't you show some respect, some common human decency for others once in a while?"

Bern cast aside my admonition.

"That Indian doctor wasn't too bad, Harley. Wasn't too bad at all, until I got his bill in the mail for $36.73. Now I can understand the thirty-six dollars. I had no problem with the thirty-six dollars. But the goddamn seventy-three cents? What's he got to nickel and dime me for like that? So during my next appointment, I had to ask him whether the seventy-three cents was for the tongue depressor or the butterfly Band-Aid. That cheap bastard! I told him I'd bring him a cup of coffee during my next office visit and charge him seventy-three cents of the total $1.73 it cost me. He's got one hell of a damn nerve charging me $36.73."

"Bern, do you actually think doctors sit in their offices at the end of the day with an abacus to tabulate an itemized bill for every patient they see? That's what their billers and coders are paid to do. The billers simply invoice you for any residual charges left uncovered by your health insurance carrier. I'll bet you $36.73 that the doctor has no idea how much you were billed."

"Still and all, Harley. It's his medical practice. His name is on the shingle outside his front door. He's ultimately responsible for the operation of his practice. I'm not going back there to that lousy crook."

"I knew you hadn't gone back to that Indian doctor because of what happened when you contracted that case of shingles two years ago."

"That was bad news, Harley. Boy was I in bad shape. My whole left flank was raw—it looked like a piece of hamburger meat. I knew I was in trouble when the whiskey couldn't cut the pain. The pain was unbearable. I couldn't take it anymore."

"Had you been an established patient somewhere, any board-certified primary care physician would have been perfectly able to evaluate and treat you for shingles. At the same time, you could have had your head examined."

"That's beside the point. I needed relief. I was desperate because the whiskey didn't help. So I walked into the first Urgent Care facility I could find. The receptionist at the front desk asked me if I was having a problem. Can you believe that, Harley?"

I believed it, because much like the Doctor Krinicke anecdote, I had heard the shingles story dozens of times before.

"Most medical practice receptionists generally expect patients to present with a problem, Bern. They assume that you're not there to have a cup of tea while unwinding in the comfort of the waiting room amid the neutral-colored chairs and cheap wall artwork."

Brushing aside my sarcasm, Bern continued. "I told her I had a problem, all right! A big problem!"

Without further ado, as the story went, Bern stripped naked from the waist up. Right in the middle of the waiting room, with all of the other patients in plain sight, he first unzipped his jacket and draped it across the receptionist's beige counter. Off went his plaid button-down, long-sleeved shirt, which he tossed next to the jacket. The receptionist just stared at him, shocked into silence at the image being burned onto her retinas as his sleeveless white T-shirt finally fell to the floor.

"I think this qualifies as a problem, don't you?" bare-chested Bern exclaimed as he turned to his right, revealing the banded vesicular rash of shingles splayed across his left flank.

He caught the unsuspecting receptionist off-guard, but she eventually regained her composure and ushered him into an empty exam room. She understood that hotheaded and bare-chested Bern could inflict more psychological damage than physical injury upon the innocent, snot-laden children in the waiting room.

"You're pretty proud of that stunt, aren't you?" I challenged.

"Well, I needed to get some relief, Harley. Once I was in the examination room, the doctor wasted no time. He took one look at me, diagnosed the shingles, gave me a prescription for Vicodin and sent me on my way. I was in and out of there in about eight minutes flat."

"You're pretty proud of yourself, aren't you?" I repeated.

"You bet I am. I learned from my past experience at St. Vincent's Hospital. You remember that story, Harley? Did I ever tell you about that time I spent in St. Vincent's?"

Remember? How could I forget? It was undoubtedly Bern's favorite medical story, based on the number of times he told it over the years. It probably took place in 1981 or 1982.

"I had a bad infection in my big toe after a fifty-pound metal plate from the printing press fell on my foot. The foreman had me working a double overtime shift. We were short-staffed; I was doing the work of two pressmen. Anyway, once the toe swelled to about triple its normal size, I couldn't wedge my foot into my shoe. I couldn't walk and I couldn't work. The toe looked like one of those link sausages. My choices were simple. I could either cut a hole in the front of my shoe to accommodate the toe, or I could go to the hospital. I chose the hospital, because the shoes were fairly new."

"Makes perfect sense to me, Bern."

Bern was admitted to St. Vincent's Hospital in lower Manhattan on a Tuesday evening. Having received a hefty dose of intravenous morphine to quiet his aching toe, his first priority upon settling into his hospital bed was to secure a cup of coffee and a solid meal. Much to his chagrin, though, his nurse informed him that the hospital kitchen was closed for the night.

"Closed? That can't be."

"Dinner is served between four thirty and five in the afternoon in this ward, sir. It's now nine fifteen in the evening."

"Well, what am I supposed to do until breakfast? Starve to death? I need some sustenance to heal, don't I, nurse?"

"I can see if there are any extra meals available, sir," the jaded nurse sighed back. I'll make a call down to the kitchen for you."

The extra meal failed to materialize, but Bern's stomach wouldn't take no for an answer. Shedding his open-back hospital gown, he started to put on his street clothes when the nurse returned to his room to administer a dose of intravenous antibiotics.

"Just what do you think you're doing?" she indignantly asked.

"Getting something to eat, as I explained before."

"Sir, you've been admitted to this hospital. This isn't the Waldorf-Astoria or The Plaza, and I'm not a concierge. This hospital is not a hotel. You can't just come and go as you please. You think I'm going to condone your wandering the city streets in the middle of the night with that sorry toe of yours, only to create a racket and wake up the other patients when you limp back onto this ward?"

"Look, nurse. I don't mean to sound disrespectful, but I have to eat something—tonight. I don't want to make trouble for you, but my health and my sanity both depend on it. The way I see it, there are two choices. Either you get me something to eat or I get it myself."

This was the 1980s, and the medical climate must have been substantially different than it is today. Maybe the nurses' union wasn't as formidable. Maybe nursing practices were more flexible. Maybe nurses were given less direct supervision and more autonomy in the care of their patients. I don't know. What I do know is that that nurse, bless her heart, put on her coat, walked out the front door of St. Vincent's Hospital in the middle of a cold February night, and returned with a pastrami on rye sandwich, a sour pickle, and a steaming cup of black coffee. The iconic Clara Barton herself wouldn't have gone to these lengths for her patients.

The next morning, the attending physician overseeing Bern's care waltzed into his hospital room to examine the afflicted toe. Bern was told that his situation looked bleak, but that efforts to save the toe with massive doses of intravenous antibiotics would nonetheless continue. If the antibiotics failed to resurrect the gangrenous toe, he was facing a field trip to the operating room for an amputation.

What followed doesn't seem possible, but Bern swore up and down a flagpole that it was the truth. The doctor reported that the hospital had recently run out of the standard supplies needed to properly dress the wounded toe. So while chain-smoking a pack of cigarettes, this "doctor" literally wrapped up Bern's foot in a wad of newspaper. The fishmongers throwing the daily catch around Pike's market in Seattle would have been proud, but then again their fish probably smelled better than Bern's foot.

"Thankfully, it was the sports section of the New York Post. I took that as a good sign, since the print along my ankle region reported that the Yanks beat the Red Sox," Bern said.

"I would have interpreted that omen similarly, Bern."

Three days and a few dozen meals later, the tide miraculously turned; the threat of amputation was averted. The doctor was stunned. After two more days had passed, the infection had cleared to the point where Bern was ready to be discharged. The doctor reminded him how very close he came to a toe amputation, if not a whole foot amputation. Bern attributed his cure to the infusion of coffee his nurse procured for him at the time of his admission. The doctor thought the IV antibiotics had more to do with his clinical improvement. They agreed to disagree on that matter. The fact remained that Bern's big toe was saved, though the mangled nail of said toe forever resembled something in between a tortoiseshell-colored conch and a walnut.

~

As I drifted off to sleep in my hotel room, I thought about the contrast between Bern's and my parents' approach to doctoring. From my vantage point in the relative median position on the bell curve of doctoring, I saw Bern on the far left and my parents on the far right. I didn't need Dr. Chin's help to see any better in this respect. A crystal ball would have been nice, so I could see if the Las Vegas emergency room doctors were having the pleasure of making my parents' acquaintance at that very moment.

CHAPTER 10

SUNRISE IN LAS VEGAS

I struggled to awaken as the morning sunlight shone through the windows of my hotel room. Bern was surely awake; he never slept late a day in his life. I imagined the sound of his keys and key chains rattling in the pocket of his pants as he dressed to begin his first morning in Las Vegas. He used a separate key chain for each key, all of which were linked together in a labyrinthine configuration. The combined weight of the metal in his pocket should have caused him to list to his right side. His keys served no discernible purpose, as we were in Nevada and Bern's car and apartment were both back in New York. I opened my bloodshot eyes just long enough to see the nightstand alarm clock flashing 6:03 a.m. in neon green. By now, Uncle Bern was surely out and about in search of his first coffee fix of the day. It was just past 9:00 a.m. eastern standard time, which meant he was three hours overdue for a hit of caffeine. His brain must have been pounding against his skull.

I tried to fall back asleep, to no avail. So I dragged myself out of bed, took a hot shower, and went down to join Bern for the largest cup of coffee I could buy. I found him sipping his third cup in a coffee shop with a French sounding name on the ground floor of the Paris Hotel. All seemed quiet and serene as I walked inside. Classical music was softly playing in the background. A few people who clearly had not slept for at least thirty-six hours were staggering and swaying in line in front of me. Croissant flakes were scattered about the surface of Bern's table in a pattern vaguely resembling a tie-dyed shirt. Brushing the crumbs aside, I sat down opposite him with my coffee.

"It's about time you got down here, Harley!"

"It's only seven o'clock in the morning, Bern."

"Yeah, yeah, but you missed all the action!"

"What action? Did someone hit the jackpot on the slots?"

"Nope. Nothing like that. I ran into a little trouble here about twenty minutes ago."

In Bern's vernacular, the phrase "a little trouble" is code for a fistfight. I shook my head in disbelief.

"I had no choice, Harley. You know I don't go looking for trouble. You would have agreed with me, had you been here."

My uncle looked absolutely unscathed and he obviously hadn't been detained in some subterranean casino jail. All was calm in the coffee shop. The tables and chairs were neatly arranged. The baristas were frothing cappuccinos. Nothing that terrible could have happened, or so I tried to convince myself.

"Really, Bern? Trouble? Twice in twenty-four hours? That has to be a record, even for you."

"Outside of my service in the army, you're probably right, Harl. But I had no choice," Bern reiterated with conviction. "My hands were tied."

The symbolism in these last few words went unrecognized by my uncle.

"Unbelievable! You're unbelievable! You need serious professional help and a whole team of psychiatric professionals working around the clock to diagnose whatever's wrong with your head."

Bern just shrugged his shoulders and laughed at my familiar joke.

"All right, Bern. Tell me what happened." I was exasperated yet utterly intrigued.

"It started when I went to take a leak."

Bern explained that the restroom was located at the end of a nondescript corridor off to the side of the coffee shop. The men's room was small, only accommodating a single person at a time.

"I took care of my business and washed up. Well, as I opened the door, a guy was standing in the hallway. He stood right in front of me, blocking my passage back to the main part of the coffee shop. He stared at me with this deranged look on his face, then indignantly stretched his arms out as if to say, 'What the hell?'"

"You didn't do anything to provoke him?"

"Provoke him? I never even saw him before."

"You're sure about that?"

"Listen, Harley. I had no reason to provoke the man. I was just taking a leak. He wouldn't let me pass. So I asked him, I said to him, 'Is there some kind of problem here, pal?'"

"I don't particularly like it when complete strangers call me 'pal,' Bern."

"He asked what the hell I was doing in the bathroom. So I told him. I told him I was taking a leak, just like I told you, Harley. Then I asked him why he was so concerned with my business."

"Sounds a little antagonistic to me so far, Bern. How did the guy respond?"

"He took this nasty, arrogant tone with me. He said, 'It became my business when you made me wait out here all this time, old man.'"

When in doubt as to whether to fight or take flight, Bern reflexively erred on the side of violence. It was the product of growing up in the rough and tumble Bronx of the 1930s, nothing more. I was therefore surprised when Bern said he tried to diffuse the situation.

"I looked away, put my head down, and tried to sidestep around the Irishman in the narrow hallway."

I never learned of the criteria Bern used to determine that this man was of Irish heritage. Stereotypes probably figured prominently in this conclusion—possibly some combination of red hair, freckles, an emerald green four-leaf clover tattoo, and a T-shirt advertising Guinness beer.

"He wouldn't give me an inch, though. The Irishman wouldn't budge. Instead, he contorted his lips into a snarl and jabbed his index finger into my chest. He called me a dirty Jew. He said, 'No one but a dirty Jew needs so much time in the bathroom, old man.'"

Fascinatingly, the bathroom Irishman and the LaGuardia airport cab driver must have both memorized the same prejudicial reference text for instantly determining a stranger's religion. Bern apparently knew the key tenets of a similar reference work that bestowed upon the reader the power to identify a stranger's ethnicity with a quick glance. What were the odds?

My uncle continued relaying the back-and-forth of his increasingly hostile conversation. "'Yeah? Is that right?' I said. 'Only a no-good drunk Irishman like you would say such a nasty thing. I didn't do anything to you. You don't know me. I'm giving you one chance to get the hell out of my way.'"

I knew Bern wasn't bluffing. The Irishman, though, wasn't convinced. They both stood their ground.

"He didn't take me up on my offer, Harley." Bern smiled a toothy grin. "He asked me what I was prepared to do. He asked if I was going to go back in the bathroom and hide."

One punch later, the Irishman found himself on the floor, blood streaming from his twisted nose. Bern did indeed go back into the bathroom, but he only needed a few seconds this time. He grabbed a roll of toilet paper and casually tossed it to the Irishman, who was still writhing around on the floor and cursing my uncle's existence.

"I told the Irishman that I had to go back into the bathroom to clean up—his bloody filth made my hand dirty. I stepped over him rather than around him to get back to my table."

Fortunately, I've never come face-to-face with the brash anti-Semitism that Bern claims to envelop him on a semi-regular basis. I'm sure it's still out there, and I'm sure I would find some evidence of it if I looked hard enough. Maybe Bern fought some of these battles so that I wouldn't have to. Maybe he made the world a slightly more tolerant place to live for posterity. Most likely he was just a curmudgeon who found trouble where none necessarily existed.

I slowly shook my head in disbelief as Bern finished his story. "Sooner or later, Bern, you're going to either lose one of these fights in a bad way or get your ass arrested. Frankly, both of these scenarios should have occurred long ago."

"Stop worrying, will you? I've only broken my nose six times since I was a kid, yet you see how good looking I still am."

Bern promised to behave himself for the remainder of the trip.

"Once I'm back home in New York, though, I can't make any promises, Harley."

The early morning hours passed quietly at the French coffee shop in the Paris Hotel without further incident. From time to time I scanned the dining area and the casino floor, looking for any signs of the Irishman returning with his posse for vengeance. Bern was perfectly content sipping his coffee and eating breakfast pastries while talking about the Yankees' spring training record. He seemed unflappable. Yet I was still incredulous that my almost eighty-one-year-old uncle had kicked the tar out of two different guys in two different states in the last two days.

～

At the previously designated hour of 10:15 a.m., Bern and I knocked on Mom and Dad's door. Gerry answered.

"Oh, it's you, Harley." This was apparently a big surprise. Was he expecting Wayne Newton, Celine Dion, or an Elvis look-alike at this hour of the morning?

"How was the rest of the night? Did you and Mom get some rest?" I asked with a false air of innocence.

Sydelle didn't give Gerry the chance to respond.

"Ugh, Harley," she groaned. "What a night. Ugh. Don't ask. It was some night. Don't ask what I went through," she said with just a mildly hoarse voice.

She had not been lost at sea, trapped in a Himalayan avalanche, or deserted in the Australian outback. It couldn't have been that bad.

"What happened? There couldn't have been anything catastrophic, because you didn't wake me up again."

"Well, let me tell you what happened." Syd settled into an armchair in the corner of the room and paused for dramatic effect. "After you left our room, I kept coughing and coughing. I never made it out of the bathroom. I couldn't stop coughing. The coughing was incessant. Finally, finally after about forty-five minutes, I threw up three white pill particles. I saved them for you. Would you like to see them?"

The Mona Lisa, Niagara Falls, the Sistine Chapel, three white pill particles, Versailles, and the Great Wall of China. Hmmm . . . which of these do you think I could do without seeing?

"That's quite all right, Mom. I think I'll pass up the opportunity to see partially degraded calcium."

"After I threw up, I went to bed. Of course, I couldn't go right to sleep. Who could fall asleep right after going through what I went through? Ugh. What I went through. Ugh. What torture."

Her melodrama made it seem like she had just delivered twins without an epidural while simultaneously passing kidney stones.

"I'm glad you're feeling better this morning."

"Thank God. I don't know how I could have gone on coughing like that. Ugh."

"Enough with all the talk," Bern chimed in. I'm hungry. Let's eat already." Thirty minutes had passed since he finished the last bite of his second pastry. The Fighting Irish incident was already filed away in the deeper recesses of his mind, taking a backseat to the grumblings of his stomach.

~

I wish I could say that the shenanigans at the Pearl the previous evening were unusual. In reality, they aligned perfectly with my dining history with Mom and Dad. Memories of eating out with my parents filled my thoughts as the four of us walked to breakfast. Our destination was Le Café Ile St. Louis.

As a kid, we ate at local diners, Italian restaurants, delis, and Chinese restaurants dotting the Long Island landscape once or twice each week. My memories of these dining experiences were generally fond, and, as much as I hate to admit it, they probably laid the foundation for my lifelong appreciation for good food. The local diners offered a consistent, welcome respite from a slew of otherwise regrettable weekend days immersed in my school homework. There's no specific diner in mind here; all of the diners had essentially the same items on their menus. Chief among them was the Hamburger Deluxe, which forever occupies a special place in my heart. While there was nothing special about the burger or the french fries and coleslaw that accompanied it, I can't replicate the experience of eating a Hamburger Deluxe anywhere outside of Long Island. (For the sake of clarity, the only things distinguishing a regular hamburger from a Hamburger Deluxe were the accompanying french fries and coleslaw.)

Their preferences in restaurants offer a keen glimpse into the larger world of Sydelle and Gerry. This shouldn't be shocking, as food and culture are inextricably linked across cultures around the globe. But within the specific context of the restaurant experience, elements of Mom and Dad's social mores, philosophy, and ideals come to light. You see them interacting with each other as well as with the public. It's not about the culinary experience, enjoying each other's company, exploring new tastes or cuisines, experiencing a change of scenery, or simply escaping the daily routine of planning, prepping, and cleaning up after a meal at home. Their idiosyncratic ideology unfolds in layers, in the style of a lasagna or baklava (just about every diner offers lasagna and baklava, by the way).

Any dining experience with Sydelle and Gerry begins in earnest long before crossing the threshold of a restaurant. Let's call this the Preparatory Phase. Multiple factors must be considered in choosing the restaurant that has the privilege of feeding my parents.

First, there is the Principal Cuisine Genre (PCG). Many PCGs are absolutely off the table, pun intended. The lowest caste of PCGs includes Indian (again, pun intended), Korean, Vietnamese, Japanese, Spanish tapas, Ethiopian, and Mexican. Bona fide PCGs are limited to Italian, American/Continental (including seafood and steak), Chinese, and Greek. French bistros lie in limbo somewhere on the outer fringes of acceptability. Fusion foods breed nothing but confusion and are forced into the land of gastronomic purgatory. The classic New York diner exists by itself as an independent subcategory within the American/Continental PCG, like the Vatican or San Marino within Italy. The diner is revered simply because Geriatricville doesn't have anything similar. A dim light shines softly on the hallowed memory of the New York diner, like the portraits of the founding partners of a prestigious law firm are illuminated in the conference room where the current partners convene.

Second, Sydelle and Gerry remember the past and consider the future as they live and eat in the moment. It's not as simple as saying, "I feel like having pasta tonight." If Gerry downed a heap of pasta within the last forty-eight hours, Sydelle can forget about baked ziti at her favorite neighborhood Italian joint. If she's planning to make spaghetti tomorrow night, Gerry would never think about ordering chicken marsala the evening before. His stomach could mutiny if presented with the same PCG on consecutive evenings. PCGs must be staggered like the individual squares on a checkerboard. This requires careful planning, since there are only four main PCGs.

The eatery's reputation comes third. If a critical threshold of six or more Geriatricville cronies recommends a restaurant, it's worth a try. Next comes the three Ps: portions, price, and proximity. We're looking for massive quantities of familiar, inexpensive food within a fifteen to twenty-minute driving radius from home base. Quantity is synonymous with quality; a pyramid of plain white rice can taste at least as good as an ounce of the finest imported caviar, on principle alone.

The choice of table format puts the final set of parental pre-dining eccentricities on display. If a reservation has previously been made, you can be certain that a booth has been requested. Booths are prized and placed on a tier above any type of table-and-chair configuration. Chair size, upholstery and padding are irrelevant. If a reservation has not been made, or if the restaurant does not accept reservations, a booth is invariably requested upon greeting the host. Visible disappointment and an audible sigh result if no booths remain. But life does go on.

A great deal of weight is placed on the tableside milieu. Sydelle and Gerry apply a mental Battleship board game grid to the available tables on the restaurant floor. For any number of reasons, Mom or Dad may figuratively "sink" a given table. The table initially selected by the unsuspecting host or hostess is merely a suggestion. Two-dimensional factors are first debated:

• Tables too close to the entrance are sunk.

• Tables too close to the kitchen are sunk.

• Tables too close to the bathroom are sunk.

- Tables too close to already-seated large parties exceeding eight patrons are sunk.
- Tables with lopsided legs are sunk.

After a prospective table fulfills the 2-D criteria, they layer in the third dimension to round out the selection process. Syd and Gerry crane their necks and scan the ceiling for fans and air conditioning vents. Combined with auditory and tactile stimuli, they look for any form of untoward airflow. Continuous drafts, intermittent drafts, inexplicable breezes, and jet stream currents are all scouted. Any table subject to any combination of these airflow patterns is instantly sunk.

Sommeliers have developed their palates to detect delicate yet complex nuances in the nose and finish of the wines they taste. Golfers toss blades of grass into the air to gauge subtle wind conditions before addressing their golf balls. Syd and Gerry assess drafts with a simple, time-honored, and battle-tested measure. They stop blinking and wait to see if a draft will cause premature corneal drying. If excessively dry eyes quickly force them to blink, the table is sunk and the process is repeated somewhere else on the restaurant floor.

Even while seated, though, if any of these malevolent airflows is underestimated, incorrectly assessed, or otherwise misperceived, all bets are off. Sometimes the foul airflow can be managed with an exchange of seats in a version of musical chairs (without the music). On other occasions, dictated by the magnitude of the perceived affront, an entirely new table is demanded in another section of the restaurant.

At the end of the day, the table seating decision just can't be rushed. Life's too short to go through an entire meal regretting a hasty choice in seating.

~

Mom and Dad took a minesweeper to the breakfast tables at Le Café Ile St. Louis. I stood at attention, hands clasped behind my back, awaiting their verdict. Bern was looking for anyone holding a fresh pot of coffee. The hostess led us to a table in the more desirable outer atrium section, where the traffic meandering through the Paris casino was a source of entertainment unto itself. However, as we passed through the interior of the restaurant en route to the atrium, Syd perceived a one-point-four-degree dip in the temperature. The atrium table was summarily vetoed in favor of an interior booth, where we had titillating views of several dozen other empty tables and booths.

Sydelle and Gerry sat down. A round of booth hopping occurred because my mother is left-handed. This meant she had to sit in the position that rendered her left arm along the outer edge of the booth. If you watch a professional football game during a time out, the cameras occasionally show the defensive coordinator furiously scribbling black Xs and Os on his white grease board to illustrate modifications to his nickel or dime defensive strategy in response to the opposing team's performance. If Syd could get her hands on a travel-size version of one of these grease boards, it could potentially eliminate the musical chairs.

Why was Syd so intent on an outside seat? Elbow room. She felt like she needed the additional elbow room that the outer edge of the booth afforded to comfortably wield her knife and fork. Bern shrugged off the seating changes; having already chugged his first cup of coffee in three minutes flat, he signaled the waitress for a refill. Bern had no problem with his spot being reassigned. The US Army reassigned him to a tour of duty in Germany rather than the infantry in Korea. Switching spots at the breakfast table just wasn't a big deal.

Now, I can understand the need for some elbow room while performing the chicken dance or when brandishing an axe in the course of chopping down an oak tree. Mom stood about five feet three inches tall and weighed 105 pounds soaking wet. How much room did she really need to fork her breakfast? She wasn't hacking open a coconut with a machete in the jungle.

I settled in with my own cup of coffee, but no one was cruising down easy street once the seating configuration had been amicably settled. Outerwear next had to be dispersed since Mom couldn't leave her Raynaud's Disease behind in South Florida. Coat racks and coat hooks were sought out, like a search party on the hunt for the yeti. Coats couldn't be checked, for two main reasons. First, one never knew when an unforeseen draft would arise;

the threat always existed on some level. Mom didn't allow herself to be lulled into a false sense of security. Just because Le Café Ile St. Louis's air conditioning vents were docile at the moment, it didn't mean they would stay that way until the end of the meal. The principles of Newtonian physics did not apply here: objects at rest may not, in fact, tend to remain at rest.

Second, my parents never trusted the coat-check person stationed behind the wooden Dutch doors of the coat-check room. They believed that every coat-check person spent their time scheming and plotting. Gerry knew that the open novel beside the three-legged stool on which the coat-check person sat was just a prop to disarm the unsuspecting restaurant patron into a false sense of complacency. The coat-check person was either a convicted felon released on probation or a compulsive kleptomaniac who hadn't been discovered by the authorities yet. Either way, Gerry's highly coveted lightweight grey jacket might have been in jeopardy.

There were usually several options for coat management. At Le Café Ile St. Louis, two coats found their way onto brass hooks attached to the sides of the booth. This was ideal. (In the event that the booth didn't have any of these hooks, a subsequent handwritten letter of complaint would have brought this fundamental design flaw to the attention of the proprietor of the restaurant.) The bulk of Sydelle's coat, stuffed as it was with feathery down, combined with the proximity of the hook, impinged on her personal eating space. One sleeve, for example, lay flush up against Mom's shoulder and hung only inches from her cheek; it prodded her each time she deigned to bring her fork or glass toward her mouth. Any normal person would not tolerate this annoyance. Yet for Mom and Dad, this was but a minor nuisance, as the proximity of the coat equated with an insurance policy drawn against the ever-present possibility of a malevolent draft.

Alternatively, if Sydelle and Gerry had been seated at a table with chairs, they would have sought out a freestanding coatrack to serve as the de facto repository, provided that their coats did not directly touch those of other patrons. Mom and Dad don't like strangers handling their coats, due to the omnipresent risk of rhinovirus transmission lurking like a cumulonimbus cloud. They viewed this as an unnecessary risk. But what's life without risk?

In the worst-case scenario of a total absence of coat hooks, racks, and closets, the algorithm is surprisingly simple. If Mom and Dad are seated at a table with chairs, the coats are simply draped over the backs of their chairs. This is obviously not an option within the confines of the coveted booth. Inside the booth, a cramming/wedging technique is used. Basically, the coats are stuffed and jammed between people or against the wall alongside the booth. Sardines are packed in water or oil, and we're packed in a wintry mixture of feather down and wool.

Once Mom and Dad suspended their coats from the tableside hooks, a quick draft check was performed. All was clear as the menus were presented. All remained quiet on the front until the innocent water server approached with his pitcher in hand. One would think that filling the water glasses should be straightforward and unworthy of mention. When thinking about the details of a fantastic dining experience, no one recollects the tap water.

The water server took my glass first and began to fill it up. The sound of ice cubes clinking into the glass triggered a dual-pronged Pavlovian reaction in my father's mind. His hands reflexively shot out to cover the mouths of his and Mom's water glasses. He shouted out in rapid fire, "Water, no ice! No ice! Two waters no ice! No ice here! No ice!" Why this emphatic, guttural reaction to ice water? Isn't ice water refreshing, better tasting, and more thirst quenching than lukewarm tap water? Who wants to drink tepid water with a nice meal?

Ice equated with anathema to Mom and—by extension after forty-plus years of marriage—to Dad. Sydelle's Raynaud's Disease again came into play here at breakfast. If she touched a glass of ice water, her fingers would turn a frigid shade of bluish-purple. The arctic sensations in her fingers would then diffuse to permeate the rest of her body, just like a medication infused through an IV line in your hand courses through your circulatory system. Coats would be mobilized in an attempt to rectify the situation, but the extent of the improvement could only be partial. She may not warm up until tucked in bed underneath a thick down quilt. Drinking ice water would be even worse than touching the glass, because the ingestion would accelerate the cold diffusion process in both duration and magnitude.

Sydelle wouldn't resurface from underneath the quilt until it was time to fly back to Geriatricville. Dad had seen this phenomenon play out time and again. The imagery has been permanently branded into his retinas, hence his urgent reaction.

Restaurant patrons quietly and politely mutter a "thank you" or more commonly say nothing at all while the water is poured. The water server just goes about his or her business, existing on the fringe of consciousness of typical diners. But after Gerry's verbal barrage, their water server was rendered stunned like a deer caught in headlights. The server stood tableside, motionless, and unsure of how to act. Beads of condensation dripped from the bottom of the pitcher onto the white tablecloth, but the temporary paralysis induced by Dad's verbal tirade kept the server's feet mired as if knee-deep in a cement block. Gerry snapped the water server back into consciousness by repeating his frenzied request.

"Water, no ice! No ice! Two waters no ice! No ice here! No ice!"

By now, enough repetition had occurred such that the synapses in the water server's brain had begun to fire. He apologetically removed two of the ice-filled water glasses and sheepishly returned a few moments later with two glasses of lukewarm water. The water was likely sourced closer to dirty dishwater than a French alpine or Pacific island spring, but that's immaterial.

Dad didn't realize the effects his actions and words had on the water server. He's been brainwashed by Sydelle to leap into action. Gerry was steadfastly loyal to Syd. He sought to protect her and defend her in any way, no matter how simple. It was the clearest way he showed his love for her. Mom's absolute intolerance for anything cold was ingrained in Dad's brain, so he acted instantaneously when he sighted the ice water. People don't consciously think about putting their left foot in front of their right foot whenever they walk. My father didn't think about spouting off like Old Faithful to stop the Ice Capades. He just reacted. It was the present day equivalent of a medieval knight spreading his cloak over a muddy puddle to protect his damsel's feet.

Another question remained. Why were two waters without ice requested? If Sydelle was the cold member of the duo, why couldn't Gerry tolerate a few cubes in his glass? Gerry didn't have Raynaud's Disease. He actually gravitated toward the warmer than average side of the spectrum, usually complaining that it was either too hot outdoors or too hot indoors. Maybe Dad had ice intolerance by association. Maybe he had sympathy- or empathy-associated ice aversion. Maybe he wished to present a unified front to the water server, a symbolic stance of solidarity with his beloved.

I let the Ice Capades go uninterrupted. It ended as quickly as it started, and I chose to keep my sarcastic tongue in my coffee cup. Humor helps me connect with people and stay connected with people in a more meaningful way. A patient may show up in my office with a potentially life threatening medical problem. A young physician may be interviewing for our fellowship program. Both of these people are nervous, anxious and, particularly in the former case, quite scared. If I've made these people laugh at least three times before each walks out of my door, I've met one key criterion for a successful visit, in my opinion.

I don't know how or when sarcasm became such a key part of my sense of humor. I suppose it's a style that just came naturally to me. Once in a while though, I realize that I can take my sarcasm too far, especially with my parents. Understandably, they sometimes think I'm ridiculing them despite the fact that it's not my intention. So when the Ice Capades antics unfolded before my eyes over breakfast at the Paris Hotel, I sipped my coffee and kept my wisecracks to myself. I had already heaped a fair amount of sarcasm into their laps and the weekend was only just getting started.

CHAPTER 11

THANKSGIVING OR THANKSRECEIVING?

A waitress appeared a few minutes later to tell us about the special omelet of the day. This was a complete waste of time. Mom and Dad never ordered daily specials. Never. The server might as well have been speaking Latin. Hearing loss combined with inattentiveness generally prevents Gerry from catching the full description of the specials. When he happens to hear an unfamiliar ingredient, his cognitive train derails. Upon request, Sydelle fills in the blanks after the server leaves the table, but the supplemental information only has about a thirty-eight percent chance of penetrating into Dad's cerebral cortex. It's a lost cause. Even when one of the specials is recognized, the usual failure to disclose the price of the dish renders it doomed.

As we waited for breakfast to be served, Mom told the story of the last time Elyse and I hosted Thanksgiving weekend for my parents and Uncle Bern in Minneapolis. I sat back quietly and listened with some difficulty to her version of the story, which was replete with "lovelies" and "wonderfuls." As nice as her recollections were, though, they were laced with guilt over the fact that it had been seven years since we had spent Thanksgiving together. I acknowledge that my parents take great pleasure in spending holidays with me; most families enjoy spending time with each other over the holidays. As you may imagine, though, my recollection of the 2005 holiday season differed ever so slightly from that of my mother's.

Thanksgiving has always been my favorite holiday. For me, it's about the November chill in the air and the warmth of the fireplace in the family room. It's about the scented candles glowing throughout the house mixed with the sweet and savory aromas wafting from the kitchen. It's about the turkey prepared the way my grandmother Anna used to make it along with a couple of new dishes I debut every year to keep the dinner fresh and exciting. It's about the last glimpses of the panoply of autumnal colors prior to the first snowfalls of the rapidly approaching Minnesota winter. It's about the busyness of the holiday season and the time off from work to partake in it with our most cherished friends and family. It's about the pro football games on TV and tossing the football outside with the kids. It's about old traditions and emerging traditions. Call me sappy. I can take it. It's just the way I feel about the holiday.

When Elyse and I host Thanksgiving dinner, I plan the dinner about four weeks in advance and spend the better part of the holiday week putting it all together. Thanksgiving in 2005 was no exception in this regard. Daphne was the main novelty on this particular Thanksgiving. She was born the previous month, and my sister-in-law was in town to both help Elyse and meet her first niece for the first time. I spent the five days leading up to Thanksgiving doing all the requisite prep work for a fairly elaborate traditional dinner. That meant putting in a full day in the operating room, then coming home to cook until 11:00 p.m. By the time Thanksgiving morning rolled around, I dragged my already exhausted ass out of bed at the crack of dawn to begin to assemble the meal. I cooked nonstop until mid-afternoon. At about 3:00 p.m., I stepped away from the oven just long enough to pick up Mom, Dad, and Bern at the airport.

While I waited the standard ten minutes for Sydelle to come out of the restroom in the baggage claim area, Elyse and her sister Stephanie called me to ask for guidance, saying that they had dropped the turkey onto the kitchen floor while basting the bird. After freaking out, I simply told them to return the bird to the roasting pan and pretend like it never happened; no one would ever know the difference. Dinner was about two hours away; the only alternatives were the microwave pizzas sitting in the freezer. Elyse's laughter gave her prank away. The turkey never hit the floor, but I confess that they did have me going there for a while.

I arrived home with my parents and Uncle Bern in tow. At the time, Elyse and I were living in a small two-bedroom condo in downtown Minneapolis that did not have a formal dining room. Instead, we had a round wooden table that could comfortably seat four and a pair of nearby barstools poised underneath a high kitchen countertop. Bern grabbed a beer out of the fridge and planted himself on the couch to watch the Detroit Lions battle the Green Bay Packers. He made no pretenses about offering to help me out, as his culinary skills were limited to the preparation of hot dogs and baked beans. That was just fine with me. I was content to have his calming influence on my father and regular updates on the score of the football game.

Dad invaded my kitchen. He stuck his nose into the pots simmering on the stove. When he thought I wasn't looking, he swiped the wooden spoons nestled in their trivets to sample the sauces and gravies. Not content to look through the oven's glass door, he instead let the heat out each time he unnecessarily cranked the squeaky door ajar to inspect the turkey.

After urinating again, Mom promptly marched upstairs, intent on watching Elyse breastfeed our newborn daughter. Elyse nipped that one in the bud (pun intended); she rightfully booted her mother-in-law out of the bedroom with the swiftness of a seasoned bouncer inspecting the cheap fake ID of a college freshman. She wanted to preserve that bastion of sanctity between mother and daughter that comes with breastfeeding. Taking a page from the Queen's Guard in front of Buckingham Palace, my sister-in-law stood sentry in front of our closed master bedroom door to guard against a repeat assault on Elyse's privacy.

That play worked to my advantage. It was more successful than the screen passes the Lions were trying to execute against the Packers' swarming defense. When Sydelle returned to the ground floor, she extracted the nuisance that was my father from my small kitchen, calling his attention to the bowls of snacks in the family room. Gerry grabbed a handful of nuts and planted himself on the couch next to Bern.

During a TV timeout, Bern threatened to stuff Dad underneath one of the beds if he kept pestering me in the kitchen. My uncle reminded my father that it wouldn't have been the first time he temporarily stored one of his relatives underneath a bed. Dad knew that the "relative" Bern spoke of was none other than the mother of his ex-wife. Bern's only marriage to a woman named Elaine ended in an annulment long before I was born. He spoke of his marriage very rarely, so I paid attention whenever the topic arose.

I first learned that he had been married when I was about ten or eleven years old. His wife had some advanced form of psychosis during an era in which mental illness was poorly understood and severely socially stigmatized. The marriage was doomed before it began, but Bern's contentious relationship with his hotheaded, self-aggrandizing mother-in-law further stoked the already simmering marital fire. Unsolicited as it was, Bern used the present TV timeout to retell the story of the denouement of his ill-fated marriage.

"Things came to a head one night during a fierce three-way argument in my apartment, Harley. The neighbors called the cops when they heard all of the hollering through the walls. By the time the police arrived, Elaine's mother had gotten herself so worked up that I had to stuff her underneath the bed in my bedroom." Bern had wedged her into the space in between the bed frame and the floor for safekeeping. "I thought this was a safer option than trying to physically restrain the lunatic until she calmed down," he explained.

"What exactly was Elaine doing while you were cramming her mother under the bed?" I asked curiously.

"She was standing catatonically in the corner of the bedroom. She didn't know what to make of the situation, Harley. Anyway, I felt that my mother-in-law was so out of control that she posed a danger to herself. More importantly, she posed a danger to me. The way I saw it, I had a choice. The choice was either to shove my mother-in-law under the bed or deposit her outside the bedroom window on the rusty fire escape. Since it was below thirty degrees outside and my barefoot mother-in-law was dressed only in a nightgown, I chose the more chivalrous option—you know I'm a gentleman at heart, don't you, Harl?"

"A true knight in shining armor, Bern. That's you."

"The cops bought my story. I talked my way out of an arrest that night and into the office of a divorce lawyer the next morning. The story didn't end there, though. The first attorney, whose name I've long forgotten, wasn't terribly motivated to get me out of my marriage. The only skill this lawyer had was delivering invoices for his services. The legal bills kept pouring in as the months kept rolling along, but the divorce proceedings never gained momentum."

"So what did you do next?"

"I was out of patience, Harl. I stormed into his office one day and called him out on his ineptitude. Still, there were no results; I had no satisfaction. But I had a couple of buddies whose family owned a pizza parlor in the city. I vented my frustrations over a couple of slices of pizza and a beer with them one evening. My friends told me to stop worrying, that my troubles would soon be over."

Bern paused for effect for a moment. He didn't need to; he still commanded the floor.

"Sure enough, a couple of my friends' 'associates' with mafia ties paid a visit to my lawyer. Within a week, my legal fees were refunded in full."

"What exactly did these 'associates' say to the lawyer?"

"It wasn't what they said, it was what they asked. They asked the lawyer if he had a vested interest in keeping his kneecaps located somewhere between his thighs and his shins."

Classic mafia, I thought to myself as Bern wrapped up the story. It was impressive, if it was, in fact, true.

"So I took my money and retained a new divorce attorney named Stanford Lotwin, this time with much better results. In a time when outright adultery constituted the only real grounds for divorce, Lotwin somehow convinced the judge to grant an annulment. Boy, was I happy to sign that paperwork."

"What happened to Elaine? Did you ever speak to her after the annulment went through?"

"She was in bad shape, Harl. Elaine spent the rest of her life in a psychiatric facility. The court ordered me to partially pay the expenses until the day she passed away. I considered it a small price to pay for my freedom. For me, Stanford Lotwin ranks alongside Joe DiMaggio and Mickey Mantle on my list of great American heroes."

Having decimated the bowl of nuts, Dad had moved on to the dried fruits and cheeses by the time Elyse and Stephanie returned to our family room. I was putting the finishing touches on dinner. In addition to the roast turkey, I had prepared all of the other traditional dishes from scratch, right down to the gravy. Thoroughly exhausted, all I wanted to do was sit back and slowly savor the meal and my daughter's first Thanksgiving over a few glasses of red wine.

Elyse and her sister "volunteered" to sit at the bar, while the rest of us sat at the table. In their minds, the bar clearly offered the more peaceful option. Changing diapers and staring at our kitchen appliances during the meal were far more preferable to watching Dad and Bern devour Thanksgiving dinner like a pack of African hyenas hacking apart the carcass of a zebra.

I carved the turkey, which did not require any special skill set. Dad and Bern nonetheless heaped on a pile of undue praise, asserting that my burgeoning surgical skills cultivated throughout the years training in residency somehow translated into an unusually high degree of turkey-carving prowess impossible for a layman to replicate.

"Look at him go, Bernard."

"He's a surgeon, Gerry. What else did you expect?"

"Look at the size of that carving knife!"

"I carried a knife like that in the army, Gerry. It came in handy."

"For what? You never saw any hand-to-hand combat in Germany."

"I used it to slice salami and cheese when we bivouacked out on maneuvers in the field. I also used it to stir the big pots of coffee I brewed for the guys every morning."

"Not me, Bernard. I only use an electric knife to carve a turkey. I should have brought it for Harley to borrow."

"Harley is managing just fine without it, Gerry. He could have borrowed a couple of scalpels from his operating room if he needed extra cutlery."

"Look Bernard! He's slicing against the grain! Or is it with the grain? I can't tell."

"Relax, will you? The turkey will taste the same either way. I guarantee it."

"You're supposed to slice along the grain, Bernard. Tell him! Tell Harley to go with the grain!"

"I'm telling you to relax, Gerry! At ease, soldier!"

"I've never seen turkey come off the backbone so cleanly, Bern. Wow, that knife must be sharp!"

"Take a look. That's what a surgeon looks like."

"Harley cut right through the joint between the thigh and the leg. He knew exactly where to make the cut! How did he know where to make the cut?"

"He knows, Gerry! He knows. A surgeon knows these things. Now stop talking for a minute and have another slice of cheese."

Elyse and my sister-in-law brought all of the other dishes to the table while I carried out my turkey dissection.

It was all over in a flash. Bern and Dad finished their meal before I sat down and picked up my fork. Literally. Elyse and her sister looked at each other dumbfounded. They had respectfully waited to start their meal until I arrived at the table. They expected a toast celebrating the holiday together, a toast to my daughter's first Thanksgiving, and a toast to me, the cook. None of that happened. So Elyse stepped up and delivered the toast herself. Gerry and Bern muttered some form of muffled assent through the stuffing that filled their mouths without looking up from their dinner plates. I didn't let that stop me from enjoying my dinner, but Elyse was outraged. She decided right then and there that we would spend Thanksgiving with her family in Santa Fe for the indefinite future.

Back at the Le Café Ile St. Louis, peace, love, and joy descended on the table the instant breakfast arrived. Dialogue halted. Sydelle replaced it with a monologue; she continued to chat away, though it was unclear to whom she was speaking. Dad shoved approximately seventy-five percent of his scrambled eggs into his mouth before Mom's pancakes cooled enough to permit a bite. When he chose to reply to Sydelle's chatter, it was in the form of a single word, grunt, hand gesture, or nod.

I enjoyed the serenity while it lasted, because the joy was fleeting. The diabolical kitchen had committed an act of omission. My breakfast failed to arrive simultaneously with the rest of the food. Most servers only had two arms, but Dad expected these people to possess the balance and flexibility of the ensemble cast of Cirque du Soleil. The fact that the server had to make a second trip to the kitchen was a hard reality for my father to face.

Additionally, we were short one fork. A search party was deployed for the missing flatware while hypotheses were voiced as to its whereabouts. Did it fall onto the floor? Did the restaurant set the table with an insufficient number of forks from the outset? Did the busboy (accidentally or intentionally) clear the fork? These questions were never answered, but they did fill the time it took to pilfer a replacement fork from one of the nearby tables.

But the show still couldn't go on. The steak in Bern's steak and eggs was too rare. On average, when dining out with my family, about one out of every three entrées is jettisoned back to the kitchen for modification. On this morning, it was Bern's steak. It was ordered medium, but it appeared to be medium rare instead.

"Send it back! Send it back, Bernard! Tell them! Don't eat it! Tell them! Tell them! Send it back!" bellowed Gerry in between forkfuls of his own eggs. Food particles spewed from his mouth like water from a rotating sprinkler head in the middle of a front lawn. You would think he was heroically foiling the attempted poisoning of a fifteenth-century European monarch.

"Waiter! Sir! Hello? Here. Over here!" Dad summoned the server before Bern had the chance to protest. His hand shot straight up into the air to attract the waiter, like a third grader eager to catch his teacher's attention. By now, the server had returned to our table so many times that the hardwood floors needed to be refinished.

By the time Bern's modified steak and eggs returned to the table, the steak looked like the sole of a shoe and the scrambled eggs looked like yellow rubber. Gerry's breakfast plate represented the culinary equivalent of a tabula rasa. It was cleaned so thoroughly that he could have flossed his teeth in the reflection. Satiated for the moment, he had some time to work with as he plotted his next move. My father was the lurking leopard perched atop a tree branch deep within the African savannah. These leopards spent their days relaxing in the trees, cooling off, conserving energy, and sleeping.

But mostly they were biding their time, waiting for the cloak of nightfall to facilitate the hunt.

Gerry was also on the prowl. He appeared to be digesting, but he wasn't. The piece of bread he used to mop up the last molecules of sauce on his plate served the same purpose as the spots on a leopard's coat— it was a camouflage tactic. All Sydelle had to do was show some subtle sign of weakness. Her consumption slowed, with 2.36 pancake forkings per minute compared with 2.73 forkings with her first bites. She spent some more time conversing. She sipped some more water. That's all it took for Gerry to pounce.

Two different pouncing strategies were used. He started with a fringe attack, snagging a pancake scrap from the perimeter of Syd's plate. It was a quick strike, similar to a frog's tongue darting through the air to snatch a bug flying by. The thin, linear trail of syrup between the two plates yielded the only hard evidence of the attack. Dad didn't ask if he could taste Mom's pancakes, yet she didn't object to his gastronomic version of guerilla warfare, either.

Then, as Sydelle took her last bites, Gerry moved in for the kill. His motivation for finishing off her pancakes had nothing to do with residual hunger and everything to do with a philosophical belief in finishing what was started. In one fluid motion, he impaled her remaining pancakes onto his fork, airlifted them off her plate, and deposited them onto his. Birds swoop down to snag fish out of rapidly flowing rivers with similar efficiency and precision.

At the apex of the arc, Dad ostentatiously blurted out, "I'm full. I don't want any more."

"Who do you think you're fooling, huh? It's only a matter of time before the rest of my eggs meet the same fate as those pancakes over there," said Bern to his brother-in-law. I enjoyed it whenever someone besides myself periodically called out Dad.

Needless to say, Dad didn't even ask Sydelle if she was finished eating. To do so would have tipped his poker hand.

Mom suppressed her craving for a little something sweet at the end of breakfast. Dessert was her favorite part of any meal. Dad's tastes aligned with the savory end of the flavor spectrum. He was more of a meat and potatoes type of gastronome and never voluntarily ordered dessert. True to character, he ordered a decaffeinated coffee with milk on this occasion. There was a cognitive disconnect here: the caloric load of the food he just devoured didn't matter to him, but the saturated fat content in one half teaspoon of cream was completely out of the question. I suppressed the desire to inquire as to whether his waistline was impervious to the fat in the twenty-two ounces of steak he just guzzled down with his eggs. Mom ordered a decaf coffee as well, so as not to inhibit falling asleep that night, a good fourteen hours from now. Apparently, getting out of bed overnight to urinate every couple of hours had no effect on her sleep cycle, but the wheels came off the bus after a few dozen milligrams of caffeine.

Our server presented Gerry with the check. He whipped out his bifocals from the front pocket of his shirt as soon as it arrived. Any shirt that didn't have a front pocket to house his bifocals was intrinsically flawed. This prerequisite also applied to T-shirts. The bill was checked and double-checked for accuracy. With the economy still recovering from the recession, the restaurant could've been trying to squeeze my father for a few extra dollars.

The frown on my father's face signaled a problem as he scrutinized the check. I scanned the restaurant to see how crowded it was, should Dad lose his composure and create a scene.

"Sydelle, what's Pet Fillet? Who ordered pets? Who eats pets for breakfast? What kind of pets has Bernard been eating over there? What's P-E-T F-I-L-L-E-T?"

My mother leaned over to examine the check.

"Gerry, it's an abbreviation. The food we ordered is abbreviated on the check. It's the steak you just ate with your eggs. It's the petite filet mignon."

This was not good. It was nothing but a source of confusion for Gerry.

"I didn't order that!"

"Of course you did! You and Bernard both had the eight-ounce petite filet mignon with scrambled eggs."

"Oh."

"What about this Seas Med printed on the bottom here?

"It stands for seasonal medley—the fruit bowl Harley ordered for breakfast."

"Why can't they just call it a fruit bowl?"

Sydelle deciphered the rest of the code, which you would think was written with invisible ink in ancient Sanskrit by the way my father wrestled with it. Bern was getting agitated, to my delight. I found it entertaining when he lost his patience with Dad. No one else could yell at Dad in a way that would shut him up, make me laugh, and avoid offending my father in the process. Considering the number of times Gerry overreacted over the years, Bern had plenty of chances to cultivate this skill.

"Sydelle doesn't make up the menu, Gerry. Stop creating problems. Stop asking her questions she can't answer. Stop knocking yourself out for no good reason! Just pay the damn bill already! Move on and pay the damn bill!"

If it had been at my father's disposal, he would have used the giant telescope at the Arecibo Observatory in Puerto Rico to inspect this bill. If Gerry worked for the federal government, the budget deficit would never have reached its present calamitous state. As the audit of the breakfast check drew to a close, his credit card reluctantly slid into the cracked clear plastic holder inside the worn bill case.

Gerry signed the check with the pen housed adjacent to the reading glasses in his shirt pocket. Writing implements furnished by the restaurant were shunned for fear that they were teeming with cholera, schistosomiasis or, worst of all, the dreaded rhinovirus. You may agree with this. The guy didn't want to catch a cold. But delve a little deeper beneath the surface of this phobia and you'll quickly see the flagrant lack of any logic. Haven't the countless prior servers and patrons all touched the same rectangular black case in which the bill resided? Did their server scrub in and glove up prior to handling the bill case like a surgeon prepping their hands for the operating room? The pen habit was so ingrained in my father's mind that it was useless to bring up these points. As for me, I've symbolically rebelled. I'll go so far as to bring a restaurant's pen home as a souvenir of a particularly memorable meal.

The morning drew to a close as we readied to leave Le Café Ile St.

Louis. A couple of years had passed since the four of us were together, and it had taken two meals over an eighteen-hour period to reestablish our equilibrium. Syd fumbled with the buttons, clasps, and zippers of her jacket as she prepared to face the sixty-three degree outdoor temperature. Dad categorized the receipts and other miscellany in his wallet. Bern and I were tired of sitting around and eager to have some fun exploring the Strip and hitting the blackjack tables and casino sports books. Taking one final swig of his coffee, he walked out of the restaurant. I followed suit.

CHAPTER 12

THE GOOCH AND THE MOOCH

Having survived breakfast without any esophageal malfunctions, we walked over to the Bellagio hotel. Admittedly, I approached the Bellagio with some positive energy. Dad was in the lead, Bern and I walked side by side in the middle of the pack, and Syd trailed a few paces behind. As we crossed Las Vegas Boulevard, my thoughts drifted back to my childhood.

When I was a kid growing up, Saturday was my favorite day of the week. Before the homework really started to pile up, I spent Saturday mornings in my pajamas watching cartoons on TV, playing on my state-of-the-art Atari 2600 gaming system, and messing with my jigsaw puzzles and Legos. Around lunchtime, I camped out in front of the kitchen window, waiting for Uncle Bern's car to pull up in front of our house on Long Island. My grandmother always accompanied him, and the two of them would spend the rest of the day with us before driving back to Queens long after my bedtime. Those visits became some of my most cherished childhood memories. Bern's objective during these visits was quite simple: he sought relaxation and fun. As a career lithographer, he spent his days commuting on the New York City subways from his apartment in Queens to the printing presses housed in huge buildings in the SoHo section of lower Manhattan. He worked long hours that frequently extended throughout the night when a strict deadline had to be met.

Unable to afford to associate with beach-house socialites in the Hamptons on the eastern tip of Long Island, Bern viewed his Saturdays at my parents' house like the equivalent of a country getaway. When it was too cold to toss a ball around outside, he taught me how to play blackjack, poker, and gin rummy. Bern didn't care for board games like Clue or Battleship. He preferred games with real-world practicality, meaning games where money could be exchanged. Dad would play with us too, albeit reluctantly on most occasions. Uncle Bern was unmistakably the driving force, and I idolized him for his eagerness to teach me these adult games. Yet I never had the chance to actually gamble with him. Medical school had created a sieve of negative cash flow through my twenties from steadily mounting tuition loans, leaving no extra money in my pockets to dump into the casinos' vaults. About twenty-six years had now passed since we first started playing cards together on the carpeted floor of my parents' den on Long Island. This Friday afternoon in Las Vegas had been a very long time in the making. I was truly excited to sit down alongside Uncle Bern at the blackjack tables, a couple of cold beers in our hands.

The last time Bern was in Las Vegas, Mario Puzo had Morris "Moe" Greene running the city in the original installation of The *Godfather* trilogy. Taking in the sensory overload that was now synonymous with the Strip, Bern watched the serenade of the trademark dancing fountains in front of the Bellagio. Venturing inside the grand casino, he stood in the front lobby, his eyes fixed on the Chihuly glass ceiling. I studied his face, surmising that he must have felt like he was in a James Bond movie considering he was used to the exposed pipes, peeling paint, and concrete floor of the basement poker room back home in his New York apartment building. But we didn't linger, as the canopied blackjack tables and scantily clad cocktail waitresses were calling. Sydelle and Gerry wandered off to play the penny or nickel slots. The way they gambled, they were slated to receive a complimentary cup of decaffeinated coffee to share in about seventeen years. After circling the banks of table games in the center of the casino floor, Bern and I selected a ten-dollar-minimum blackjack table and sat down. My hands were clammy and my heart pounded against the inside of my chest wall as I reviewed some of the finer points of basic strategy while arranging my stack of chips at the table.

As the dealer paused to refill the automatic card shuffler, my years of anticipation were dashed in a moment. The disappointment had nothing to do with the cards subsequently dealt as the new hand started.

From his spot at the table immediately to my left, Bern said, "I forgot my ATM card back home in New York."

"What? Seriously?"

"Yeah. I forgot it, Harl. It's not in my wallet."

"Okay, but I assume you brought some cash, right?"

"Yeah, I have some money, but not that much. I figured I'd use my ATM card when we got here."

"What about a cash advance on your credit card?"

"I had a credit card, but it expired last year."

I caught the unmistakable glares of the other blackjack players penetrating over the rims of their cocktails as the deal continued. I quickly lost the first hand. This was not surprising because my first two cards average 14.8 at the Vegas blackjack tables. Gathering my chips in my fist, Bern and I left the table and regrouped in the center aisle of the casino floor.

"Let me get this straight. Your ATM card is in New York, your credit card has expired, and you have just a little cash on you?"

"Yeah."

"Perfect. Why on earth didn't you renew your credit card?"

"I never use it. Those companies are all full of crooks."

Bern inherently feared credit card companies. His worries stemmed from his prior battles as a victim of identity theft. He preferred cold, hard cash for the vast majority of his transactions. Personal checks were written for the remainder. Forget about electronic bill pay. You'd see Bern walk barefoot on Mars without an oxygen mask before he paid a bill online.

"Everyone should have a valid credit card for emergency use if nothing else. I'm not suggesting that you maintain a balance and pay exorbitant interest rates."

I felt that weird feeling that comes from giving a life lesson to a person who has previously given you many lessons in life. I took a quick, deep breath.

"Okay. Forget about the credit card. Forget about the ATM card. It's no problem."

"How do you figure, Harley?"

"We're here to celebrate your eightieth birthday. I have plenty of cash, an ATM card, and about six perfectly valid if not overused credit cards in my wallet. I have you covered. Your gambling is on the house this weekend."

"I can't do that," Bern replied. Always proud, he was never one to accept any form of charity, even if it came from family.

"Oh, come on Bern!" I implored. "It's your birthday, well, kind of. Would it be so bad if I treated my only uncle once in his life?"

"No, thank you. I appreciate it, but I can't let you do that, Harley." Bern's wall of pride was impenetrable.

"Okay, fine. I'll loan you as much cash as you want. You can pay me back after the trip."

"No, thank you. I don't want your money. You work too hard for your money."

"Bern, it's a loan. You'll pay me back. It's not a big deal."

"It may not be a big deal to you, but it's a big deal to me!" Apparently, the wall of pride was made of concrete three feet thick.

I made him an offer that I thought he couldn't refuse. "How about this scenario: I'll loan you the cash now, and you can pay me back along with some interest when you get back home. I've waited my whole life to play a few hands of blackjack with you in a casino. Be reasonable!" I pleaded.

"I just can't do it, Harl. Really, thank you. I just can't do it."

I begged him. Then I begged him some more, to no avail. As it turned out, the wall of pride was made of concrete with steel reinforced to withstand a nuclear holocaust. I spent the rest of the trip dejectedly gambling by myself while forcing casual conversations with complete strangers making idiotic decisions like doubling down on an eight with the dealer showing a face card. Still worse, Bern hovered behind me, his hands stuffed into his pockets, watching me gamble in silence. Making a few bucks at the tables offered no consolation. Twenty-six years of anticipation were gone in a flash due to a rectangular piece of plastic left sitting in a faux crystal dish in Bern's New York apartment.

I've never created a bucket list of things to accomplish before I depart this earth. But if I had one, gambling with Uncle Bern would have been on it.

Instead, Bern and I spent the remainder of the morning sipping Bloody Marys and debating the pros and cons of Texas Hold 'Em, five-card draw, and seven-card stud. In between, Bern gawked and commented on the cocktail waitresses walking the casino floor. We wandered over to the sports book and window-shopped a few boutiques before meeting up with Syd and Gerry as they exchanged a few chips at the casino cashier.

Since we had been within the windowless confines of the casino for a few hours, we decided to have lunch al fresco at the poolside café of the Paris Hotel. Still reeling from the frustration of my uncle's financial situation, I wasn't particularly in the mood for cheery conversation. Bern lightened the air by levying an unsolicited series of disparaging comments against Sydelle's cousin and his arch nemesis, The Gooch. Gerry egged him on and I couldn't help but laugh, stoking my mother's ire. Sydelle's utterly predictable reaction, in turn, incited Bern to continue his tirade against The Gooch.

I'm technically related to The Gooch via my maternal grandmother, but the exact branches on the family tree are obscured by a bunch of long-deceased relatives whose names I have trouble recalling. Cousin Shirley is The Gooch's real name and I know that my grandmother was quite fond of her. At least ninety-one or ninety-two years old, she still lives by herself in Tampa, Florida. But even though Bern and Shirley are geographically separated and never speak with one another under any circumstances, The Gooch remains his one and only arch nemesis. Bern hates The Gooch to the core.

Bern nicknamed her The Gooch long before I was born, though I don't know when or why. Whenever I press Bern to divulge the nickname's origins, he never gives a clear answer. All I've learned is that the nickname is designed to portray the essence of Cousin Shirley's black constitution and convey the utter disdain and contempt my uncle has for her. The word "gooch" does sound derogatory, which of course is Bern's full intent. It sounds like a cross between a goblin and an ogre. Over the years, I learned that the term "gooch" actually refers to a small but sensitive area of the body called the perineum—the strip of skin located precisely between the genitals and the anus. I have no plans to test Bern's anatomical knowledge of the perineum, because I'm afraid of the answers he may offer up. For me, Bern's idea of The Gooch as "she-devil" works just fine.

Verbally vilifying The Gooch is one of Bern's life missions. It was a vivid, continually resurfacing conversation topic throughout my childhood. Along with my parents and grandmother, Bern and I would sit around the kitchen table after dinner talking about the extended family. To me, these characters were mostly a collection of jumbled names without faces. I sat there listening for the pure entertainment value because inevitably, Bern or Dad would find a reason to mention Cousin Shirley, each egging on the other to the eventual disgust of my mother. The Gooch's name was figuratively wired to a fuse and the fuse, in turn, was linked to a keg full of gunpowder positioned directly underneath Bern's chair.

Mom reflexively tried to come to Shirley's rescue, but the more she defended The Gooch, the more intense Bern's scorn became. Sydelle inherited her fondness for The Gooch out of a sense of loyalty to my grandmother, just as I inherited my scorn out of loyalty to Bern. As a kid who looked up to his uncle, I thought The Gooch nickname was nothing short of hysterical, so of course I regularly used it despite Mom's disapproval.

Shirley and Mom normally chatted on the phone once every few months. These were two-hour-long conversations, recurring battles of who liked to hear the sound of their own voice more, without a clear winner ever emerging. Once, about an hour or so into one of these exchanges, on a day when my six-year-old mind was in a particularly devious mood, I picked up the kitchen phone. Sydelle was on the line in the master bedroom, likely hunkered down for the long haul underneath her electric blanket. Without any hesitation, introductions, or lead-ins, I yelled out at the top of my lungs, "You know what? You're The Gooch!" Proud of myself, I promptly cradled the phone back onto its hook without waiting for a reaction and settled my wise ass in the den for a few rousing games of Pac-Man on my Atari.

The stunt cost me a week of dessert and a week of Pac-Man. It was well worth the sacrifice. Learning of my bold declaration a few days later, Bern told me that he was never more proud of his only nephew. Not even my graduation from medical school nineteen years later trumped this triumph in Bern's mind. Initially embarrassed and furious, Mom relented with time and will now reluctantly admit the humor of my offense.

I've only seen Shirley twice in my lifetime, most recently during my bar mitzvah in 1988. Cognizant of the fact that liquor would be flowing during the reception that followed the synagogue service, Syd sought to minimize the potential interaction between Bern and The Gooch. Like a boxing referee directing the fighters to opposite corners of the ring, my mother purposefully seated Bern and Shirley on opposite sides of the ballroom separated by the dance floor. A waitress was charged with keeping Bern's whiskey glass full, so that he wouldn't accidentally run into Shirley as he crossed over to the bar on her side of the reception hall. Bern threatened to start a brawl in the weeks leading up to my bar mitzvah, but he ultimately behaved and the party went off without a hitch.

That was the last time I came face-to-face with The Gooch. It wasn't a particularly memorable meeting. She simply played the role of a generic, distant, elderly relative. I recall that she was thin and rather tall for her age. Her makeup was overdone, with thickly applied lipstick that left a telltale red ring on every cheek she kissed. We exchanged a few pleasantries, but it was neither the time nor place to vet her side of the stories. Having only heard Bern's versions, I was in no objective position to say whether any or all of his disdain for The Gooch was justified. Unfair as it may have been, it still didn't mean that I had to like the woman.

~

The tirade now spewing forth from between Bern's lips snapped me back into the present. As we sat at the Paris Hotel's poolside café, Bern showered us with a fountain of saliva and a hailstorm of food particles.

"Shirley! That she-devil! That whore!"

Never before and never since I have ever heard any woman over the age of fifty-five referred to as a whore.

"That woman is sheer evil personified!" he continued.

"Oh, cut it out, Bernard!" Mom tried valiantly to cut him off, knowing full well the futility of her entreaty.

"I hate that woman! She has got some damned nerve!" Bern persev-erated.

"Stop it, Bernard! You're going to give Harley the wrong idea."

"Never mind that, Sydelle! It's my duty and my obligation to make sure Harley knows the truth about The Gooch!"

Even though I was a thirty-six-year-old man, my mother was still worried about my uncle's biased influences on my apparently impressionable mind.

"That cheap bastard! You know Shirley owes me a lot of money, Sydelle."

Never before and never since have I heard of a woman referred to as a bastard.

"Oh, Bernard! That was so many years ago."

"So? So what? I could really use that money! You remember the winter of 1956, don't you? During the winter of '56, I drove all through the pitch-black night in the middle of a raging blizzard for that lousy ingrate. I hit a pothole the size of a meteor crater that cracked the differential on my car's undercarriage. But I still delivered her merchandise to her on time. Shirley didn't offer me a nickel to get the car repaired. It was a new Oldsmobile, damn it! She didn't even give me a cup of coffee for my troubles! Half a century has passed and she still hasn't repaid her debt to me. What did she do instead? She bought herself a beautiful brand-new Buick a couple of years ago just to spite me."

"Did you ever think that she bought the Buick to replace her last car, rather than to spite you? This may come as a surprise to you, Bernard, but I don't think Shirley thinks about you nearly to the extent that you obsess over her."

Bern ignored this insinuation, true as it probably was.

"I'd take that Buick, Sydelle! The next time you talk to The Gooch, tell her to make damn sure she leaves me that Buick in her will when she finally drops dead. That's if she drops dead! That vampire is probably 647 years old and will probably live for another few hundred years. But that's the very least she can do for me. You know I'm a generous man. I'd be willing to call off the rest of her debts if I get that Buick."

I knew Bern was just warming up, so I stoked the flames a little. "Doesn't The Gooch also owe you some money from that courthouse incident?"

"That's right, Harley! You're damn right she does! See? You see, Sydelle?

Harley remembers. Harley knows how that witch of a shrew of a woman has robbed me all of these years."

Mom dismissively waved him off with a broad swipe of her hand through the stifling hot air.

"You don't know what I went through, Sydelle! You were still a baby at the time. Don't forget I've got eleven years on you. I was a teenager looking to earn some honest pocket money. I slaved away for The Gooch all day in that sweltering courthouse that Saturday in August. I must have dropped five pounds from perspiration alone busting my balls for The Gooch! You remember what she gave me for that full day's worth of backbreaking labor? Huh? Remember? One lousy, warm tuna fish sandwich. That's how she compensated me for my efforts. That's how she treats me, her family, her own flesh and blood. That's the kind of cheap son of a bitch she is!"

Never before and never since have I heard of a woman referred to as a son of a bitch.

Bern paused for dramatic effect, then pushed on.

"So at the end of the day, I made sure I had the last laugh. I went into the second floor bathroom of the courthouse, clogged the toilets with every last square of toilet paper I could find, and flushed away. I kept flushing and flushing. When the water cascaded down the marble staircase onto the main floor, I got into my car and drove away."

"Where was The Rat when this courthouse scene went down?" I asked Bern, not wanting the story to end.

"I barely saw him that day. He was probably snaking through the sewer system of the courthouse, looking for a way to permanently escape from The Gooch's tentacles and claws."

The Rat was Shirley's husband Nathan. After you abbreviate Nathan to Nat, it's but a small step to arrive at Nat The Rat. The nickname was another product of Bern's work. Nat never figured prominently in Bern's stories of The Gooch. He typically played the role of a second-tier sidekick. Not Robin—he was too valuable an asset to Batman. Kato vis-à-vis the Green Lantern was probably a more accurate comparison. If The Gooch was the root source of evil, The Rat was guilty by association. Aside from being short, squat, and markedly obese with multiple dark brown moles sprouting hair on his face, Nat didn't otherwise bear much resemblance to a rodent. Bern nicknamed him The Rat for two reasons—the smooth way in which the nickname rolled off the tongue and his criminal acts.

According to Bern, The Gooch and The Rat had hidden portions of their business income from the feds. The tax fraud went undetected for years. Eventually, one of their disgruntled employees reported their shenanigans to the IRS. A few weeks later, a pair of federal agents showed up at their front door wearing matching navy blue suits, dark sunglasses, and holstered handguns. The Gooch and The Rat had boxes of documents confiscated as part of a formal audit that concluded with a five-figure tax bill due upon receipt.

"You know, the feds compounded that interest quarterly!" Bern exclaimed in elation, as he finished his story.

"Come on, Bern! That scene with the IRS agents sounds like something you stole out of some old spy movie or TV show."

"You don't believe me, Harley? What's wrong with you? When have I ever told you anything besides the truth about that Gooch?"

"It just sounds a little far-fetched to me, Bern. Like something out of an old episode of Dragnet."

"Get me a Bible, Harley! Old Testament. You produce a Bible and I'll gladly swear upon it right now!"

"You may have to improvise, Bern. I don't see any Bibles stacked along the poolside towel racks. This is the wrong place and the wrong city to go looking for a plethora of religious reference material. You can't blame me for questioning the bit about the IRS. According to your own words, you were not physically present when the IRS showed up at The Gooch's door."

Bern didn't say anything to me by way of a reply. Instead he stood, looked skyward, and stretched out his arms. His upturned palms were shaking a little from the tension running up and down the length of his arm muscles as he exclaimed to his maker, "Please, God! Strike me down right now! Strike me down with a great bolt of lightning if I'm lying about The Gooch! I don't need to live anymore if I can't tell the truth about something so vile as that woman!"

We were in the wrong city for this weather pattern, but Bern couldn't have cared less.

"So help me God, I solemnly swear that one hundred percent of the content of one hundred percent of my stories is true. It's all true. If anyone else wants to challenge me any further about the truth, we can take it up in God's court as soon as I drop dead!"

"Okay, Bern. You win. I'm satisfied." It was difficult to force the words out through my laughter.

My father and I were enjoying a good laugh at the expense of The Gooch, to the point where I temporarily forgot my squandered chance to gamble with Bern. I even caught two waiters chuckling when Bern stood up like the statue of Christ the Redeemer in Rio de Janeiro and asked to be struck down by lightning. Gerry's laughter distracted Sydelle's wrath from Bern and onto her own deceased in-laws.

"You have no right to laugh about my family, Gerry! No right. What about that fuck father of yours, Eugene. Huh? What about him, the man who accused me of putting too much meat in my sandwiches?"

Gerry just shrugged.

"And how about that other beauty, Nettie? You know, that fuck mother of yours who burned four hundred dollars in cash in the oven?"

Syd used this expletive so rarely that it was a testament to just how strongly she felt about her in-laws.

"Yeah, what about her?" said Gerry defensively.

"Stop talking about my family. Just shut up and cut it out."

As for Nettie and Eugene, the other two characters about to be lambasted poolside by Sydelle at the Paris Hotel, there's not much to be said. Officially, I have met both my paternal grandparents. I have no recollection of either, as they both passed away prior to my first birthday. So what I know of them comes exclusively from my mother, their daughter-in-law. Dad never speaks of his parents in my presence. Whenever the subject arises, usually by Mom in response to one of Dad's many inherited, irksome shortcomings, reticence is his default response. To call a spade a spade, Syd hated her in-laws and she chose not to disguise her loathing. So her disdain was always out there in plain sight for me to observe. Maybe that's why it still seems so natural to hear of these two long-deceased people consistently referred to by Mom as "that fuck Nettie" and "that fuck Eugene." Can you feel the love in my family?

I didn't know Nettie and Eugene as people, as human beings. I only know of them as nefarious entities that cast aspersions on Mom and the righteous life she purported to lead.

~

Classic fondue would have been a fitting lunch to set the tone for the vintage 1970s story Syd was about to tell. Instead, the waiter brought me a steak Cobb salad. Bern and Dad each ordered turkey burgers with fries and Syd opted for a chicken avocado wrap with a side of fresh fruit. It was a warm Friday afternoon poolside in Vegas as Syd launched into her well-worn description of one glorious Saturday morning in early 1970s Queens, New York, a story I refer to as the Accusation of 1972. The sun was shining, the coffee was brewing, the pigeons were crapping, and the taxicab horns were blaring. Sydelle and Gerry had decided to invite Nettie and Eugene for lunch in the duplex home they occupied before moving out to Long Island. Never excited to entertain guests in her home, and even less excited to cook for the wicked pair she was expecting, Mom nonetheless expended the effort necessary to assemble the meal. It was billed as a deli-style fete, highlighted by sliced corned beef and salami sandwiches with the traditional accoutrements purchased with money she earned teaching in the trenches of the New York City public school classrooms. Quite the spread was laid out on the Formica, such that barely any of the underlying vintage 1970s lemon yellow countertops could be seen. Having reluctantly gone through this effort, how was she then supposed to feel when her father-in-law Eugene nonchalantly waltzed into the already cramped, unair-conditioned kitchen and unabashedly accused her of putting too much meat in the sandwiches?

My eyes had drifted over to the bikini-clad women in the pool, as this was not the first time I heard the deli sandwich story. I took no issue with Mom's reaction to Eugene's critique of her sandwiches. Placed in a similar situation, I would have been equally ticked off. What the hell kind of a criticism was that? New York City's legendary Carnegie Deli serves the only sandwich I've ever eaten that has too much meat in it. Homo sapiens' evolution has not caught up with the Carnegie Deli. The average human's jaws can open a maximum of forty-five degrees. This opening excursion makes it anatomically impossible for the human mouth to fit around the mid-portion of a Carnegie Deli sandwich. Only snakes that swallow their prey whole by dislocating their jaws to an angle of one hundred fifty degrees have a shot at tackling an intact Carnegie corned beef on rye, from top bread to bottom bread.

Back to the scene in Sydelle's kitchen, Eugene held court like a fat cat with his ass stuck to the orange, brown, and yellow floral-print vinyl chairs of the dinette set. If there's supposedly no such thing as a free lunch, and Sydelle had invited her father-in-law into her home to mooch a free lunch, shouldn't Eugene just have sat down, shut up, smiled, and expressed his thanks? As far as critiques go, there were certainly more harmful ones out there than accusations of overstuffing deli sandwiches. Sydelle wasn't accused of being a racist or a Communist. But she took particular offense to the whole deli lunch episode, holding a grudge that she never relinquished even decades after Eugene's death.

Whenever Dad acts too frugally, Mom is quick to remind him that he is the product of Eugene and his too-much-meat-in-the-sandwich mentality. Mortally offended by the Accusation of 1972, to this day, Sydelle defensively and reflexively points out the rampant waste that pervaded the lives of Nettie and Eugene whenever Gerry commits a miserly act.

Still upset at the joy Dad took from the disparagement of The Gooch, Syd wasn't finished condemning her in-laws. She seamlessly transitioned from deli meat to cash as we digested our lunch. Maybe it was the wad of twenty dollar bills in the center of our table that we had collected to pay for lunch that reminded her of the four hundred bucks Nettie once torched.

For some unknown reason that contradicts logic, it seems that Eugene thought his kitchen oven was a fantastic place to store four hundred dollars in cash. For more unknown reasons, Eugene didn't think he needed to inform Nettie that the money was being stored in her oven. Nettie cooked just as often as any other 1970s-era housewife, and there was only one oven in her kitchen. Eugene never cooked, and there were no cooks or other domestic servants employed in the household. Most normal people don't make a preliminary minesweep of their kitchen oven before they preheat it, and Nettie proved (at least on this one occasion) to be normal in this regard. So on a random weeknight, Nettie turned on her electric oven to prepare it for whatever roasted or baked entrée was on the docket. About ten to fifteen minutes later, a non-foodstuff odor wafted into her nose as thin grey smoke drifted in front of her eyes. Nettie had lit up the four Benjamins, rendering the currency into unrecognizable char. When Nettie later asked Eugene to justify his decision to store the four hundred dollars in the oven, the fiasco inevitably spiraled downward into a perpetually unresolved he-said-she-said fiasco.

Even though Gerry wasn't home when the four C-notes went up in flames, the end result was such that Dad could never accuse Mom of waste. Mom had a lifetime free pass on this issue, as Gerry was guilty by association.

"You know, Gerry, dinner last night didn't cost four hundred dollars. If we had the money your beauty of a mother burned, you and I could have paid for everyone's dinner last night and still had plenty left over to play the slots this morning. And did you notice the proportions of meat in the club sandwich you ordered for lunch? What do you think? Would your father have been satisfied or would he have criticized the restaurant for putting in too much and overcharging you?"

Mom didn't wait for Dad's answers. Signaling to our waiter, Syd took a momentary hiatus in her diatribe to order a cup of hot herbal tea. It was only about eighty-eight degrees outside in the Vegas shade, so a cup of piping hot tea naturally capped off her lunch. Having refueled on coffee while Syd was in the throes of her invective, Bern added that divine intervention and the federal government should have conspired to prevent The Gooch from bearing children and thus propagating her gene pool. Dad laughed, I laughed, and Mom's lips stiffened with a resolve to not let us have the last laugh. I was perfectly content to sit back and enjoy the show. Syd slalomed up and down the generations of Dad's relatives with a verbal dexterity she could never replicate in the physical world.

"We talked enough about those two winning parents of yours, Gerry. What should we do next? Do you want to discuss your dead Aunt Edie who housed a modest school of live carp in her bathtub at the expense of her personal hygiene until they were ready for the dinner table?"

Dad finally replied, albeit briefly.

"I thought she put whitefish and pike in the bathtub."

"Does it really matter, Gerry? Would whitefish in the tub have made Edie normal?" Mom then adjusted her position and crossed her legs as she settled in to lambast Robert and Steven—Gerry's two younger brothers.

"How about Robert and Steven? Remember how they treated you when Nettie and Eugene were on their deathbeds? The money they screwed you out of could also have paid for dinner last night—and a brand-new condo in the Las Vegas suburbs."

"I don't think about them anymore," was all Dad could sheepishly reply. He tried his best to shrug off the remainder of Mom's onslaught.

The last I heard, Robert and Steven were both alive and residing somewhere in Colorado. In fact, everything I've ever learned about them started and ended with Syd and Gerry's recollections and opinions. Put simply, it was their version of the truth, not mine. The last time I physically saw them was thirty-five years ago, when i was about a year old. At the time, these two paternal uncles of mine were both flat broke, unemployed, and strung out on hashish. I didn't know if the hash made them chronically unemployable or whether their unemployment left them with nothing else to do. The only physical feature of this duo that Mom and Dad consistently described was their hair. There was an abundance of it—dark, greasy, curly, beyond-shoulder-length, 1980s disheveled rocker hair. Standing side by side, you couldn't tell where one mane-mullet combo ended and the other began, like a dense forest of weeping willow trees. At any rate, these two uncles pooled what little resources they had and hitchhiked down to Florida, intent on convincing my dying paternal grandparents to cut my father out of their will. (Nettie and Eugene retired to Florida sometime between the deli meat fiasco of 1972 and my birth in 1975.) Along with the munchies, the hash must have conferred unusually strong negotiating powers on Robert and Steven. My paternal grandparents passed away within a year of one another, as the ink was still drying on their revised wills. The duo promptly absconded to Colorado, having successfully cut my unsuspecting father out of his inheritance.

Listening to Mom reminded me of the life of Billy the Kid, who tried desperately to reach Old Mexico before Pat Garrett caught up with him and brought him to justice. With the recent legalization of marijuana in Colorado, I suppose it's a natural fit for Robert and Steven.

Dad wasn't bothered by the insults Mom brought down upon Robert and Steven as our lunch ended. He swore off his brothers' existences after his parents' estate was settled, vowing never to speak with them again. He was thirty-five years into this oath and still held on to his grudge with the force of a vice grip. As for me, I adopted Dad's oath out of allegiance. Showing solidarity with my father, I permanently walled off whatever remained of my father's side of the family in my mind. These relatives never generated so much as a fleeting thought in my head, with two exceptions. I thought of Robert and Steven whenever Sydelle criticized these putative misfits. I also thought of them when Elyse, of all people, mentioned them. Understanding with perfect clarity the myopic perspective that Sydelle used to generate her self-serving opinions, Elyse thought that my attitudes about my paternal relatives were the product of maternal brainwashing. Until proven otherwise by an objective third party, Elyse thought there could be dozens of wonderful aunts, uncles, and cousins somewhere out there just waiting to be discovered. However, Mom's impressions of my father's family were set in stone. The emotional damage inflicted by Nettie and Eugene was irreparable. For Syd, it boiled down to one key black-and-white point: her family was good and destined for heaven and Dad's family was bad and destined to sail down the River Styx on the way to hell. These were her feelings, this was her grudge to bear, and she was determined to have this imagery perpetuated in my mind.

How should I have reconciled these drastic differences of opinion? I reasoned that until I saw a Nobel Peace Prize, Congressional Medal of

Honor, or *Time* magazine "Person of the Year" award bestowed upon Robert and Steven, I was satisfied maintaining the status quo.

The relentless mid-afternoon desert sun was taking its toll on me, as I sat roasting at the poolside café while Mom, Dad, and Bern traded shots at dead and almost-dead relatives. The temperature outside remained in the high eighties, but even in the shade it felt like it was about 105 degrees. Dry heat be damned, it was hot. After some careful deliberation, I suggested a swim to kill off the three hours until dinner. There were less than ten other guests in the pool at the time. One presumably newlywed couple was off in the corner, trying to maximize their body contact. A family of four at the other end of the pool was lathering up in sunscreen. Another couple was in the middle of the shallow end performing some form of aquatic Jazzercise that Richard Simmons would have loved to bring to market. (Mom and Dad would probably have a lot in common with this last couple.) I figured I could potentially incorporate a workout while the rest of the family cooled off. The endorphin rush from half an hour of laps would fuel me through the rest of the day.

"Why don't we all go for a dip in the pool?" I proposed.

"Oh, I don't know, Harley. I'll get a chill in a bathing suit. It's so windy up here." Sydelle extricated herself. Mind you, we were on the third floor of the hotel, not the summit of Mount Denali.

Gerry was next to bow out. "My medication—I can't be out in the sun."

"What are you talking about, Dad?"

"My medication! My pills. Some of my medication makes me susceptible to sunburn. I'm not supposed to be in direct sunlight for more than thirty minutes at a time."

"Seriously?"

"Yes, Harley. It's clearly written in black and white among the list of potentially serious side effects."

"Is it listed before toenail fungus or after spontaneous salivation?"

Dad's answer was decisive. Humor was not going to make my father let down his guard. I recollected the skull and crossbones slide that my professor showed on the first day of my medical school pharmacology course. It drove home the point that all medications are potentially poisonous and that physicians should always have a good reason supporting each prescription they write. I was about to ask Dad about the ramifications of thirty-one consecutive minutes of sun exposure, but concluded that I lacked the mental fortitude to deal with whatever response he would muster.

The prospects of a workout were fading fast. I tried to convince my father to be reasonable.

"Okay, Dad. Susceptibility does not equate with inevitability. Why can't you slap on a generous layer of sunscreen, jump in the pool to cool off, and then sit in the shade with a hat and a towel?"

He shook his head emphatically from side to side as he said, "No."

"Why the hell not?" I shot back, summoning some of the mental fortitude I previously thought absent.

"Because I'm not supposed to be out in the sun!"

"Look around, Dad. There's no giant magnifying glass above the pool frying you like an ant on an equatorial sidewalk. Jump into the pool and cool off for fifteen minutes. It won't kill you."

"I don't want to take any chances, Harley."

Neil Armstrong took a chance. Jackie Robinson took a chance. Benedict Arnold took a chance. Some obviously worked out better than others, but they were all made with much higher stakes at play and under considerably more trying circumstances.

"You can reapply sunscreen as soon as you get out of the water while you towel off in the shade," I reasoned.

"No! Not for me!" Gerry was out.

"Where's the diving board?" Uncle Bern asked.

"I don't see a diving board, Bern."

"How can you put a nice swimming pool in a luxury hotel without installing a diving board? It's like manufacturing a Ferrari without any tires."

Bern voiced a similar dissatisfaction with the setup of the Geriatricville pool. Each dive there would come with a 38 percent chance of a hip fracture, so I understood its absence.

"Most people vacationing poolside in Vegas aren't thinking about a reverse two-and-a-half somersault in the tuck position from a ten-meter platform, Bern. They're main concern is whether to order a piña colada or a margarita."

"Well I need a diving board. An ice cold brew wouldn't hurt, either."

"What if I tempt you by dangling a couple of beers off the edge of the pool to lure you into the water?"

"I only swim in pools that have diving boards, Harley."

I threw in the towel, defeated. We lingered and loitered at the poolside café for the next couple of hours. Sydelle updated me on current events, meaning the happenings in the lives of her closest friends and the friends of her friends. I also received unsolicited updates on everyone three-degrees-of-separation-removed from these innermost circles of compatriots.

"You remember my friend, Sylvia, right?"

"Sure, Mom." I wouldn't know Sylvia if I fell over her. If Sylvia's driver's license fell out of her wallet into my lap during the fall, I still wouldn't know who the hell she was. But knowing how much my mother enjoyed to share a juicy item or two of gossip, I let her keep talking.

"Well, Sylvia had to come back early from her trip to St. Petersburg—Russia, not Florida. Her cousin's daughter's eight-month-old baby had a bad ear infection. It was a double ear infection, in fact. Imagine that. She had to come all the way back from Russia in the middle of her trip. How awful is that?"

"Rough break for Sylvia." How much did Syd really expect me to care about her friend's cousin's daughter's baby's routine ailment?

"And did you hear what happened to Ellen?" she continued without pausing.

"No, Mom. How the hell would I hear about what happened to Ellen?"

"I don't know, Harley. I thought that you might have spoken with Phil because you two used to be so friendly."

"Phil hasn't called me in eleven years." I sadly confessed the extent to which my childhood friends and I drifted apart since I moved to Minneapolis.

"Oh, well in that case, let me tell you." Mom was more concerned with her gossip than my fading friendships. "Ellen's nephew got engaged to a shiksa last month. They live in a nice suburb in northern Virginia. He works in the D.C. metro area, so living in northern Virginia makes sense. She doesn't know what to do about the wedding. Should she go? Should she not go? And what about the gift? What do you do about the gift? For Jews you give cash. What do you do for shiksas?"

"How about something off the happy couple's wedding registry?" I proposed, trying to be helpful.

I fumbled with the few loose casino chips in my pocket, thinking of the activity I would rather be doing.

"That's fine for the girl, but it might offend the groom."

I thought that if anyone were to be offended it would be the groom's mother, not the groom, but I chose not to call Mom out on this point, lest the story divert along another pointless tangent.

"How about some cash and a smaller item off the registry? Shouldn't that satisfy all parties?"

"Two gifts? That's too much for Ellen. She's already incurring all the travel expenses to go to the wedding in the first place."

Having exhausted my reasonable solutions to Ellen's conundrum, I resorted to sarcasm.

"I recommend lingerie, in that case. Maybe a nice his-and-hers matching set? A combination of leather and lace may be nice."

"Very funny, Harley."

"Look, Mom. I have every confidence that Ellen won't show up at her own nephew's wedding empty-handed. She can always haul a Kitchen-Aid mixer across the country as a last resort."

Two and a half hours later, we got up from the poolside table to leave. I couldn't decide if my butt or my mind was more insensate. I liked juicy gossip as much as anyone else; most operating rooms are rife with it (which is what invariably happens when a small population of coworkers spends many uninterrupted hours together). But this talk of possible wedding gifts for a stranger's nephew hardly qualified. I would have been far more engaged if Dad had spoken of a rumor about a geriatric porn movie being produced in Geriatricville, or if Bern discussed the ways some of his friends were still connected to the New York mafia, or if Mom had learned of a quasi-legal way to smuggle cases of gin to me at bargain prices by resurrecting a fabled underground network lying dormant since the Civil War. Those topics would have piqued my interest a hell of a lot more.

Back in my air-conditioned room, some relief came with a long shower—efforts to conserve water in the desert be damned. A hot yoga class would have complained about the heat in the steam room I created by the time I turned off the water. I mustered the mental fortitude to prepare for the evening out. Two events were featured on the docket that fine Friday—dinner and a show to follow.

CHAPTER 13

HENRY FORD WOULD HAVE HAD A STROKE

"We'll take the car tonight," remarked Dad as the four of us convened for dinner on Friday evening. We had reservations at Rao's, an Italian restaurant across the street at Caesars Palace. However, as anyone who's been to Vegas knows, the hotels on the Strip may look like they're right next to each other, but they're monstrosities; it takes a good long while to get from one to another.

My heart skipped a couple of beats before fluttering into a short run of premature ventricular contractions.

"We have plenty of time, Dad. I'd rather walk over to Caesars."

"I'm not letting that rental go to waste, Harley. We've been here for two days now, and the car hasn't been used since we left the airport."

"I pleaded with you not to rent a car in the first place, Dad." I backed away from the offensive, trying to maintain an even keel. The decision to rent a car was his prerogative, absurd as it was. I thought of the extreme agitation guaranteed to consume my father while driving amid all of the car and pedestrian traffic maniacally weaving between the lanes of Las Vegas Boulevard.

"What's wrong with walking? You and Mom like to walk. So what if it takes twenty minutes to get from one hotel to the next? It would take at least that long to park and re-park the rental car."

"Nothing. But what if we want to go to a casino or a restaurant on the opposite end of the Strip? It could be too far for us to walk."

"Ever consider the possibility of a taxi? You know, those ubiquitous yellow vehicles available for hire?"

Dad felt most secure when he was behind the wheel. Similar to the coat check person at a restaurant, he inherently distrusted taxi drivers. He thought their meters were all rigged to elevate the fares and drain his wallet. His systolic blood pressure rose each time the red digital numbers on the meter jumped.

"Yes, yes, Harley. Your mother and I are familiar with taxicabs. We did live in New York, you know. I paid for that rental and I want to use it, tonight! I called the valet ten minutes ago and I'm going down to pick it up, right now." With that, my father promptly turned and left us standing in the middle of the hallway.

"It's too hot to walk tonight, Harley. Who wants to perspire before a nice meal?" Bern was apparently on board with the car ride.

"You sit in the front, Bern. I don't want to catch a draft from the air conditioner." My mother had been planning on a car ride all along, as she emerged from her hotel room with her coat fully zipped to her chin.

~

I had no choice but to acquiesce, even though it entirely contradicted my better judgment. Gerry's track record with cars, and with rental cars specifically, meant that the drive, however short, would be studded with problems. But with plans to spend the evening together, I couldn't abandon my family and walk over to Caesars by myself.

Gerry maintains a unique relationship with cars that borders upon idolatry. He cherishes his cars as possessions that demand constant coddling. A car is as precious and delicate as a priceless, one-of-a-kind Fabergé egg. As a kid, I would intentionally burrow underneath his skin simply by repeatedly opening and closing the ashtray built into the rear door handle on whichever side of the car I happened to be seated. The rhythmic snaps and slams of the ashtray door got Dad all riled up, and he would crane his head to holler and shoot me looks of horror. Sydelle usually talked him down by forcing him to admit that my ashtray antics would not cause the engine to fall out of the car.

Gerry is not a car collector in the style of, let's say, Jay Leno. If you're looking for an Aston Martin, Bugati, Bentley, Maserati, or Lamborghini, don't bother to peek in Gerry's garage. What you will find instead is a late model, four-door sedan in a neutral color manufactured by Toyota, Honda, or Hyundai. No exceptions. Yet he obsesses over his cars in much the same way as a professional baseball player oils his glove, the way a hockey player tapes the blade of his stick, or the way a quarterback studies film of an opposing defense. At the end of the day, a rental car is nothing more than a hunk of metal, a bucket of bolts, a means to an end. But in that moment, it was the epicenter of Dad's world. Despite this obsession, Dad went out on a limb by allowing the Paris hotel valet to park and retrieve his rental car.

Gerry despises valet parking attendants; as a lot, they are even worse than coat check people. He only uses valet parking services under dire circumstances. Missing the opening curtain of a musical, for example, fails to meet this criterion. The reasons for this enmity are twofold. First, why spend a few dollars on a valet, when you can park the car yourself? Second, how could you possibly trust the valet attendants? In Gerry's mind, these people will improperly handle his car with a daredevil's wild abandon. What if they depressed the accelerator while the gearshift was in neutral? What if they failed to allow the engine sufficient time to warm up? And what if they altered the position of the driver's seat? My father thinks that once he hands over the keys, the attendants have carte blanche in the style of the vintage Ferrari taken for a joyride by the valets in the classic 1980s movie *Ferris Bueller's Day Off*.

Taking the Paris Hotel valet aside and into his confidence, Dad verified the rental car's identification number printed on his claim ticket with the valet—twice. He confirmed the color, make, and model of the car with the valet—twice. As the valet ran off to retrieve the car, Dad craned his neck, watching until he disappeared from sight around the bend of the ridiculously long, curved driveway. In the tense moments that followed before the car appeared, Dad tried his best to act nonchalant. But I recognized the stress he assuredly felt and accordingly cut him some slack. Nonetheless, as we waited for the rental car, I couldn't help but recall some of the more memorable automotive experiences I shared with Dad.

~

Most Saturdays throughout the course of my childhood were highlighted by a visit from Uncle Bern and my maternal grandmother Anna. Each fall, Gerry hijacked one Saturday as the day to change out the antifreeze in our cars. Forever emblazoned in my mind as "Antifreeze Saturday," this day was highly anticipated by Dad and dreaded by everyone else. The date was designated and confirmed about one month before, then re-confirmed with Bern on a weekly basis thereafter.

"We're going to do the antifreeze on the third, right Bernard?"

"Yeah, yeah, Gerry. The third."

"That's Saturday, November third, Bernard."

"I already told you that I'd be there, Gerry. Take it easy!"

"The antifreeze has to be changed before Thanksgiving. Has to. It gets too cold after Thanksgiving."

Bern would clearly be getting agitated at this point.

"Damn it, Gerry! I got nowhere else to be. The US Army has no need for my services these days. I'm retired. They're not sending me to Korea. There are three whole weeks between the third of November and Thanksgiving. Israel fought an entire war in six days for Christ's sake. Don't you think we can pour a few lousy bottles of antifreeze in less time than that? What's the matter with you, huh?"

"Okay, okay, Bernard. Easy now." Dad understood he needed to dial it down a notch before my uncle blew a gasket.

Always an early riser, my father would scurry around the house on Antifreeze Saturday. As a nine-year-old kid, I was content to sit back on the couch with a bowl of Cheerios and a lineup of cartoons on TV. At the crack of dawn, the yellow containers of Prestone antifreeze were neatly arranged along the curb along with the other paraphernalia including funnels, measures, screwdrivers, and rags. Dad bolted out of the house as soon as he saw Bern's car pulling up curbside. With a series of yells and gesticulations, he guided Bern into a parking spot directly behind our own two cars in the assembly line. Air traffic control paid less attention to landing aircraft compared with Gerry's precise arrangement of the three cars parked in front of our house.

Bern wanted a cup of coffee before starting to work on the first car. Dad denied his initial request. He only relented after Bern reminded him that even prisoners were entitled to a phone call and three square meals daily. However, Bern had to drink the coffee outside, as time was of the essence. I wanted to help, if for no other reason than simply to be included. Instead, Dad quickly marginalized me to the periphery like a backup quarterback on injured reserve. My role was limited to the uncapping and recapping of the yellow antifreeze containers. Bern was permitted to go inside on two occasions during the affair, once for a bathroom break and once for a sandwich.

Standing outside like a schmuck for seven hours on Antifreeze Saturday gave me plenty of time to observe my family. First of all, why did it take seven hours to change out the antifreeze for three cars? Seven hours is a long time. Surely the process could have been streamlined over the years. Dad could have finished one car while Bern started on the second car, for example. I suspect, though, that Dad would have been uncomfortable granting Bern this level of autonomy.

Second, all of our neighbors were of fairly similar socioeconomic means. How come none of the neighbors ever changed their antifreeze in the middle of the street? I saw them wash cars, rake leaves, and water lawns, but I never saw anyone else change antifreeze in the middle of the street. Were they ignorant of this vital car maintenance task? Were they shirking their responsibilities out of laziness or indifference? Presumably, everyone else had their antifreeze changed when their cars went in for routine servicing. I found out later that Bern brought his car to a service station owned and operated by one of his friend's friends in the mafia, to be sure that it would pass its yearly inspection with no questions asked. He knew that there would be no repercussions if he let his brother-in-law have the satisfaction of changing the antifreeze once a year.

Lastly, Gerry and Bern never collected the old antifreeze in any kind of receptacle. Rather, they just let the neon green fluid ooze into the street.

Once released onto the asphalt, the old antifreeze would drain downhill and ultimately disappear into the curbside storm grates. Out of sight, out of mind, right? Maybe. However, if the populace within a ten-mile radius of my childhood home ever starts to glow in the dark or grow extra fingers and toes, Dad and Bern would have a lot of explaining to do.

~

Dad spotted the rental car as it rounded the bend of the driveway into his sight. A late model Nissan Sentra cruised to a stop outside the lobby of the Paris Hotel. A stretch limo, a red Lotus, a Ferrari, and a black Corvette were also parked nearby, but there was no mystery as to which of these cars my father would be piloting. He dove into the front seat as soon as the valet emerged and verified that the odometer reading and the gas tank levels hadn't changed one iota. Impatient as he was, he simultaneously honked the horn no fewer than seven times to signify that it was time for the rest of us to approach the vehicle.

~

As we piled into the car, I recalled the last time my parents rented a car in Minneapolis. They were in town for a long weekend during the autumn of 2011.

Sydelle and Gerry did not stay in our home when they visited. Elyse and I imposed the "hotel rule" from the time we were first married. Facts were facts: due to space limitations, our first apartment in Minneapolis could not comfortably accommodate an extra pair of adults. So they had no choice but to embrace the Minneapolis hotel industry from the time they first came to visit us in the autumn of 2001. A more significant factor in our decision, though, was the sheer stress the uninterrupted presence of my parents would have created for us.

Our house was certainly large enough to host a couple of extra adults for the visit planned in the autumn of 2011. But as the stress of a visit from Mom and Dad was no less in 2011 than it was a decade earlier, we simply had no desire to break from precedent. We recognized that this was not the normal dynamic that exists in most families, but it worked for us. So with the hotel rule still enforced, we thought it best for Mom and Dad to rent a car for their weekend visit.

But just because I recommended they rent a car, it didn't follow that I could wash my hands of the decision. Dad called on the eve of their departure, just as I arrived home from work. I should have known that there was trouble brewing, because he never called just to say, "Hi." Elyse and I were deep in the typical semi-controlled chaos of weekday evenings with Daph and Zach. The kids' dinners were ending within a background of whining for no particular reason. There was still violin practice, baths, bedtime stories, and lunch preps for the next day to be done. This was to say nothing of the incomplete medical charts, unopened mail, phone calls to return, and the review of surgical case notes that still hung in the balance. Somewhere in between, Elyse and I selfishly felt entitled to a little dinner, too. I don't mean to imply that our weekday life was any more difficult than the average American nuclear family. I simply include this minutia to illustrate my lack of time for an unnecessary phone conversation with my father.

"Hi, Dad. What's up?" I innocently asked.

"I want to go over the directions to your house from the airport."

"Seriously?"

"That's right."

"You've driven into downtown Minneapolis from the airport several times a year for the past ten years."

"I still want to go over the directions with you."

"Christ, Dad! You laminated a custom handwritten card with the directions. It's the same route every time."

"I said I want to go over the directions!" Gerry yelled back in a tone reminiscent of a three-year-old on the brink of a tantrum.

"The state of Minnesota has not relocated the highways since you were last here. There are no construction detours. And we've been living in the same house for the last three years. But fine, Dad—let's go over the godforsaken directions again in painstaking detail. Take as much time as you need." So we did.

By the time we finished, Dad felt vindicated and I felt like I was robbed of fifteen minutes of my existence. It was a prototypical example of *mishegas*, the way business is transacted in my family. Yet I should have expected Dad's request to review the route from the airport to my house. I should have seen it coming from a mile away. I knew all about the *mishegas* and still it took me by surprise. That's the thing about *mishegas*. It can lull you into a sense of complacency, then rear its ugly head to bite you right in the ass without more than a moment's notice.

~

Before we left the Paris Hotel, Gerry verified the directions from the Paris to Caesars with two different valets and a street mime. Fortunately for all of our sakes, the routes they proposed were identical: turn left. Caesars will be on your right.

"Had a big problem at the Budget office in the airport, Harley. Big problem."

"Oh, really?" I could feign a little surprise every now and then. "What happened? Did they lose your reservation?"

"No, no! There's no help around there. I couldn't find anyone to help me out. No one! The place was deserted, a ghost town. I don't know what kind of operation they're running over there."

"What the hell happened, Dad?"

"I couldn't figure out where the windshield wiper controls were located."

"Who cares? We're in the desert, Dad, and there's been no rain in the forecast for days now."

"I know that, Harley." I'm sure my mother checked and relayed the weather forecast hourly preceding their departure from Geriatricville. "Listen, this rental car is foreign to me. I've never driven a Nissan before. I need to know where the controls are located."

Apparently, my father searched the parking lot at Budget high and low for an attendant. Unable to locate one, he left Sydelle in the car, marched right back into the office, and retrieved an unsuspecting employee. Let's call this employee Bob; let's give him a name to personalize him and at least partially reverse the impending violation of his Eighth Amendment rights. Gerry explained that Bob was not particularly knowledgeable about the operation of the rental cars in his lot. But like any normal licensed driver, he sat his ass down in the driver's seat, glanced about the steering column, and promptly located the windshield wiper lever about six seconds later.

Gerry stuck his head through the driver's side window and confirmed a positive visual ID of the wiper control lever. Still unsatisfied, he held Bob captive. Evicting Mom from her seat, Dad plopped himself down on the passenger side and forced Bob to orchestrate a custom fifteen-minute guided tour of the other controls. When he tried to extricate himself from the cabin, Bob was tackled one more time. Gerry made him complete a couple of laps around the car, looking for evidence of dings, dents, scratches, patches of rust, and paint chips.

Back inside his office, I wouldn't be surprised if Bob spent some time curled up in the fetal position before putting in the paperwork for short-term disability coverage. I hope it was approved.

~

We set off for the five-minute drive over to Caesars. I closed my eyes and leaned back against the headrest while I answered Mom and Dad's typical litany of questions about the progress of my medical practice, the progress of Elyse's medical practice, the weather in Minneapolis, and the supply of assorted deli meats in my refrigerator. Suddenly, though, the interrogation halted.

"Ooh, Sydelle! Look Sydelle! The dome light is on!"

"What's a dome light?" my mother replied.

"Come on, Sydelle! The dome light here inside the car! The light above your head! It's on!"

"So, what does that mean?"

"It's on, Sydelle! It's not supposed to be on! Don't you see? It should turn off when the car doors close and the engine starts!"

"So, what do we do now?" she asked.

"I say we go and eat dinner. How about that, Gerry?" There was Bern, the voice of reason. Dad ignored him.

"This is no good, Sydelle! It's no good!" Gerry lamented. "Why are you just sitting there? Look for the controls! Don't just sit there!"

I kept my mouth shut in the backseat alongside Bern. I knew how anxious my father became when anything mechanical or electrical malfunctions. I sat there quietly, hoping for a quick fix to descend upon us like manna sent from the biblical heavens. But when the car swerved between the right lane and the shoulder of Las Vegas Boulevard, I could no longer ignore the situation. I tried to grab the bull by the horns.

"Dad. Calm down, Dad! Take it easy, Dad. It's just a cabin light."

"At ease, soldier!" Bern echoed my sentiments in his own way.

"Stop talking army nonsense, Bernard! The dome light won't go off! Harley! Do something!"

Like so many times and situations past, my initially calm entreaties failed to register with my father when he was in the throes of a subjective crisis. I felt compelled to kick it up a notch to convince my father that we were not facing a sequel to the Cuban Missile Crisis.

"I am doing something, Dad! I'm trying to prevent hurtling to my premature demise when this death trap you're recklessly piloting jumps the median into oncoming traffic!"

"Bernard's just sitting there hungry in the back seat and your mother doesn't know what she's doing, Harley! You figure it out. We've got to get that dome light turned off!"

The Cuban Missile Crisis wasn't diffused with a single phone call from Kennedy's Oval Office. Maybe I was the problem. Maybe I just needed a little more time and patience to avert this clear and present dome light fiasco. I dialed my emotions back down a notch.

"There are no controls on the roof of the cabin, Dad. The knob has to be located somewhere on the dashboard. We'll figure it out. Just calm down. Please!"

"This is a big problem, Harley! Don't tell me to calm down!" Dad was in no position to be consoled with rational thought. I remembered that the Cuban Missile Crisis lasted thirteen days, but the millennial Y2K threat ended in a flash, essentially at the moment 12:00:01 a.m. ticked off on the clock. So I reverted to fighting fire with fire while keeping events from world history close at hand to draw upon. Maybe a quote from Churchill would come to mind and carry along with it a wave of inspiration.

"Relax and keep your eyes on the freaking road, Dad! We're not taking hostile enemy fire on Normandy Beach in 1944. It's just a lightbulb! Calm down right now before you get us all killed!"

Unfortunately, the Nazis didn't abandon Normandy Beach during the D-Day invasion, and my father showed no signs of heeding my admonitions from the back seat of the car. He shot back, "We're going to have a dead battery on our hands and I'm in a rental car here! This is no good! No good at all!"

"We're going to have an empty stomach on our hands if we don't make our dinner reservation, Gerry! Concentrate on the road, will you?" Bern's focus remained on the menu he was slated to review in a matter of minutes.

"Holy hell, Dad! Is that why you're so worked up?" The light bulb in my own brain suddenly became illuminated. "Are you honestly trying to convince me that the car battery will be dead if the dome light stays on for a few hours?

"I want that damn dome light off!"

I pictured a single soldier, outmanned and outgunned, spraying his last string of ammo from the barrel of his machine gun in a final barrage before being forced to flee for cover.

"Just get us to the damn restaurant in one piece! We're already late for our reservation! We'll figure it out later—I promise. The control knob has to be located somewhere on the dashboard. It's not going to be in the trunk or on the undercarriage. In the worst-case scenario, you can always whip out the owner's manual from the glove box. It just can't be that hard, Dad."

After he parked at the restaurant, I bolted out of the car and mentally kissed the ground, thankful that I was still alive. Gerry was lured out of the car, hypnotized as he was by the prospect of aromas wafting from the front door of the restaurant. He also recognized the fruitlessness of looking for the dome light controls in the darkness of the parking lot. As we walked toward the restaurant, I caught Dad looking forlornly over his shoulder, back in the direction of his forsaken rental car. The dome light was still shining, calling to him like a beacon in the night.

CHAPTER 14

DINNER AND A SHOW
AT RAO'S AND O

We arrived at Rao's in Caesars Palace a few minutes late for our reservation. Uncle Bern and I ordered cocktails—a couple of matching Manhattans— at the first available opportunity. I hoped my father would be able to cast aside the issue with the dome light and enjoy his meal.

"What a tremendous restaurant!" said Syd. "I wonder what it must cost to heat this place?"

"I'm guessing they spend considerably more on air-conditioning, given that it gets up to one hundred ten degrees in the desert," I said.

"Who needs so much space? How can they afford the rent?" echoed Gerry.

"The restaurant is practically empty. We're one of the only ones here," Bern added.

"That's because it's not even six o'clock on a Friday night," was all that I replied. I would have much preferred to comment on the absence of signs on the Strip advertising early-bird specials, the absence of A-list celebrities like Beyonce and Jay-Z, and the absence of Vegas stalwarts like Wayne Newton in the restaurant. But as the night was young and the meal was just beginning, I kept my sarcasm in check. Mom, Dad, and Bern were enjoying the (empty) restaurant's atmosphere, and that's what really mattered.

Bern and I probably downed our first cocktails a bit too quickly for our own good before we ordered dinner. I selected a Caesar salad to start, followed by the chicken cacciatore. We were eating in a traditional Italian restaurant and I craved traditional Italian fare. Since I cook chicken fairly regularly at home, I rarely order it when dining out. Despite this fact, the cacciatore appealed to me this evening.

As soon as the word "cacciatore" rolled off my lips, my mother's cold hand shot out and grasped my left forearm.

"Harley, wait a minute. Are you sure?"

"Sure about what?" I couldn't possibly fathom the reason for her concern.

"Didn't you read the menu?

"Yeah, I read the menu. What's the matter?"

"The chicken cacciatore is served on the bone." She slowly emphasized each of these last three words. "Look—it says 'bone in' right here on the menu."

"So? What's the problem?" I still couldn't figure out the reason for the hard stop.

"I, for one, would never order chicken on the bone in a restaurant."

"Why the hell not?" I countered. The bourbon in the Manhattan was starting to percolate through my veins.

"It's too much work to negotiate the bone."

"Negotiate? What are you talking about?" I wondered if dinner came complete with a side delegation from North Korea looking to open up the demilitarized zone.

"Why work so hard during dinner?"

"Work so hard doing what?" There remained a level of confusion separating me from the point Mom was trying to make.

"Why, cutting the chicken off the bone, of course." She was surprised that I hadn't instantly recognized the error of my ways. I wondered if the workers constructing the Great Pyramid of Giza had to worry about chicken bones after a full day of backbreaking labor under the searing Egyptian sun.

The waiter was surprisingly patient, his curiosity keeping him tableside rather than tending to his other patrons.

My composure, on the other hand, was faltering. "Jesus Christ, Mom! I'm a surgeon. I've been cutting people open for the past eleven years with all kinds of scalpels, scissors, dissectors, saws, and clamps. At this stage in my career, I've amassed just enough skill to confidently negotiate a piece of chicken." It was my turn to emphasize a word or two, as well as to use my mother's own words against her.

She relented. "Okay, Okay. Order the chicken. Just know that I would never order cacciatore in a restaurant. But it's your vacation; you do what you want."

"Thanks for granting me permission. I'm going to forge ahead and stick with the cacciatore. I'm going to roll the dice on this one, since we're all in Las Vegas."

Sydelle glared at me out of the corner of her wandering eye with a look that clearly said I had been duly warned of the consequences of my entrée ordering decisions.

Turning to the amused waiter, I asked, "Does Rao's have dinner knives with serrated edges?"

"Yes, of course sir," came his formal reply.

"Well then, Mom. That settles it. Eleven years of surgical experience, an ample supply of serrated knives, and the decade of orthodontics you subjected me to make up a sure-fire recipe for success." I turned back to the waiter. "I'd definitely like the chicken cacciatore, please." I ordered a second Manhattan to accompany my Caesar salad.

"Very good, sir," answered the waiter.

When the food was served, I kicked that chicken cacciatore's ass, and I let my mother know it.

"Look, Mom. Chicken's all done. Didn't need poultry shears, a bowie knife, or a machete. The knife the restaurant outfitted me with proved invaluable in securing the victory." I envisioned parading the defeated bones around the restaurant on a horse-drawn chariot like the victorious Julius Caesar returning home to Rome following a successful season of military conquests.

"Very funny, Harley."

"Check out that sign on the wall over your shoulder, Mom."

"What sign?"

The sign that says, "It's been fifty-six days since our last customer cacciatore catastrophe." I couldn't resist the alliteration.

Bern was laughing pretty loudly at this point. Showing her annoyance with this torrent of sarcasm, she dismissively waved me off with her hand as she finished her own entrée.

Our waiter had earlier explained that Danny DeVito had personally delivered a vat of his own homemade limoncello to Rao's a couple of weeks prior to our visit. Apparently, it was some long-standing tradition of his. I ordered a glass as I prepared for the long night that was still forthcoming. There was plenty of time to drink it, as Sydelle had not yet urinated since we sat down at the table.

Silent throughout the meal, Gerry downed his dinner with unusual gusto. The taste buds on his tongue were superfluous, as his tongue generated a series of mechanical waves that propelled food from his lips directly into his esophagus. As soon as Sydelle laid her fork to rest, he paid the bill without even double-checking the itemization. The dome light still consumed his thoughts. My father even managed to compute an approximate 20 percent tip without consulting his pocket calculator.

After dinner, Gerry would have relished the chance to run out to the rental car to make sure enough power remained to start the engine. He didn't want the dome light to think it had been forsaken like a lost love. But there was simply no time to spare. We sauntered next door to the Bellagio Hotel to catch the evening performance of the aquatic-themed "O" show by Cirque du Soleil. To commemorate the birthdays of my mother and Uncle Bern, I had purchased a set of four prime orchestra seats in advance. I dropped over $600 on these tickets, appreciating that Sydelle and Bern turned seventy and eighty, respectively, only once. They were clearly excited, talking about the famed agility of the acrobats on the walk over to the Bellagio.

We thumbed through the playbills while awaiting the start of the show. However, the dimming of the theatre lights turned out to be choreographed with the dimming of Dad and Bern's consciousness. As the red velvet curtain rose, both pairs of their eyelids descended. That's right. They were both fast asleep five minutes following the opening scene. Out cold. I was incredulous. They awoke in time to partake in the round of applause that heralded the arrival of intermission. I wondered whether their dreams or the troupe's costumes were more vivid.

Not to be outdone, Dad and Bern rallied for an encore performance. They slept throughout the second half of the show as well. I kid you not. I pinched myself to make sure I was truly witnessing history repeating itself. The artistry, choreography, and theatrics were completely lost on Gerry and Bern. Equally fated to oblivion were the costumes, lighting effects, and sound effects. As the cast linked arms to soak up the final round of applause, Gerry and Bern awoke and enthusiastically contributed to the audience's adulation. As we rose to leave, I couldn't restrain myself.

"Did you enjoy the show?" I asked my father and uncle.

"Oh, yes. Very much, Harley. Great show, marvelous show," they each replied in turn.

"Glad to hear it. What were your favorite parts?" My curiosity was getting the better of me.

"The water part," said Gerry.

"Me too," said Bern.

I could have analogized the fate of the "O" show tickets I purchased to the fate of the four hundred dollars Nettie unknowingly lit up in the oven. It certainly would have fallen under my purview to do so. But what good would it have done? What good would have come from making my father and uncle feel badly at having played identical Rip Van Winkle roles in their seats while the acrobats were performing on stage? So all I said was, "That's understandable. I found the water parts to be spectacular as well."

Unlike the dome light's draining effect on the rental car's battery, Dad's siesta rendered him fully energized. The characteristic Friday night panoply along the Strip was on full display during our sprint back to the rental car. Some guys were covered in tattoos from head to toe. Others sported more facial piercings than fingers and toes combined. Among the women, it was virtually impossible to differentiate between ultra miniskirts, bikini bathing-suit bottoms, and lingerie. It was sometimes even difficult to distinguish the men from the women.

Within this sea of humanity, Sydelle, Gerry, and Bern first insinuated and then distinguished themselves. Falling January snow, Ivory soap, and angels cloaked in flowing robes at the gates of heaven were not as white as the tennis shoes my parents and uncle sported during this walk. The glare attracted more attention than a pair of couture Jimmy Choo stilettos worn by a six-foot-tall woman with hot pink spiked hair.

But that didn't stop Dad from pointing his index finger directly toward the Amazonian wearing the Jimmy Choos with the hot pink spiked hair while exclaiming, "Look at that one, Bernard. How 'bout that job?"

"What's the big deal, Gerry? Haven't you ever seen a hooker before?" said Bern in an all-too-audible voice.

"Hooker? You think so?" questioned Gerry with obvious excitement in his voice.

"Well, sure. What else? You think she's a nun on her way home from donating a pint of blood at the Red Cross or handing out free meals at the soup kitchen?" Bern said with some of his own sarcasm.

"Shhh! Shhh! Stop pointing and quiet down!" I snapped, as my eyes darted back and forth between Dad and Bern. "Don't you see the two huge guys with shaved heads flanking her?"

Dad and Bern paid no attention to me, and continued to mercilessly ridicule anyone who looked even remotely different than a suburban kindergarten teacher wearing a pastel-colored cardigan sweater set accessorized with a strand of pearls and hair wound into a tight bun. I decided to start up a game of Pot Calling the Kettle Black.

"How about you two? I must have missed the issue of *GQ* magazine when you both posed together on the cover." Glaring first at Dad, I pointed out his bald spot, forehead lipoma, short-sleeved dress shirt tucked into pants hiked up toward his nipples, and black socks paired with the aforementioned puritanically white tennis shoes. Uncle Bern was a veritable Don Juan in his own right, for those of you attracted to a nasal bridge contorted from six prior fractures.

Distancing myself from the pack to avoid further embarrassment, we made it back to the parking lot at Caesars unscathed.

Drawn to the animal magnetism of the dome light, Gerry hurled himself back into the car with the fervor of reunited lovers following a prolonged military tour of duty. Turning the key in the ignition, the dome light dimmed ever so slightly for an instant as the engine came to life.

The car battery wasn't dead, but that damned dome light stayed on like the eternal flame marking Kennedy's grave in Arlington National Cemetery. Gerry was not pleased, and took no solace in the fact that the car battery had not been drained by the wattage required to keep the dome light illuminated during dinner and the Cirque du Soleil show. He wasted no time resuming his pre-dinner tirade. I made one brief attempt to head him off at the pass.

"Dad, the dome light control switch has to be located somewhere on the dashboard. There is no other possibility. It has to be there. We'll figure it out when we get back to the Paris."

"This is terrible, Harley! I can't leave the car like this overnight. It'll be dead in the morning! Then what will I do? I'll have some problem on my hands."

"That's the same thing Harry S. Truman said when he learned the details of the Manhattan Project right after taking the oath of office in the spring of 1945." A healthy dose of perspective came, courtesy of Bern. It was highly apropos at this moment. If there was ever a prototypical case of perseveration, this was it. Out of ideas, I sat back and let the scene play out.

"Sydelle! Call Budget."

"What?" Mom replied. She was busy applying lipstick with a handheld makeup mirror by the soft glow of the dome light.

"Call Budget up on your phone. Ask them how to turn the dome light off."

"What number should I call?"

"Any number. Look at the brochure. Call the number on the brochure. There has to be a number printed for customer service. You're a customer— get some service. Come on, Sydelle! Use your head, will you?"

Dad spoke to Mom like a boss berating a dim-witted, under-performing employee. An outsider would perhaps be dismayed, but this verbal dynamic between my parents was quite typical. Mom took no offense, as she knew after four decades of marriage that no offense was meant. Without raising any objections, she found a toll-free number on the jacket of the rental car agreement. However, some precious time was lost powering up her mobile flip phone.

I never learned the name of the poor bastard who had the misfortune of answering the phone at Budget that evening. Let's just call him Tony. I'm certain that Tony could make, modify, and cancel a reservation. He could review prototypical car makes and models within the various rental classes in Budget's fleet. Optional enhancements like infant car seats, insurance coverage, and Global Positioning Systems would have fit right in his wheelhouse. On the other hand, Tony probably didn't know how the Chinese yuan was trending against the US dollar or the number of snow leopards remaining in the Asiatic wild.

So what do you suppose happened when Sydelle asked Tony to tell her the exact location of the dome light control switch in Gerry's rental car? One thing that didn't happen: the solution to the dilemma. While only privy to my mother's half of the conversation, my father had no trouble chiming in from the driver's seat.

"Dome light! Tell him it's the dome light, Sydelle!"

"He doesn't know what a dome light is, Gerry."

"Come on, Sydelle! Stop busting my chops! The dome light! The light on the roof of the interior cabin, the dome light! Tell him, Sydelle!"

"What are you getting yourself so worked up for, Gerry?" Bern stepped into the fray. "If you had had a couple of beers at the restaurant like I suggested, you might be able to think straight for once."

Dad ignored him. Bern shook his head and shrugged his shoulders, indicating that Gerry was a lost cause.

"He says he doesn't know what you're talking about, Gerry." Syd resumed her role as intermediary between Dad and Tony.

Of course Tony didn't know, I thought from the back seat. Rain Man wouldn't have known, either. Stationed in some windowless cubicle halfway across the country, this one random guy was supposed to have memorized the precise location of every knob, button, and lever in every car within Budget's nationwide arsenal of vehicles? He had a greater chance of predicting the winning numbers of the next Powerball jackpot.

"Nissan, Sydelle! Nissan! Tell him we're driving a 2012 Nissan."

Bern turned to me and said, "We could be driving a Maybach or a Mitsubishi—the poor schmuck still wouldn't be able to help that lunatic father of yours."

Mom repeated the make of the car to Tony like a faithful junior-level employee.

"That doesn't help him, Gerry. He still has no idea. He put me on hold."

Five interminable minutes passed before the connection died. I wouldn't be surprised if Tony intentionally disconnected the call. Simply by hanging up the phone, he disavowed himself of the situation, saving the memory only for some water cooler conversation during his next work break.

"What's happening, Sydelle? What's going on over there?"

"I lost the call."

"What? Come on, Sydelle! How did that happen?"

"I don't know, Gerry. These things just happen sometimes. Maybe I should call the phone company and ask them for an explanation?"

It was good to see Mom flash a little sarcasm of her own. I noticed it, even though it flew right over Dad's head. While the dropped call was a harsh reality for my father to face, I struggled to suppress a laugh.

"Maybe I should call a psychiatrist and ask them to explain what the hell is wrong with you!" Bern wasn't finished ridiculing his brother-in-law, knowing that Gerry wasn't paying him any attention.

"Well why are you just sitting there, Sydelle? Don't just sit there! Call them back! Ask for the same customer service representative!"

"You've been talking to me, Gerry. You haven't given me the chance to hit redial yet."

"Let's go, Sydelle! You're wasting time! Time to call back! Call back! Call them back, will you?"

Sydelle dutifully called back. Of course, she was attended by a different customer service agent who was in no better position than Tony to extinguish the dome light.

"Stop fooling around, Sydelle!" Gerry interjected. "Ask for a manager! Or a supervisor! A manager or a supervisor! Stop wasting time with these morons! These people can't help you! Tell them you want a supervisor! Supervisor!"

I really had to concentrate to prevent myself from bursting into laughter at this point. I wished Elyse could witness the scene firsthand to avoid being accused of embellishment. She expected the unexpected when watching my parents stumble through the throes of one of their perceived crises. Yet she was still surprised to find herself stunned whenever an outburst hit without warning. Her facial expression at these times said it all; she knew what was happening but didn't want to believe it. After the fact, when a semblance of normalcy returned to the family dynamic, she found the *mishegas* just as ludicrous as I did.

Another few minutes passed while Sydelle awaited the arrival of the Budget administrative messiah. But guess what happened next? Another dropped call. The folks at Budget hung up on her again. Maybe these people were smarter than I was giving them credit for.

Gerry was clearly beside himself with rage. I was now becoming angrier by the moment as well. Whatever humor and patience I had accumulated from the satiety of a full stomach had evaporated. I catalogued my position in the car at the moment; it was powerless. Powerless to ease my father's nerves. Powerless to prevent a ten-car pileup from his distracted driving. Powerless to apologize to the unsuspecting Budget agents on the other end of the phone for Dad's behavior. Powerless to make my father speak to my mother with a modicum of decency. And powerless to turn off the dome light, at least until I took a turn in the driver's seat. Unwilling to accept defeat, Sydelle dialed up customer service a third time and requested to speak with yet another supervisor. At "Hello," Gerry erupted again.

"We're paying customers! We want a supervisor! Who's in charge? Get me a supervisor!" There was no speakerphone on Sydelle's cell phone, but that didn't matter.

My feelings of powerlessness combined with the helplessness of reliving the Budget phone calls proved intolerable. The humor of Tony's first dropped call was replaced by a sudden urge to escape my present situation. I had to get out, even if it meant resorting to tactics like those portrayed in movie jailbreaks where the prisoner painstakingly scrapes through the concrete wall of his prison cell with the edge of a dull spoon. I had to get out. I couldn't stand it any longer. Our car was inching forward at a snail's pace, mired as it was in Friday night Strip traffic. I conjured up a preliminary extraction plan. A momentary lull in the phone conversation occurred, as Sydelle Rosetta-Stoned Gerry's gibberish into English for the supervisor. We came to a four-way stop at an intersection. Without thinking through all of the ramifications of my actions, I put the extraction plan into effect.

"Pull over! Let me out!" I yelled from the back seat. The outburst caught my parents completely off guard; I think I surprised Bern as well.

"Out? Don't be ridiculous, Harley. We're right in the middle of the street," my mother replied.

"I want out! I'm getting out of this godforsaken car right now!"

"Oh, Harley. We're almost back at the Paris. Don't be silly."

"I can't listen to another second of these inane phone conversations, Mom! I can't take it anymore! You people could bring a pack of well-hydrated camels to its knees! I'm done!"

The "Chinese fire drill" games we played as teenagers began as soon as a traffic light turned red. Yet I jettisoned myself out of the car just as it turned green. And that was it. I jumped out in the middle of the Las Vegas Boulevard traffic.

"Let me know how this all works out for you in the morning!" I said as I slammed the rear door shut. The slow pace of the traffic afforded a modicum of safety as the cars around me had all stopped and were just beginning to move forward with the green light. Most of the cars simply stopped in their tracks, the drivers waving me along toward the curb. A few honks and a couple of hostile gesticulations were the only prices I paid for my freedom.

When the rare convict attempted a jailbreak from Alcatraz, he kept his eyes fixed on the prize that was the California coastline while swimming frantically against the frigid Pacific current. He didn't pause to take in the sea lions on Pier 39 and the other scenery along Fisherman's Wharf. Burying my hands in my pockets, I weaved through the pedestrians and focused on the Eiffel Tower replica marking the façade of the Paris Hotel. I never looked back, fearing I would turn into a pillar of salt in the Old Testament style of Lot's wife if I did.

As I drifted off to sleep that night, I confess that my curiosity about the ultimate state of the dome light lingered. Just because I was curious, don't for a second think that I paced the halls all night long. I don't think I turned over in bed even once.

CHAPTER 15

EVEN A BLIND SQUIRREL FINDS A NUT ... SOMETIMES

The next morning, I knocked on my parents' hotel room door at 10:00 a.m. sharp. Gerry opened the door and I didn't see any jumper cables in his hands, which I interpreted as a good sign.

"Hey, Dad, how was the rest of your evening?" I casually asked as I walked inside.

"Huh? Oh, fine. It was fine, Harley."

"Well . . . what happened after I jumped out of the car?" The suspense was killing me. "What's the status of the ol' dome light?" I took a sip of my morning coffee. Unlike Uncle Bern, I somehow managed to avoid a fistfight while ordering my coffee from the lobby café on the way to my parents' room.

"Turns out the control button was located on the dashboard after all."

"You don't say," I replied dryly. "I, for one, am absolutely astounded."

"Yeah. It was on the left-hand side, near the knob for the dashboard lights." He said this so nonchalantly, he could have been talking about the day's forecast or the pitching matchups for the Yankees' next few games.

"Amazing, Dad! I didn't see that one coming from a mile away. I figured the switch would have been conveniently placed alongside the muffler by the left rear axle."

"Oh, Harley. Don't give us such a hard time so early in the morning," Syd chimed in. "Especially after that stunt you pulled in the middle of the street last night."

"Really, Mom? I'm giving you the hard time? It's not as if I suggested taking a gander at the dashboard to find the damn control knob before you incessantly barraged the car company on the phone last night. Exactly how much more time did you waste on the phone with Budget after I extricated myself?"

"About forty-five minutes. We kept holding and holding. We just sat there in the dark in the hotel parking lot. I had to go to the bathroom, of course. Luckily, my bladder held out. Finally we were transferred to a well-spoken man in Columbus, Ohio who knew something about the car. He told us how to turn the dome light off."

"Wonderful. Can we all get on with our lives now?"

If I could go back in time, I would have gladly paid for one of those chauffeur-driven stretch Hummer limousines instead of allowing my father to rent a car in Las Vegas. Bern would have loved riding in a Hummer; he undoubtedly would have retold a bunch of Korean War stories during the rides.

The retelling of the dome light saga over, Gerry was chomping at the bit. Literally. The man was famished. Before the trip, one of his esteemed Geriatricville cronies had raved to him about the splendor of the breakfast buffet at the Paris Hotel. Insider trading information hand-delivered by Warren Buffett himself would not have carried more weight in Dad's mind. Stock shares in Buffett's Berkshire Hathaway firm could have been on the verge of splitting three-for-one, but somewhere deep in the kitchens of the Paris Hotel, short order cooks were scrambling up irresistible eggs in industrial-sized skillets. In reality, though, Dad needed little convincing, for he never met a buffet he didn't like. Part of the allure surrounded the prospect of a bargain, which in this case meant out-eating the entry price. The more he thought about the buffet, the hungrier he got. The more his stomach grumbled, the more he thought about the buffet. Bern fantasized about a never-ending supply of coffee and Mom imagined a mountain of fresh sliced fruits and berries as high as the pyramid of the nearby Luxor Hotel.

I, on the other hand, had as many reasons to avoid buffets as my family had to seek them out. Gorging myself on mass-produced food of mediocre quality was not in my best interest. I had to think about my long-standing pre-dawn exercise routine mixed with my more recent decision to restrict my carbohydrate intake. With my weight down and my coronary arteries unclogged, buffets were my caloric adversaries. Handling the same bacteria-laden serving utensils as dozens of other patrons with uncertain standards of cleanliness was not exactly a comforting thought, either. Moreover, conversations at buffets were unsustainable due to the repeated trips to and from the food stations. Call me a snob. Buffets just weren't my style. But subscribing to the psychologically proven model of learned helplessness, I went along without a word of discontent.

Elyse called me craving gossip during the fifteen minutes we spent in line waiting to be granted entry into the hallowed halls of the Le Village Buffet. I turned away from earshot to mute her laughter as I described the potbellies of the diners ahead of us in line that could easily balance cafeteria trays loaded with food. Elyse derived unmistakable yet understandable pleasure from my misfortune. I cut the conversation short after she asked me to estimate the percentage of patrons in the line wearing pants with elastic waistbands. I promised to call her later as the hostess ushered us inside.

Gerry didn't say much as we meandered through the aisles of the buffet; I suspected he was strategizing. Sitting down at the table, I ordered some orange juice and coffee. Dad didn't have time to order any beverages. He was a man possessed. I blinked and he was gone, off like a shot. He didn't even sit down. Dad was on a reconnaissance mission, familiarizing himself with the layout of the food stations like a rescued pet exploring a new home upon jumping out of an animal shelter crate. Kids in candy stores didn't show this degree of ebullience. I sat back, content to sip my coffee and enjoy some solid people watching. Fanny packs, T-shirts adorned with corny slogans and Velcro-strapped footwear abounded on the men and women carrying about mountains of food precariously stacked like a tower of Jenga blocks.

My father returned with a mountain of salad. He moved with a distinct spring in his step that stopped just short of skipping. This roughage would insulate his gastrointestinal tract. Otherwise, the grease that was to come would have overwhelmed the capacity of his digestive enzymes, resulting in a hole torn straight through the wall of his stomach. Six more courses followed in rapid-fire succession: cheese and crackers; pancakes, French toast, and a medley of mini breakfast pastries; a three-egg vegetable omelet with bacon and potatoes O'Brien; tuna salad on an everything bagel; fresh fruit; and finally, selections from the meat carving stations.

Some of the details were irretrievably lost, for this eating bonanza passed by in a blur. I don't think a court stenographer could have catalogued everything that passed through Dad's mouth. I learned a few things while watching the man eat. He could swallow mini muffins in one bite if they were first dunked in maple syrup. Ordering the cheese omelet with egg whites tempered his overall cholesterol intake and paved the way to double his bacon consumption. Eating bacon and other blatantly non-kosher items was permissible when Dad hid them from plain view, for example, buried underneath an omelet and potato avalanche. Fruit acted as a smoke screen to cloak the true amount of saturated fats he ingested. It also mesmerized Sydelle into thinking that the topics of nutrition and health were actively percolating somewhere in the depths of Dad's mind.

Dad found casual conversation during the buffet to be superfluous. I reasoned that it was probably safer for him to remain quiet. He periodically choked from failing to properly chew and swallow his food. Extra talk could have resulted in a tableside Heimlich maneuver. To his credit, he took a short break in between courses; I overlooked the fact that the break was for the express purpose of waiting for the next course to be doled out. He kept his plate hovering in front of the meat carver, like Oliver Twist asking for some more soup, until it was loaded up into a teetering mound. When the prime rib and roast turkey had been carved down to their stumps, he waited until the carver offered him the whole bone.

Only one controversy occurred during the buffet. It surrounded lox, the holy grail of Jewish brunch foods. Gerry coveted lox like a leprechaun covets a pot of gold at the end of a rainbow. So imagine his consternation when Bern returned to the table with a slab of lox and a full complement of pumpernickel toast points. He couldn't believe it. How could he have missed the lox? Impossible. Unthinkable. The lipoma on the left side of

Dad's forehead usually throbbed like an irritated bunion before a rural summer thunderstorm whenever he came within a two-and-a-half-mile radius of lox. He demanded an explanation.

"Lox! There are no lox here! Where did you get lox, Bernard?" Bits of egg flew out of Dad's mouth.

"Over there in the far corner, Gerry. I didn't take it out of my suitcase."

"Come on! I didn't see any lox over there."

"You calling me a liar? What the hell's wrong with you? I'm not making it up, Gerry."

"Show me."

"I'll show you all right, right after you put a hundred down on the table. You want to put a hundred dollars on it? Come on, Gerry! You want to put your money where your big mouth is?"

Bern was putting himself in a position to earn some gambling money. Realizing this, I encouraged my father to slap a Benjamin down on the table. The confidence in Bern's voice indicated that he had about a 99 percent chance of winning the bet.

"That bastard Gooch would never have the guts to bet me, but how about you, Gerry? You want to make it interesting? Come on, it's only a hundred! Let's put a hundred on it!"

Dad also sensed that Bern was wagering a strong position. He wanted nothing to do with the bet. He knew Bern well enough to forego the wager, as Bern would have had absolutely no qualms about collecting from his brother-in-law. Leaving his fork impaled within his half-eaten omelet, Gerry silently rose from the table, turned, and walked in the general direction of the purported smoked salmon. Sonar, a minesweeper, and a GPS device would have been invoked if any of these technologies were at his disposal.

Less than five minutes later, a radiant Gerry triumphantly returned to the table, lox secured. What remained of the omelet was temporarily cast aside, allowing the lox to take center stage. He extracted the fork from the omelet like King Arthur drawing Excalibur from the mythical stone. Once the lox were no more, Dad reacquainted himself with the forlorn omelet, bringing it back into the fold of his good graces.

"Hey, Gerry! Gerry!"

Dad's face was buried in the omelet. It wasn't easy for Bern to get his attention.

"Gerry! Damn it, Gerry! I'm talking to you!"

With his head and neck fixed in position hovering over the omelet, Dad made eye contact with Bern.

"Good thing you didn't put a hundred on it," Bern jeered. "Was I bullshitting you or telling you the truth about the lox, huh?"

"Truth."

"Put a hundred on it next time, will you?"

"Right, Bernard," was all he could say in return.

Dad's failure to sight the lox distinctly reminded me of another time when his vision failed him in a restaurant. This debacle occurred about eight months prior to the Vegas trip, so the memories were quite fresh in my mind. Mom and Dad had strategically planned a Minneapolis visit in between the kids' birthdays so that they could monopolize face time with Daphne and Zachary. They didn't want pre-birthday party planning, the logistics of the birthday parties, or the unwrapping of gifts that followed the parties to encroach upon their visit. We decided to go out for a family dinner on the Friday evening of their stay. Elyse foreshadowed a tempest before the first storm clouds approached on the horizon. She had less than no desire to accompany us and deftly sidestepped the meal with an excuse conceptualized many days prior.

I suggested a restaurant called Buca di Beppo since it was nearby, served massive quantities of easily recognizable, traditional, inexpensive Italian fare, and offered enough options to keep Daph and Zach happy. Gerry had frequented this restaurant on multiple occasions, thereby satisfying two of the all-important criteria for a successful dining experience: past precedent and menu familiarity. The restaurant was fairly large, with the dining area divided into multiple rooms. The ambiance was completely casual, the service was family-style, and the background noise was such that patrons could converse but definitely not hear a pin drop. Plastic models of pontiffs past, nostalgic photos of Americana, and Vatican-themed memorabilia lined the walls.

We arrived about eight minutes late for the reservation as Sydelle had announced that she had to urinate as we were about to leave the house. The smiling hostess grabbed some paper and crayons for the kids and then promptly seated us at a round wooden table for five. Immediately thereafter, a party of eighteen began to filter in at the next table. This was no ordinary party of eighteen, as they were all visually impaired. By visually impaired, I mean completely blind. Dark sunglasses, walking stick, guide dog blind. Placed in the context of a loud, busy restaurant with narrow aisles, irregular room layouts, and tables of varying sizes and configurations, one can naturally surmise that blindness can pose some logistical issues.

And then, it happened.

The red tip of a blind woman's white walking stick lightly glided across the pleat of my father's left trouser leg at ankle level. Twenty-six seconds later, the hip of another blind patron grazed the back of Dad's chair. That's all it took. With wild gesticulations of his arms flailing about seemingly independent of cerebral control, Dad summoned our waitress. A young waitress who probably still possessed some faith in the righteousness of mankind dutifully approached our table.

The first words out of Dad's mouth were, "This is no good! No good! We're not comfortable here! I'm not comfortable! Table's not acceptable! It's no good!" Phrases such as, "Excuse me " or "I'm terribly sorry to bother you" were nowhere to be found.

Naturally shell-shocked by this salvo, the waitress did not immediately reply. I intervened both on behalf of the waitress and on behalf of human decency.

"Dad. Dad! Please calm down."

"Table's no good, Harley! No good. We're getting manhandled here! Got to move!"

The waitress continued to stand mutely beside our table.

"Will you acknowledge the fact that these eighteen people are blind? Perhaps they deserve just a little bit of tolerance as they negotiate the combined seventy-two chair legs scattered around the perimeter of their table?"

"Why do I have to sit here and be physically attacked?" Gerry replied. "We're packed in here like sardines!"

I tried to reason with my father.

"You're not being physically attacked. No one's attacking you. The blind people presumably came here for pasta, not a military sortie sanctioned by the army." Bern would have been proud of me for referencing his beloved US Army. "I would say with a fair amount of certainty that their primary motive for making the reservation was not to treat you like a human piñata."

I caught the beginning of a smile emerge from the corner of the waitress's mouth. She wisely continued to remain silent.

Gerry didn't say anything in response. I temporarily held the floor. Like a US senator beginning a filibuster, I suggested that we physically push our table a couple of feet off to the side. This would widen the common aisle in the dining room and theoretically allow the blind folks to find the way to their table with greater ease.

Like piranhas seizing prey, the waitress and I clamped down on the table edge with our hands in white-knuckled vice grips. Before Gerry could object, we slid the table across the hardwood floor about two and a half feet to the side. The waitress and I exchanged appreciative nods, much like doubles partners in a tennis match recognize a cross-court winner that just catches the edge of the baseline. Gerry remained unscathed for the rest of the evening and the blind party of eighteen had safe, unencumbered passage to their seats.

Several moments passed in relative silence as the kids began to color and play games of Tic-Tac-Toe that never yielded a winner. The cocktail I ordered came compliments of the house. The first sip was glorious and the second was even better. I didn't get to the third before all hell broke loose again. The source? Gerry.

"Sydelle, where are my reading glasses?" he asked in a clearly worried tone."

"How should I know where your reading glasses are? Aren't they in your shirt pocket?"

"No, they're not in my shirt pocket! Why would I be asking you where my glasses are if they were in my pocket?"

"Did you leave them at the kids' house?"

"I don't know! I thought I gave them to you. Check your purse, will you?"

Mom rummaged through her purse, excavating and replacing the contents of the thirty-seven separate compartments as if she was the lead detective investigating an undisturbed crime scene. No reading glasses were discovered, although she was pleased to find an unexpired coupon for a free half-dozen bagels with the purchase of a full dozen at the local deli back in Geriatricville.

Gerry's mind was running rampant with possible locations of his reading glasses, including the house, the courtyard, the garage, the passenger-side front seat of my car, the passenger-side front floor of my car, the sidewalk between the parked car and the restaurant, the path to our table from the front door of the restaurant, and the dark side of the moon.

"Dad, I'm sure your glasses are safe and sound in my house. As soon as I get home this evening, I'll search high and low for them. If I have to, I'll dig through the kids' Lego bin, block by block."

Gerry was skeptical, retracing the sequence of events between my house and the restaurant over and over again in his mind. The magnitude of his skepticism showed in the furrowing of his brows and the tightening of his lips. If it had been available, he would have forced me to seal this promise with my hand atop the Lincoln Bible and then sign a photograph of my right hand on the Lincoln Bible in the presence of a notary.

"How can I see the menu without my reading glasses?"

"You've been to this restaurant before, Dad. The element of mystery has been taken out of the equation. It's basic Italian food. Spaghetti and meatballs. Baked ziti. Chicken marsala. We're not dealing with offerings of puffer fish written in Japanese calligraphy."

"Gerry, I'll read the menu to you," Sydelle chimed in. "We'll all share a salad. You remember how large the salads are here. The three of us can also share a pasta dish and an entrée." It was assumed that we would share the meal, given the gargantuan portion sizes that could feed a small battalion. At the age of thirty-six, I wasn't given the option of ordering for myself.

The recitation of the menu began. It resembled the manner in which a second grade teacher calls attendance at the beginning of each school day.

"House salad." Pause. "Caesar salad." Pause. "Caprese salad." Pause. "Chopped salad." Pause. The cadence of a metronome was not this accurate.

Gerry called his first time out. "Caprese? What's Caprese?"

"Oh, Gerry." Sydelle waved a dismissive hand in his general direction. You know what's in a Caprese salad. You've had it a hundred times before. It's sliced tomatoes and mozzarella."

"Well, I don't remember. Where does it say tomatoes and mozzarella? I don't see tomatoes and mozzarella!"

"You've had it, and you like it. What's not to like? You like tomatoes and you like mozzarella cheese. Trust me."

"It just says Caprese here!"

"Dad, a traditional Caprese salad has alternating slices of tomatoes and mozzarella with basil and a balsamic vinaigrette."

"I don't want it. Caesar salad for me."

How could Gerry turn around and select the Caesar salad with such conviction? The menu made no mention of croutons, parmesan, eggs, and romaine lettuce. I considered pointing out the flaw in his logic, but decided to avoid getting him further riled up.

That was it. The salad course was decided. Game, set, match. Not wanting to disrupt the progression to the pasta course, I continued to entertain the kids. To their credit, Mom and Dad promptly selected linguine with a medley of mixed vegetables in a red sauce. Onward to the recital of the entrée course options.

"Chicken piccata." Pause. "Chicken marsala." Pause. "Chicken parmigiana." Pause.

"What?" Gerry replied. "Can't hear you!"

The relief I gleaned from pushing the table to the side a few minutes prior was fading. Sydelle repeated herself in a slower and slightly louder voice. Gerry leaned forward, craned his neck toward Sydelle, and cupped his right hand over his right ear so as to funnel the sound of her voice into his ear canal. "Chicken piccata." Pause. Pause. "Chicken marsala." Pause. Pause. "Chicken parmigiana." Pause. Pause.

"Chicken? What chicken? Where's the chicken? Chicken? It's too loud in here! I don't see any chicken! Where's the chicken? It's too loud in here! I can't hear!" He spat out the phrases as fast as his tongue and lips permitted.

The Richter Scale in my mind began to register the tremors from the fault lines etched into my father's wincing, squinting, furrowed face. Trouble was brewing. Daphne and Zachary sensed it as well; they asked me why Grandpa was yelling. I threw myself into the conversation at this point, since I was seated next to my father.

"Dad, they have chicken. All kinds of chicken. It's all over the place. Piccata, marsala, saltimbocca, and parmigiana. Trust me on this one." He finally got the message.

Sydelle dutifully continued. "Veal piccata." Pause. "Veal marsala." Pause. "Veal parmigiana." Pause. You get the idea. A labyrinthine network of impenetrable brick walls figuratively sprang up in the center of the table to reflect the new wave of confusion in Dad's mind. He abruptly and arbitrarily truncated the veal list.

"Veal parmigiana? Where's veal parmigiana? Where's the veal? I thought they only had chicken in this joint! You just said chicken parmigiana! Where do you see veal parmigiana? So loud in here! I don't see veal parmigiana!" He spit out these phrases even faster than his tongue and lips permitted. I pieced them together into some semblance of coherence based on past precedent.

I thought of Yogi Berra's famous quote: "It's déjà vu all over again."

"It's on the right side of the menu in the middle of the page," Syd wearily replied.

"No, it isn't! I don't see it! No veal!"

"Gerry, it's right here in the middle of the page. I'm not making it up. It's right next to the chicken marsala."

"Where? I can't see it!" Gerry was now clearly distressed; he was still officially speaking, but his amplitude was on the verge of yelling.

Sydelle attempted to again define the available veal options, but

Gerry stopped listening. Truth be told, he did have the mild-to-moderate high-frequency hearing loss that oftentimes accompanies people who log almost eight decades on the planet. But the larger issue at hand pertained to his impatience and general unwillingness to listen.

I interceded again. Leaning over, I pointed to the exact location of the veal parmigiana on the menu. In a moment of sheer clarity, Dad found it. Indiana Jones had an easier time nailing down the precise location of the Ark of the Covenant in the Map Room.

Some less-than-playful banter ensued as the remaining entrée choices were reviewed. It was like a covered pot of boiling water. The cover was still technically in place, but the overflowing water was streaming down the sides. A quick survey around the room showed that none of the other patrons was staring at us, yet. The decision eventually boiled down to either chicken parmigiana or veal parmigiana. Mom asked Dad to make the final call. Sandra Day O'Connor may have been the swing vote during her tenure on the Supreme Court, but I wondered if Chief Justice Rehnquist ever put her on the spot when dinner was on the line for the nine justices.

Now rhythmically pounding his fist on the table, Gerry frantically shouted, "I can't see! I can't see! I can't see a thing in here!" The flatware was bouncing around, the stainless steel knives and forks clanging together. His face was beet red.

Daph and Zach looked up from their coloring. They stared blankly at each other before looking inquisitively at me. A green crayon may have snapped; a blue one slowly rolled off the table and onto the floor. Dad's demonstration of fury had to end, from the standpoints of showing the kids how to behave in a restaurant, proper courtesy to the other patrons, and pure embarrassment. Mom's face was still buried in the pages of the menu, hoping to passively ride out the storm of Dad's tantrum. The responsibility to end the tirade fell squarely upon my shoulders.

"Calm down right now, Dad! Relax! Just relax and stop yelling! Cut it out! Stop it right now!"

I addressed my father in much the same tone I used to speak to Daphne and Zachary when they lost self-control.

"I understand that you can't see the menu. Do you really think we're all fabricating the existence of veal parmigiana in this place? Do you think we're making it up? Do you think the restaurant just puts veal parmigiana on the menu to tease and mislead their customers? Take a quantum leap of faith—accept that we're actually telling the truth about the veal parmigiana!"

I was on a roll, so I continued. My blood pressure was on the rise and I'm sure my cheeks were starting to flush. Still speaking rather loudly I said, "Take a look around you! Look right over there! Look!" I motioned toward the party of eighteen next to us. "There are eighteen completely blind people sitting right next to us! They're smiling. They're laughing. They're enjoying each other's company. They're speaking civilly to one another. Look at them!"

Gerry complied. He glanced over at the table and then returned his focus onto me.

"That's right, Dad! There's food on their table! They're eating the food that they ordered! The blind people are all enjoying the food that they were somehow able to order through some miracle of their maker!" I was borderline yelling, so I slowly and carefully enunciated my words. "The eighteen blind people had no trouble ordering their food, yet you're screaming at the top of your lungs that you can't see! Don't you think there's a problem here? Isn't there something totally screwed up with this situation?" Then, taking it down a notch, I said, "Is any of this resonating in your brain at all?"

Having done all of the dirty work to extinguish this forest fire, it was now Mom's turn to stamp out the remaining glowing embers.

"Oh, Gerry. Why do you have to get so worked up all the time? Why make such a fuss?" she asked.

"Okay, okay," Gerry finally acquiesced. "Chicken parmigiana."

Game, set, match.

The anger I felt in the moment quickly dissolved once I fully recognized the irony of my father's figurative verbal claims to blindness with respect to the literal presence of the eighteen physically blind diners.

Peeking over the edge of Buca's cocktail menu, I stole an occasional furtive look at the table of eighteen sitting alongside us. While I couldn't be certain, there was no conclusive evidence that they overheard our menu interpretation fiasco. I saw smiles, laughter, and pleasant conversation.

How wonderfully normal, I thought; it must be nice. Instead of burying my head in the sand, I found the bottom of my glass.

The waitress arrived with the Caesar salad in a bowl so large a small child could bathe in it. I ordered another cocktail before she had the chance to set the communal bowl down. For some reason not meaningful enough to explore, Dad always preferred oil and vinegar dressing on just about every type of salad—even Caesar. Heaping salad onto his plate, he inverted each bottle in turn, squirting a few dashes of oil and a few dashes of vinegar directly into his open palm to gauge the patency of the spouts and the relative rates of dressing egress. He considered the potential impact of a draft from the overhead ceiling fans on the dressing's fluid dynamics during this experimentation phase. Once satisfied, he doused his salad with oil and vinegar. The garlic croutons plunged to the bottom of the plate, submerged by the liquid weight of the dressing.

Dad inhaled his salad before I finished turning the pepper mill over my own Caesar. He wielded his salad fork with a shoveling-stabbing motion. The technique involved a lot of wrist action crafted and honed over years to optimize efficiency. Some fallout around the plate consisting of lettuce bits, crouton crumbs, and shaved parmesan was duly collected during a secondary sweep of the table with a bimanual fork-and-fingertips loading method. Gerry then wolfed down a second helping of Caesar as he simultaneously announced that he didn't want any more salad.

Daph and Zach were happily engrossed in their macaroni and cheese and buttered spaghetti noodles when the linguine primavera and chicken parmigiana were served. Other than Daph's simple request for extra parmesan cheese, the kids were as silent as kids get. Gerry, on the other hand, heralded the arrival of the plates with an emphatic cry of, "Sydelle! Watch out, Sydelle! Here we go, Sydelle!" Did my father really think that Mom was completely oblivious to the arrival of massive plates of food to the table? Having finished her salad, she had to figure that the entrées were due to arrive. Sneak attacks, guerilla warfare, and scare tactics were generally not part of the dinnertime experience in midwestern Italian restaurants. As the servers set the platters down, Dad withdrew his hands from the table, positioning them chest-high and parallel to one another with palms facing outward. He used the same hand position as an emergency room team that stands "clear" by halting chest compressions during an attempted resuscitation from a cardiac arrest a few seconds before the defibrillator device deploys.

"I see, I see, Gerry," Mom replied. "Oh my God! Will you just look at the portions? Such huge portions! Who can eat so much food?"

A rhetorical question with an obvious answer. Dad. My father is the person who can eat this much food.

"It'll be good, Harley," Syd continued. "You'll have leftovers for next week, so you won't have to cook so much. You can maybe have a few moments to relax rather than having to worry about cooking a whole dinner after working so hard all day long."

"I'm not worried about next week, Mom. Eat however much you wish."

Grasping the serving utensils, I transferred the pasta and chicken from the large serving platters onto the individual dinner plates. This mundane task should have generated absolutely nothing worthy of comment. But Syd remarked that my years of painstaking surgical training enabled me to twirl the pasta forks with virtuoso skill. There must have been an imaginary soprano singing a sweet aria into her ear as she watched me twirl those pasta forks. Gunslingers in the Wild West twirled their still smoking pistols around their index fingers before holstering them. Professional hockey players bounced pucks on the blades of their sticks before expertly flicking them to the referees in between play stoppages. Me? I handled a couple of pasta forks. While Syd showered me with compliments, Dad precisely directed the amount of food I dished out. When exactly 90 percent of the surface area of his dinner plate was occupied, his hand shot up with his elbow bent at a ninety-degree angle, much like a police officer directing oncoming traffic to halt in the center of a busy city intersection.

For Gerry, the consumption of pasta differed in several key respects from salad. Painters place tarpaulins over furniture and rugs to protect against inadvertent spills, splashes, and spatters. With similar intent, Dad unfolded his dinner napkin, tucked it securely inside the front collar of his shirt, and then fanned the remaining cloth out across his chest. By the end of the meal, the marinara sauce transformed his white napkin into something resembling a Jackson Pollock painting. To set himself up for success, Dad flexed his neck and upper back. This enabled him to bring his face into striking range, which was two to four inches between the food and the tip of his nose. His dinner fork then plunged into the peak of the linguine mountain. As I watched the fork impale the pasta, I thought of the classic arcade game where the player uses a joystick to position a mechanical claw arm over a bed of stuffed animals before deploying the claw with the push of the joystick's little red button. With a scooping-sweeping motion, Dad shoveled the forked pasta toward his mouth. His oral sphincter sprang into duty. As his lips engulfed the pasta, a sucking mechanism started in a manner akin to the tentacles on the arm of an octopus. A continuous, uninterrupted stream of linguine steadily passed through his oral aperture. According to basic Newtonian physics, objects in motion tend to stay in motion. This law was heretofore confirmed, for Gerry's face didn't surface for air until the plate was clear. Dolphins, porpoises, and my father all need to come up for air only once every couple of minutes.

Along with the linguine, Gerry's chicken parmigiana had also vanished. I knew the coordinates of the chicken initially, because I had personally placed it on his plate prior to the arrival of Mount Linguine. But it disappeared, presumably somewhere within the sea of pasta that served as a carbohydrate smoke screen.

After replenishing his blood oxygen and glucose levels, Gerry began Phase Two. He took the proverbial bull by the horns at this stage. Tilting the edge of the serving platter toward his plate, he used the serving fork to mudslide the pasta along. After announcing that he didn't want any more pasta, Gerry downed a second helping of linguine primavera.

With the linguine primavera mountain now reduced to rubble, Gerry went on a reconnaissance mission. The mission took some planning and some time. The objective was to amass a third helping of food. The mission was accomplished in waves as he compiled food from several sources during a circumferential survey of the tabletop. By this time, Zach and Daph had finished eating their mains and were clamoring for dessert; Dad funneled their leftover macaroni and cheese onto his plate. Sydelle's plate provided some offerings as well. Stretching across the table, Gerry extended his fork to harpoon a remnant of chicken parmigiana off of her plate. He next claimed what was left of the remaining linguine from the serving platter in the center of the table, taking care to leave several stragglers of pasta behind to give the illusion of temperance. When it was all over, a fallout of scraps too large to be cleared by the waiter's table crumb sweeper surrounded his dinner plate.

"Boy, am I full," Syd was first to exclaim. "I am gaining weight on this trip. I overate."

A general state of satiety had gradually descended upon the table. Gerry leaned back in his chair. Daph and Zach, however, were still clamoring for dessert. Syd ordered a decaf coffee and I ordered a slab of decadent chocolate cake for the table to share. Dessert was never Dad's favorite course, but the allure of the cake proved too tempting to resist. He frowned after a few forkfuls.

"Sweet. It's too sweet," he complained. I was quite familiar with this criticism, having heard it levied dozens of times in the past when dessert was on the table.

"What did you expect, Dad? It's chocolate cake with chocolate icing."

"I know that, but why do they have to make it so sweet?"

"It probably has something to do with the fact that it's chocolate cake with chocolate icing. Do you see the kids complaining?"

"No."

"Exactly."

As soon as I wiped the smeared chocolate off of the kids' lips and chins, Gerry began craning his neck around in search of our waitress. Spotting her about twenty feet away, he summoned her with some form of crude hand signal. "Check" was all he said to her when she arrived. Despite this rather rough request, she got the message and returned with the bill. At Dad's request, I verified the accuracy of the bill to ensure that the restaurant was not unfairly swindling him. His pocket calculator nonetheless plopped down onto the table to aid in determining the proper tip. Forget about doubling the tax. Forget about just adding a straight twenty percent to the bill. Dad used some combination of Euclidean geometry, integrals, and derivatives to ultimately arrive at a gratuity of $19.34.

Gerry was eager to leave as soon as the bill was paid. Having sat relatively still for the better part of two hours, Daphne and Zachary were whining to go home. Their four- and seven-year-old attention spans were both spent. I certainly had no desire to prolong the ordeal any longer. But we couldn't just stand up and leave. Mom had to urinate. The lukewarm glass of water and four sips of red wine she drank during dinner had run their course. She couldn't wait until she returned to her hotel room to relieve the mounting pressure in her bladder. We were and will always be hostages to the demands of her bladder. Ten minutes of our lives passed, never to be reclaimed. Gerry started to yawn and sigh while rubbing the stubble on his jawline. The kids started to provoke one another through a mutual exchange of pokes, prods, and nudges.

Upon returning from the restroom, one final order of business remained. Mom had to reapply her lipstick. It was about sixty-three degrees outside. She was going from the restaurant to the car and then directly from the car to her hotel bedroom. Nonetheless, she excavated her lipstick and handheld mirror from the depths of her handbag. A generous double layer of some vibrant shade of red was applied. Whether the majority of the lipstick ended up on her lips or on her upper incisor teeth is debatable. Gerry yawned some more as he massaged the fatigue out of his face. After one final check in the mirror, Sydelle announced that she was ready to leave.

We erupted out of our chairs and headed toward the door. Gerry was in front of me, leading the way. As we left, Gerry's right hip inadvertently slammed up against the chair back of one of the eighteen blind patrons. For the record, the blind guy didn't so much as flinch.

~

Seven solid courses and two full hours later, we left the Le Village Buffet. Several members of the Paris Hotel culinary staff followed us out, intending to borrow a few pallets of lox from the neighboring hotels to tide them over until their next shipment arrived. There may have been a domestic smoked salmon shortage. I intentionally walked several paces behind Dad to avoid a gut-busting button exploding off of his shirt and rabbit-punching me in the back of the head. Please believe me when I tell you that my father walked out of brunch licking a multi-scoop strawberry ice cream cone.

CHAPTER 16

THE FASHIONISTA

Since dinner was a mere seven hours away, Sydelle thought it would be a grand idea to "walk off brunch" with a Saturday afternoon stroll along the Strip. It was a pleasant walk, but at her pace, we burned about four calories per hour. Bern and I discussed the present state of the Yankees (a subject that never grew old) and the New York Giants' prospects for a playoff run later in the year. I made sure that I didn't mention the Vegas sports books as we passed the Venetian Hotel, as my disappointment about playing blackjack with Bern still lingered.

My uncle occasionally gambled on the NFL playoff games with a bookie near his home in Queens named Louie the Mole. With putative ties to the New York mafia, Louie the Mole operated out of the back of a candy shop in Queens. According to Bern, he sat behind a little wooden table, presiding over two stacks of incoming and outgoing Benjamins. The incoming stack was always the taller of the two. Flanking Louie the Mole were two henchmen in gaudy three-piece suits, their intentionally unbuttoned jackets sending a clear message that they carried—but did not care to conceal—handguns. But Louie was of no use to me at present; I just had a fleeting thought that if he magically materialized in Las Vegas, Bern would have let him front the cash to play a few hands of blackjack with me.

We walked up to the front of the Wynn Hotel, caterpillars and tortoises lapping us in the process. Appreciating some of the high-end finishes in the atrium, Gerry sauntered up to the front desk to inquire about room rates. Mind you, he had no intention of ever staying there. It was furthermore futile for him to ask a general question about prices given the extreme variability in rates by room type, dates of stay, major sports events, large conventions, etc. that routinely make Vegas the destination city that it is. Still licking my wounds from the check-in fiasco at the Paris, I kept my distance from the front desk personnel.

"Six bills a pop, Sydelle," Gerry declared on his return, pointing his thumb back at the employee from whom the rate was solicited. "They want six bills a night for this joint, Sydelle." Translating Gerry's vernacular, each night at the Wynn cost approximately $600.

"This isn't exactly the Motel 6, Dad. Steve Wynn is one of the most prominent and most successful business magnates in the history of Las Vegas."

"I would never stay here for six bills a night. Never."

"I know, Dad. Luckily, no one is forcing you to stay here against your will. Come on, let's go."

We passed some time meandering through the sculptured gardens at the Wynn. Casual window-shopping proved to be our next pitfall. Gerry had purchased a beige Members Only brand windbreaker jacket for the grand sum of sixty-five dollars about a year and a half before the Vegas trip. However, he refused to cut the tags off the jacket, fearing that he had overpaid. So the jacket remained unworn in his closet collecting dust. Dad was biding his time until he came across a cheaper windbreaker. Time was on his side.

A mannequin in the window of Brioni was outfitted in a lightweight beige jacket. This stopped my father in his tracks.

"Look, Sydelle! A beige windbreaker, just like the one I bought." He stood transfixed directly in front of the plate-glass storefront.

"Oh, Gerry. You've been searching high and low for a jacket for the last two years. Isn't it time you just wore the one you bought?"

"Don't tell me that! It's the same jacket, Sydelle. Look at it!"

"It's similar Gerry, but it's not the same."

"I've got four or five beige jackets in my closet," Bern said. "All brand names. You know I only wear name brands. You can have them all."

"Who needs five beige jackets?"

"Presents, Gerry. I got them all as gifts. I don't even put on a jacket until there's snow on the ground. They're as good as new."

"How come you get so many gifts?"

"From my girlfriends, Gerry. My girlfriends gave them to me."

"Girlfriends? Come on, Bernard. What girlfriends?"

"Never mind my girlfriends. I'm allowed to have a social life, aren't I? Let me worry about my girlfriends. We're talking about you and your wardrobe here. Do you want my jackets or not?"

"Where did you buy your jacket, Dad?" I asked.

"Macy's."

"Well, then I recommend that we move on," I said. I dress for work every day, wearing either a full suit or a sport jacket and slacks to see patients in my office. When I invest in a new suit, I tend to buy from the high-end lines, as a single well-made suit lasts a lot longer in my wardrobe than a few poorly made ones. That said, I would have to have one hell of an extraordinary run at the craps tables to afford the full-price merchandise adorning the walls of the Brioni boutique. Elyse bought me a Brioni necktie a few years back. While it remains my favorite tie, it's the only item in my closet made by Brioni. Cognizant of both the price tags in the store and the contents of my father's wardrobe, I knew that there was absolutely no chance anything made by Brioni would ever come into direct contact with my father's body.

"How come?" Dad wasn't ready to abandon his find without a suitable explanation.

"Let's see, Dad. Where did you buy your jacket?"

"I just told you, Harley. Macy's. Why?"

"Because this is Brioni."

"So what?"

"Have you ever heard of Brioni before?"

"No."

"That's what I thought. To put it mildly, you are not going to like the price point at Brioni."

"How do you know, Harley?"

"Because Elyse and I have previously shopped at Brioni."

"Don't tell me that! I want to see how much this jacket costs!" His obstinacy didn't surprise me. Frankly, I didn't really expect him to go quietly. To do so would have been to underestimate my father.

"Trust me, Dad. That jacket is way out of your price range."

"We'll see about that. I want to see how much it costs."

"Dad, there's no way that jacket costs less than one thousand dollars."

"A thousand? You're crazy, Harley!"

"I wouldn't be surprised if it sells for two thousand," I replied.

"I'm going in to find out."

"It's a waste of time, Dad."

"I want to know! I'm a customer just like anyone else that walks through that door." He was not to be dissuaded.

"You're right, Dad. You are indeed a paying customer. Go ahead, then. Suit yourself." No one else recognized my pun, but it made me happy to say it standing in front of Brioni. "I'll wait outside. Let me know how it goes."

Gerry actually went inside the store. He commanded the undivided attention of the sales team, as he was the only patron at the time. He exited within sixty seconds, never to return.

"I don't see any garment bags over your shoulder, Dad. Did you have the jacket shipped directly to your house in Florida?" I asked.

"No. It was exorbitant."

"Really? You don't say? Did I exaggerate the price?"

"No."

Bern started to laugh. "You can have all of my jackets for two hundred total, Gerry. It's a bargain. Think of all the money you'll save compared with the Brioni."

"Knock it off, Bernard!" Dad didn't appreciate Bern's taunts, coming on the heels of his defeat inside Brioni.

"Can we please go now?" I begged.

Sydelle and Bern echoed my sentiments. With strength in numbers, we left the Wynn. Finance figured prominently in Mom's mind as we walked out onto Las Vegas Boulevard.

"You know, Harley, we just replaced the wall-to-wall carpeting in the house. It wasn't cheap; I picked an expensive pattern."

"That's great, Mom. I hope you and Dad thoroughly enjoy it."

"I just hope a little something is left behind for your inheritance when your father and I are no longer around, if you know what I mean."

I knew exactly what she meant. Double entendre was not exactly Syd's forte. Nonetheless, I refused to take the bait.

"Maybe if you had chosen a cheaper option, Dad's beige windbreaker budget could have been liberalized."

That ended the conversation. We killed the afternoon drifting through the other hotels in the vicinity—The Mirage, The Venetian, and The Palazzo. We wandered through the Fashion Show Mall and then caught the now-defunct pirate show outside Treasure Island. Bern remarked that the visage of one of the mechanical pirates bore a distinct resemblance to The Gooch. Back at the Paris, we changed our clothes and printed out our boarding passes for the flights home the following morning. Gerry used the hiatus to register a formal complaint with the hotel's in-room dining service. Apparently, he was displeased that a breakfast tray left outside someone else's room the previous day had yet to be cleared. Sydelle urinated a few times and Bern caffeinated himself. I spent the time alone at the blackjack tables, trying to win enough cash to buy a beige windbreaker.

CHAPTER 17

ACCOUNTING 401—HIGH FINANCE

I had a good run at the blackjack tables, winning on a few well-timed splits and double downs. By the time I cashed in my chips and joined my family, I had collected enough of a profit to buy the zipper on the Brioni windbreaker. Instead of returning to the Wynn Hotel, though, we walked into a kitschy gift shop just down the block from the Paris. It was one of those classic tourist traps that sold all kinds of Vegas-themed junk along with over-the-counter remedies for every kind of hangover known to exist. The store was perfect for my needs at the moment: a couple of small mementos to bring home for Daph and Zach.

As I meandered through the aisles, Mom and Dad decided they needed to buy Daph and Zach some toys as well.

"We'd like to buy the children a few trinkets, so that they can keep us near and dear to their hearts," Mom said sighing, guilt dripping from every word. "After all, we're so far away in Florida and so much time passes in between visits."

"Me too. I'm in," Bern added without a hint of guilt in his voice.

We reached the checkout line after a solid hour zigzagging through aisles stocked with the kind of crap you only buy if you're drunk, high, or both. By that time, the store's air conditioning system had turned Sydelle's fingers a ghastly shade of plum despite the thick wool coat and turtleneck she had donned. Bern was ready to leave as well, as he was due for his pre-dinner coffee.

I was working on getting us all out of the souvenir store before sunset. We switched cashiers after Gerry calculated that the wait at the initial checkout line would have delayed our departure from the store by about fourteen seconds. After I had paid for my purchases, Mom, Dad, and Uncle Bern laid their toys on the counter. The cashier found the bar codes on each of the items, scanned them into the cash register, and presented the total bill to my father. This was all pretty mundane and barely worth mentioning. But the action quickly picked up, like a shooter in the middle of making eight consecutive points at a $50 craps table.

"Split bill, please. We want separate bills," Gerry told the cashier as she robotically scanned the barcodes into her cash register.

At this point, I had been on the phone confirming our dinner reservation, but my ears pricked up upon hearing Dad ask the cashier to split the bill. Finishing my phone call, I shifted my position to catch a glimpse of the scene unfolding at the register.

"Excuse me, sir?" the cashier asked my father.

"Split the bill."

"I don't know how to do that."

"What?"

"My register doesn't let me split a bill after all of the items have been rung up."

"Come on, now!" Gerry was getting riled up. "Just split the bill, will you?"

"I can cancel out the transaction and start over again if you would like, sir."

"No, no! I don't want to cancel it out! We want to purchase these items. Can't you just divide the bill in two parts?"

"I'm sorry, sir. As I already explained, I don't think I can do that. I can ring up your items as two separate transactions, if you would like."

One look at the unfortunate cashier revealed that she may have been all of fifteen years old and weighed about eighty-two pounds soaking wet. She looked like a sweet kid who divided her time between homework, baking chewy chocolate chip cookies, and babysitting. Obviously flustered, her cheeks flushed in response to Gerry's antagonism. But to her credit, she remained composed. After all, she was dealing with a lunatic.

"Come on! Who's in charge here? I'm not playing games. What kind of games are you people playing with me?"

If I could have gotten a word in here, I would have pointed out to my father that the store was filled with all kinds of games, from playing cards to toy slot machines to travel checkerboard sets.

"Sir, I'd like to help you, but I just don't know how!" she exclaimed, now sounding exasperated.

"Then get me the supervisor! We're wasting time. I want a supervisor! Who's in charge here anyway?"

The supervisor dutifully approached post haste, having been conveniently within earshot. He may have been two years older than the cashier. Unshaven with oversized metallic eyeglass frames and a golf shirt partially tucked into his trousers, I could instantly tell he was ill-prepared to deal with the likes of my father.

Dad pointed his way through a not-so-brief synopsis of the events to the supervisor, who remained speechless. I couldn't tell if his stoicism was due to incredulity or his inability to understand Gerry's rapid-fire verbal barrage. When Dad finished hollering and no reply issued forth from the mouth of the supervisor, I stepped in.

"Dad, do you have any idea how absurd you sound?" I said in a voice that could easily be heard on the other side of the store. "We're not in a restaurant and this cashier is not a waitress. You're being ridiculous! Who the hell asks to split a bill in a souvenir store? Do grocery stores split bills? How about hardware stores or gas stations? Cash registers in stores like these don't have the software capabilities to split bills."

Once I started, I didn't stop. I couldn't stop. I felt badly for the poor cashier, who had done absolutely nothing wrong to incur my father's wrath. Similar to the scene in Buca di Beppo with the eighteen blind diners, I was again watching a senior male relative act inappropriately in a public place rather than serve as a role model to me.

"What exactly do you expect the cashier to do, Dad? Whip out a pad of paper, pencil, and calculator to itemize the bill by hand, add up the individual totals, and determine the state tax that should be applied to each item? Even if the cashier expends this heroic effort on your behalf, you won't have the patience to wait for her to figure it all out. Be realistic for a second."

Dad actually waited until I finished speaking my mind before responding.

I gave him credit for this needle of patience buried within the haystack of unreasonable discourtesy he showed the cashier. However, it was obvious that he was refusing to listen to reason.

"Now just wait a minute, Harley! It's simple math, and I'm the customer. The customer is always right. If I want her to split the bill, she should split the bill!" Turning so that he could address the manager while continuing our own argument, Gerry shouted, "Otherwise, I'll take my business elsewhere!"

This manager obviously didn't give a damn if my father spent $46.18 at his store or another souvenir shop in the area. Of that fact I was certain. He surely wished that my father had never set foot in his store.

"How can I get some satisfaction here, Harley? What's your bright idea?"

"You want my advice? Fine, Dad. I'll tell you exactly what we're going to do. Listen up. I'm going to break this down for you, step by step. Listen carefully, because I'm only going to say this once."

Gerry stared back at me, as did the manager and the cashier. I felt the gaze of other customers in the checkout line as well.

"First, I'm going to apologize to the cashier and the manager for your outrageous behavior." Unfortunately, I had become quite accustomed to this role, and in this case, familiarity did indeed breed contempt. The way I apologized to the cashier wound up being quite similar to the way I made amends with the Paris Hotel's receptionist at the start of the trip.

"Second, you're going to pay for the entire purchase with the credit card of your choice." Dad was fortunate that I granted him the option of selecting his card of choice. No other payment options were to be considered.

"Third, we're going to leave this store and hope that we'll be granted entry the next time you decide to buy Daph and Zach a couple of toys. Lastly, when we get back to the hotel, you and Bern can settle up. You'll have options, Dad, lots of options. Bern can pay you back for his half of the purchase in cash or personal check. He can convert his dollars into Euros so that you'll have some pocket change for your next European cruise down the Danube. He can treat you and Mom to lunch tomorrow. You can arrange monthly installments, with or without interest compounded quarterly. Hell, you can even arrange a layaway plan or have Bern perform odd jobs around your house until he fulfills his financial obligations. Whatever you want to do is fine with me, as long as I never, ever hear about this godforsaken bill again."

Dad stared at me for a few seconds after I fell silent, frowned, and then sheepishly slid his credit card across the counter toward the cashier. As we walked out of the store, I sent Elyse a text message to please have a stiff cocktail waiting for me upon my return home.

Gerry thought I should have defended him against the evil souvenir store management empire that conspired against his bill splitting request. His silence during the walk back to the hotel said as much. In his mind, his only son should have stood by his side in solidarity, if for no other reason than to pay my respects to the DNA we shared. Maybe he was right. Maybe I should have insisted that the cashier split the bill. Maybe I should have acknowledged that sometimes in life, you have to lean in a little and force the issue to get what you want. Furthermore, the odds were that I would never see this cashier again. She would have probably forgotten the whole incident by the next morning. Even if the stars aligned during a future visit to this same souvenir shop, it would take one fantastic memory to recollect the bill splitting incident. But who knew for certain?

What I did know was three basic things. First, I knew that I was a loyal person at heart, especially with regard to my family and close friends. Second, I firmly believed in calling a spade a spade. Third, I had no problem admitting when I was wrong. On this occasion at the checkout line in the souvenir store, when I was in the heat of the moment, my gut told me that Dad was issuing an inappropriate demand and behaving in a manner that was embarrassing, undignified, and uncalled for. I did what I thought was right. If that meant sacrificing some loyalty to my father, so be it.

I had picked up a couple of small trinkets for Daph and Zach—some pens and other miscellany that had the words "Las Vegas" flashing in multicolored lights. These gifts had life expectancies of about thirty seconds in the kids' hands, but that was immaterial. What mattered was that I brought something home to prove that Daph and Zach were in my thoughts while I was away from home. What mattered even more was the fact I needed to rally, as the hour of our third and final evening meal was rapidly approaching. This was slated to be the dinner during which we would formally raise our glasses and toast to Sydelle's seventieth and Uncle Bern's almost eighty-first birthday.

CHAPTER 18

SUNSET IN LAS VEGAS

The venue for the trip's grand finale was set at the Palm Restaurant inside Caesars Palace. The original Palm in Manhattan is a quintessential New York steakhouse, exuding an old boys' club ambiance that only Peter Luger in Brooklyn surpassed. Elyse and I were dating the first and only time we ate in the flagship restaurant, so being at the Palm in Las Vegas conjured fond memories of our pre-married life together. The dimly lit dining room, timeworn creaking hardwood floors, crisp white tablecloths, traditional steakhouse fare, and boisterous wait staff created a memorable scene. Caricature portraits of the restaurant's most famous patrons adorned the walls.

Compared with the rest of us, Mom's mood was a bit downtrodden. She recognized that the weekend was quickly drawing to a close.

"It's been such a lovely weekend," she remarked.

Bern naturally agreed and Gerry grunted some presumable form of assent.

"Oh, yes," I compulsorily agreed. To suggest otherwise would have deeply offended my mother. When a gift is received, the giver is automatically thanked, even if the gift itself is hideous or useless. A married guy instinctively remembers to put the seat down after he finishes using the toilet in the master bathroom. Some things in life are automatic. You do them because it's part of basic human decency. So when Mom said that the time she has spent with the three most important people to her on the planet has been lovely, I immediately agreed even as the melting clocks depicted in Salvador Dali's *The Persistence of Memory* came to mind.

"You know, we really should do this more often," continued Sydelle. "Isn't it nice to be all together like this, enjoying each other's company?"

"Of course, Mom," I reiterated, mentally clutching the boarding pass for my flight home to Minneapolis. Despite the nearly three full days we had spent together, it still didn't feel quite right to be on a trip as an adult with my parents. Las Vegas was a contrived city essentially manufactured out of desert nothingness, but being there without Elyse didn't feel natural.

"Why don't we commit to another family vacation next year?" she continued.

"That's out of the question." As I've lived my life, I've grown increasingly appreciative of living in the moment and living for the moment. We were in the midst of celebrating two milestone family birthdays and Mom was already moving on to next year.

"Why?" she asked. Syd was clearly taken aback by my answer.

"Because I refuse to pledge myself to another trip without my wife, especially without speaking with her about it first. How many other married men that you know of go on multiple vacations by themselves with their mommies and daddies?"

"Okay, okay," Syd relented. "I just thought it would be nice."

Extracting myself from the conversation, I let my mind wander while gazing upon the signature caricatures blanketing the paneled walls of the restaurant. Looking at them reminded me of the charcoal portrait of Daphne hanging on her bedroom wall at home. I missed the kids and I missed Elyse, despite only being away for three days. I returned to reality when our bottle of wine arrived. Trying to be friendly, the waiter innocently asked from where we were visiting. Gerry pounced on the opportunity to partake in one of his favorite hobbies—striking up small talk with complete strangers.

"How did you know we were tourists?" Gerry said with a broad grin.

"Oh, after you've been waiting tables around here for as long as I have, you figure it out pretty quickly."

"Really? Did you hear that, Sydelle? He figured out we were tourists." Dad was impressed with the waiter's acumen. With the wall caricatures hovering above and glaring down upon us, I wondered if the French Polynesians recognized that Paul Gaugin wasn't a local after he landed in

Tahiti from his native France in the late nineteenth century. Determining that we were not born and raised in Las Vegas was about as difficult as figuring out that the Dalai Lama didn't hail from Australia.

"We came all the way from South Florida, in Palm Beach County," he proudly told the waiter. You would have thought he had just completed the Iditarod race barefoot with only half of his regular sled dog team.

"Palm Beach is very nice," the waiter politely replied.

"We live in a town outside of West Palm Beach. We caught a direct flight from Fort Lauderdale. There's only one direct flight a day to Las Vegas, so we had to take it. Otherwise, we would have had to make a connection. Who wants to make a connection? Why should we make a connection? We took the direct flight. We've been here for three days now, staying at the Paris hotel across the street."

Dad pointed his thumb in the general direction of the Paris. The waiter's eyes glazed over a bit before he scanned the restaurant, looking for an excuse to escape the conversation. He shifted his weight from foot to foot, as if standing barefoot on a bed of coals that was growing gradually warmer.

"Dad, please understand that the details of your travel itinerary are completely irrelevant to this nice guy's life. Don't you think he has better things to do than pretend to care about the time you check out of your hotel tomorrow?"

My rescue attempt imperviously boomeranged off Dad's chest and landed somewhere across the dining room.

"Oh, yeah, that reminds me, Harley. We have to check out tomorrow morning, right after breakfast. Boarding passes too, thank God we already printed out our boarding passes." Now placing his hand on the waiter's forearm, he asked, "How much time will it take us to get to the airport?"

Gerry clearly missed my point, so I feigned ignorance about one of the steaks listed on the dinner menu. The waiter quickly described the nuances of the dish and then took our dinner orders without pausing for a breath. Sydelle asked if the kitchen could allow some time in between the salad course and the entrée, so as to facilitate digestion (and prolong the meal).

"Of course, ma'am."

The waiter would have agreed to just about any request, as long as it permitted him to leave our table. I didn't see this guy again until he presented the dessert menus. A rotating corps of servers attended to us instead. They kept their feet moving at all times, like a running back caught among a pile of offensive and defensive tackles at the line of scrimmage. The servers took care not to linger so as to avoid falling into Gerry's sticky web of tedium.

Ideally, the breadbasket should have arrived within five minutes of placing the dinner order. It didn't. Gerry recruited some employee of the restaurant, who was not a member of the wait staff, with an obscure hand gesture and took him to task. Dressed in a full suit, I suspect he was the restaurant manager.

Mom and Dad shared a salad. The salad dressing was ordered on the side, per usual. Dad wanted some fresh ground black pepper on his salad. Mom passed the salt and pepper but the black pepper granules were not visible through the walls of the pepper mill, so he couldn't readily discern the salt from the pepper. He manipulated them in his hands and stared at them like an unsolvable Rubik's Cube puzzle. No luck. So he dumped a few granules of each mill into his open palm, using trial and error to ultimately divulge the secrets of the salt-and-pepper shaker mystery.

The salad talk started.

"My God, the portions! Would you look at the size of this salad?" said Sydelle as she watched Gerry shake out enough black pepper so it resembled an ant colony perched atop his lettuce.

"Yeah, what about it? So what?" replied Gerry.

"Who can eat this much salad? I'm not going to have enough room left for my steak."

"Oh, I don't know, Sydelle. Eat it. Don't eat it. I don't care."

"You know, it's a good thing we shared," declared Sydelle with conviction. You would think she had narrowly avoided some calamity like backing up her computer's hard drive fifteen seconds before it was struck by lightning. "Who needs so much salad? They could give a little less, and they could charge a little less."

"Oh, I don't know Sydelle! I don't know!" whined Gerry. He was heavily invested in his salad and didn't appreciate the distraction my mother was causing.

Each portion of salad was optimized via a vegetarian bartering system that unfolded in rounds, similar to the National Football League Draft. Onions were first transferred over to Dad's salad. In exchange, several broccoli florets migrated over to Mom's side. Broccoli florets were especially coveted; they were considered a first-class vegetable in Sydelle's mind. Gerry claimed all feta cheese, olives, and chickpeas. In return, Sydelle inherited the lion's share of the fruit—any combination of strawberries, cranberries, and oranges. The third and final round consisted of mop up. Dad forced some extra salad miscellany onto Sydelle's plate while he ate all of the remaining "grass" (his vernacular for any form of lettuce). He then retrieved the miscellany from her plate when she refused to eat it. Ultimately, the salad was completely finished. Where my father was involved, leftovers occurred more rarely than the sighting of a live snow leopard strolling through the Sistine Chapel.

At this stage in the meal, a mini debate flared up.

"Oh, God. I'm already full! I can skip the steak and move right to dessert," Sydelle exclaimed with a toothy grin that showed her receding gum lines. "It's nice to have some time in between courses to digest."

Gerry had a diametrically opposed viewpoint on the spacing between courses. Keeping his eyes transfixed on the doors separating the dining room from the kitchen, he impatiently exclaimed, "What are they doing back there? What's taking so long?" He was still famished. He needed to replenish a substantial percentage of the caloric load he lost sweating the price of the Brioni windbreaker.

Truth be told, the rest of the dinner passed uneventfully. We shared a nice bottle of wine, ate some great steaks, and capped the meal off with slabs of chocolate cake decorated with the obligatory birthday candles for Syd and Bern. An off-key chorus of the obligatory "Happy Birthday" song accompanied our four forks clanging together.

"Here, Gerry. Try it. It's good."

"I don't want any Sydelle!"

"Oh, come on! Just have one small taste."

You might as well tell a cocaine addict to take just one small hit from a crack pipe.

"I already told you I don't want any!" came his agitated reply.

I pictured my father as the hunter perched all day in his deer stand waiting for the ideal buck to take with his bow and arrow. I waited for it. Waited for it. Waited just a little bit longer . . .

About two minutes later, Gerry picked up the fork and steadily plunged and stabbed his way through the alternating layers of sponge cake and icing.

It was late by the time we got back at the hotel, at least by septuagenarian standards. My flight home was scheduled to depart early the next morning; there was no sense awakening either my parents or Bern to say good-bye in the pre-dawn hours. It was time for the obligatory round of hugs and kisses combined with Mom's waterworks. "Don't get so emotional, Mom. Your ninetieth and Bern's one-hundredth birthday are a mere twenty years away. I'll organize a nice quiet celebration in Rio de Janeiro during Carnival. That way, you'll have something to look forward to."

"Oh, Harley. Can't you ever give it a rest? Why do you always have to give me such a hard time?"

"Because the sarcasm just oozes out of my pores without control during moments like these. I try to control it, but sometimes it just oozes out, following the path of least resistance. It's kind of like your mucous tide, Mom. I know you can relate to that."

"That reminds me, I need to take my Mucinex before bed tonight."

"Glad I could be of service, Mom."

"If I forget to take the Mucinex, the plane ride will make my ears clog for the next week."

"Christ, Mom. I'm not discussing your eustachian tube dysfunction now. I was trying to say a legitimate goodbye to you, Dad, and Bern. You and Dad already have reservations for Minneapolis in a couple of months. We'll see each other again in about eight weeks. It's not like I'm about to take a vow of silence in a Tibetan Buddhist monastery for the next decade."

Bern chose this moment to break his silence.

"A hundred years old? I don't have to worry about living to one hundred, Harley. All I have to do is survive one day longer than The Gooch."

"Cut it out, Bernard! Cut out the nonsense! Why do you have to make trouble about Shirley again? We had such a nice night—don't ruin it now."

"I'm just telling Harley how I feel, Sydelle." Bern tried his best to sound innocent; his performance did not merit an Academy Award. "I just want the satisfaction of shoveling a little dirt onto her casket. I want to physically see that Gooch in her rightful place—six feet under—with my own two eyes. That way, I know she won't be able to hurt me or anyone else anymore. Harley will be safe from her talons. At that point, I can go to my own grave in peace."

"Relax, Mom. Bern is just trying to keep me out of harm's way. It's his duty. He's a modern-day equivalent of the Knights Templar who swore an oath to protect the Holy Grail. You wouldn't want any unnecessary misfortune to happen upon me, your one and only child, would you?" My innocent tone was as genuine as the Eiffel Tower at the front corner of our hotel.

Bern winked at me, acknowledging my allegiance. He wasn't crying in his coffee over the trip's imminent end. He handled farewells much better than Mom.

I turned around to give Dad a hug, but he had vanished. I suspected that he was retrieving his boarding passes from the room safe, where they had been stowed to prevent potential tampering by the hotel's maid service.

~

On the flight home, I reveled in the sheer bliss of anonymity and solitude. I enjoyed a large coffee, a good book, a nap, and the anticipation of seeing Elyse, Daphne, and Zachary at home in Minneapolis.

For entirely different reasons, Gerry also enjoyed his flight home to Geriatricville. The air conditioning on the plane was blasting. Sydelle hunkered down in her turtleneck sweater, wool coat, and several layers of complimentary airline blankets. Dad required nothing more than a thin cotton T-shirt. All the inner warmth he needed was nestled in the back pocket of his pants. It had nothing to do with indigestion and everything to do with the paper voucher for a free night he scored upon checking out from the Paris Hotel.

Mom and Dad couldn't wait to share the details with me. They called as soon as they crossed the Geriatricville threshold. Apparently, the bathroom toilet in Mom and Dad's hotel room had overflowed in the middle of the night. Yes, this was unpleasant. Yes, this was something that they didn't expect to deal with while on vacation. But this was not a biblical flood requiring the navigational capacity of an ark filled with a male-female pair of every animal species on earth and captained by the Hebrew equivalent of the Gorton's Fisherman. Nor was it akin to the relentless flow of the Atlantic into the sinking Titanic that required the doomed passengers in steerage to seek out the temporarily dry high ground of the ship's deck from which the lifeboats were deployed. There was just a little toilet water on the subway-tiled floor of the hotel bathroom.

A frantic Gerry called the hotel front desk. The urgency in his voice made it seem like the sky was falling. The front desk staff called housekeeping. Housekeeping, in turn, called the plumber. The plumber knocked on their door about eighteen minutes later. Thus far, it sounded like a sensible sequence of initial events that could reasonably be expected to produce a viable solution to the toilet problem. When Dad opened the door to receive the plumber, reason went down the drain. Visibly disheveled with a stained, partially untucked gray workman's shirt and a severe case of bed head clearly indicating that he had been jolted awake by the call from housekeeping, the plumber grinned an almost toothless smile and handed Dad a plunger (wood shaft end first, to his credit). The plumber wished him goodnight and left, never to return.

Standing utterly stunned in the threshold of the door, Dad mentally weighed his options. While he could follow the plumber down the hall and holler out a demand for his return, he was dressed in nothing but his threadbare boxer shorts and the plumber was already long out of sight. Alternatively, he could call down to hotel management, chew out the unsuspecting night manager, and restart the plumber request process. This would likely consume a longer chunk of time than the twenty minutes that had already elapsed, and the night manager would first have to calm Gerry down enough to understand his pressured barrage of verbiage before relocating the plumber (assuming that the hotel didn't have an army of on-call plumbers at their disposal). Passing the plunger to Sydelle was never in consideration. Aside from being the antithesis of chivalrous, Sydelle had no idea as to how to properly engage a plunger into the murky depths of a clogged toilet. Even if she knew the key maneuvers of rudimentary plunger use, she lacked the upper body strength required to unclog the bowl. So Dad was left with the final option of keeping the plunger and taking matters into his own hands—literally and figuratively. Under the circumstances, this proved to be the only practical option. About five minutes later, the toilet was flowing with born-again vigor. The toilet water on the bathroom floor was mopped up with the extra set of towels requested at check-in. A still seething Gerry crawled back into bed, though it took him a good long while to nod off.

With the first rays of the sunrise poking through the slits in the drawn polyester window drapes the following morning, Dad jettisoned himself out of bed, threw on some mismatched clothes, and presented himself to the daytime crew behind the counter at the front desk. Without offering any explanation to the clueless hotel staff, he thrust the mostly dry but nonetheless used plunger toward the first perplexed hotel employee with whom he made eye contact.

"Sir?" was all that the guy behind the counter said as he begrudgingly accepted the plunger.

Dad spared no repulsive detail as he unloaded on the front desk personnel with wild abandon. To his credit, the employee behind the counter took it all in stride, maintaining eye contact despite being on the receiving end of spittle flying from Gerry's foaming and frothing mouth. When Dad paused to catch his breath and bring his blood pressure down, the front desk clerk excused himself behind a nondescript, unlabeled door.

Upon his return, the clerk triumphantly presented Dad with an ironclad voucher for a free night's stay during a subsequent trip. This voucher was as valuable as a check made payable to "bearer." Dad snatched it up and proudly paraded through the center aisle of the casino floor en route to the front door. He stood tall, chin and chest thrust forward, much as Caesar returned to the adulations of Rome following a productive season replete with carnage and territorial expansion of the Empire. The only problem with this outcome was that Mom and Dad had no plans to return to Vegas anytime in the near future to redeem the voucher.

If the plunger incident went down as Dad described it, I have no problem with the way in which he reacted. The hotel management clearly mishandled the clogged toilet situation, and my father's anger was clearly justified in my mind. He deserved more than an apology from the unprofessional nighttime staff. He deserved a free night, and he got one. I duly congratulated him on the outcome, adding to the sense of vindication he already felt with the room voucher in hand.

~

The Palm restaurant missed its opportunity to immortalize caricatures of Sydelle, Gerry, and Uncle Bern on its walls during our weekend in Las Vegas. That didn't make the trip any less significant in my mind. Never before and never since has the *mishegas* in my family life been so densely concentrated, both in scope and in time. That fact, in and of itself, made the trip indelible in my soul.

In a three-day period, I came to appreciate the power of *mishegas* and its prominence in my family life. Perhaps more so than ever before, I learned to both fear it and embrace it. I developed a love-hate relationship with it. I certainly didn't crave new *mishegas*. It wasn't as if I went to bed saying to myself, "This day was pretty damn good, but it would have been better still if a little more *mishegas* occurred. At the same time, though, I would never give back any of it. Not even one bit.

For me, much of the magnetism of *mishegas* rested with its utter chameleon-like quality, transforming itself through time rather than color. In the thick of it, *mishegas* ranged from put-your-head-through-a-wall ire to bust-a-gut-rolling-over-on-the-floor laughter. But given time, all of it funneled down into a common denominator that was heartwarming, priceless, and irreplaceable in the end.

Acting like a master puppeteer, the *mishegas* tugged at the strings governing my emotional world, eliciting bursts of laughter as when Bern vilified The Gooch to bursts of fury when Dad offended the Paris Hotel receptionist. It allowed my emotions to soar, like when we formally celebrated the two birthdays over a fantastic steak dinner at the Palm Restaurant. It also caused them to nosedive, as from the disappointment of missing my highly anticipated chance to gamble with Uncle Bern. Impressive, no? Yet it didn't stop there, as *mishegas* was as physically versatile as it was emotionally virtuosic. The *mishegas* spanned the gamut of the physical world, from the microscopic chemical warfare Sydelle waged with her antibacterial wipes to the macroscopic fistfight between Bern and the Irishman in the Paris Hotel coffee shop. Powerful stuff, this *mishegas* was.

Mishegas played tricks on my mind, acting like a cultural trompe l'oeil. As the weekend unfolded, I saw the *mishegas* convert one person's theory into another's reality. According to Dad's theory, the rental car customer service representative stationed halfway across the country should have been easily able to extinguish the eternal flame of the dome light via telephone. According to my reality, I knew the switch controlling the dome light was easily identifiable to anyone possessing a little bit of patience. According to Bern's theory, the cabbie in the LaGuardia parking lot provoked a fistfight with his anti-Semitic words. According to my reality, the fistfight resulted from Bern's hearing loss mixed with his inherently combustible personality.

Finding evidence of the seven deadly sins in Sin City is not surprising. Finding them all within your family, on the other hand, is more worthy of comment. The seven deadly sins played out before my eyes during the trip. There was lust: Bern gawking at the casino cocktail waitresses. I saw gluttony: Gerry's eating performance at the Le Village Buffet was an archetypical example. Greed showed up through Dad's efforts to grab free hotel rooms. Sloth appeared when Dad and Bern fell asleep at the "O" show. Wrath was obvious in Bern's animosity toward The Gooch, and in Gerry's outburst with the hotel receptionist. Envy, in contrast, was subtle yet still present—Dad would have loved that beige windbreaker in the Brioni store. Lastly, there was pride, manifested by Bern's inability to accept my offer of cash when he forgot his ATM card at home in New York. How do you find solid evidence of the seven deadly sins in your family in three days? *Mishegas,* that's how.

CHAPTER 19

THE CRUISE TO NOWHERE

What do you do when you turn your ankle while going for a rebound during a pickup basketball game? You shout out an expletive or two. You shake it off. You walk it off. Most importantly, you play on. As my plane took off from McCarran Airport, I was plucked from the quicksand of *mishegas* I had been sinking into with Syd, Gerry, and Uncle Bern. I was saved, extracted in the nick of time. I compared myself to a kid who accidentally gets his head stuck between the rails of a staircase—for three days. After days of writhing and squirming, twisting and turning, one final, emphatic yank sets him free. The kid lands on his butt, feeling off balance from the sudden change in momentum. He's stunned and sore but relieved to know that he's fundamentally okay. So when my plane touched down, I started to shake off the Vegas trip like a dog just in from the rain. I optimistically closed the book on that brief chapter in my life and the emotional maelstrom that it was. I had survived a bona fide family trip to Las Vegas, with receipts, photos, and souvenirs to prove it. Now home in Minneapolis, I was back on the concrete footing that was my life with Elyse and the kids.

A welcome blast of normalcy hit me as I walked through the front door of my house. The toilet in the powder room wasn't flushing properly. One of the cats had puked on the Oriental rug in the living room again. Daph and Zach were battling over whose turn it was to select a movie to watch. But I was back. Back where I belonged. Twenty minutes of whining and melodrama later, I was still just as pleased to be home. Home in Elyse's warm embrace. Returned to the comforts of my favorite pillow, my favorite coffee mug, and my favorite spot on the den sofa. The next chapter of my life was waiting to be written.

I took a scalding hot shower, changed into my favorite college sweatshirt with the crisscrossed hockey sticks of the Cornell men's ice hockey team, and prepared for the upcoming week. Relaxing in bed with Elyse that evening, I recounted the saga of the entire trip, bringing what I thought was final closure to the ordeal.

How very wrong I was. As it turned out, the book I closed on the Vegas trip was bound only by one of those cheap little clasps on the side of a kid's diary.

The following week saw the return of my routine phone conversations with Mom and Dad. Results of a few medical appointments were disclosed, early-bird dining experiences were reviewed, and upcoming standing-room-only events in the Geriatricville clubhouse were previewed. Lulled into a state of semi-consciousness, Sydelle blindsided me with a bombshell like a bird flying happily along until it smacks unwittingly into the center of a clean plate-glass window.

"You know, Harley. We all had such a lovely time in Las Vegas, brief as the weekend was."

"I'm glad you enjoyed the trip, Mom."

"So, we were thinking."

"You were, huh?"

"Yes. We were thinking. Your father and I were thinking about taking a Disney cruise this winter with you, Elyse, and the children. What do you think?"

I didn't need to think.

"I think that idea is God awful, Mom." My tone was calm and pleasant, yet firm and confident.

"Why?" Sydelle replied in horror as her voice rose an octave, astonished that I was anything less than instantly smitten with the idea.

"Well, let's see," I countered. "First and foremost, did you forget that Elyse gets violently seasick whenever she's on a boat? Don't you remember how I had to drug her up to a nearly comatose state when we ferried between the Greek islands a couple of summers ago?"

"Yes."

"And how about last summer, when we took the kids whale watching in Vancouver? Elyse spent six of the eight hours on the boat doped up, asleep, and drooling. She spent the remaining time trying to keep the horizon horizontal."

"Now that you mention it, that sounds vaguely familiar to me."

"So you want Elyse to voluntarily put herself on a cruise ship in the middle of the ocean for the better part of a week? How do you think that's going to go for her? Perpetually dizzy and dry heaving is not the way most people want to spend their vacation."

"What if just you and the children were to come on the cruise?"

"You know, Mom, cruising has never been our thing—it's just not our style of vacation. Plus, the kids are not interested in anything Disney these days."

"Oh, Harley. Cruising is lovely, just lovely. It's such a luxurious way of traveling. All you have to do is try it once and you'll be able to see that for yourself. There's nothing not to love about cruising."

"Be that as it may, I have to think long and hard before I take a second vacation without Elyse in less than twelve months."

I thought about it. Elyse and I thought about it together. Then I thought about it some more. We decided that the cruise could theoretically happen, if the dates coincided with the kids' school holiday schedules and if the cruise would take the place of our obligatory annual winter trip to Geriatricville.

Armed with these non-negotiable talking points, the cruise conversation resumed the following week with Mom and Dad. I wasted no time disclosing the two key stipulations Elyse and I had discussed. Syd and Gerry were given three options: Martin Luther King Jr. Day weekend, President's Day weekend, or the last weekend in February (the kids had a four-day weekend for parent-teacher conferences). Sydelle agreed to research the possible cruising options and get back to me. As sure as the sun rises in the east and sets in the west, she followed through in short order by the next time we chatted.

"I spent all day on the phone with the Disney cruise people yesterday. It was only sixty-eight degrees yesterday, which, combined with an afternoon thunderstorm meant that it really wasn't a great day to be outdoors. So we really didn't miss much with all the time we spent on the phone."

"On with it, Mom. I'm not the Walt Disney Company. I have patient charts to finish and dinner doesn't cook itself in my house. What did you learn?"

"Based on the dates and availability, there's really only one good option. We would sail from Fort Lauderdale on the morning of February sixteenth, and return on the morning of February twenty-first. So you and the kids would have to fly down and spend the night of February fifteenth with us as well."

"You're kidding me, right?"

She'd completely disregarded our previous conversation. I might as well have been talking to a wall.

"No, Harley. Those are the best dates. Not only that, but the space on the ship is filling up fast, so we made a reservation and put down a deposit. We reserved three staterooms—one for you and the kids, one for Bern, and one for your father and I."

"Holy shit, Mom!" I was pissed off. "What about everything we discussed?"

"I remembered the dates. But the cruises that leave on those dates are either fully booked or exorbitantly priced. This was the only reasonable option."

"Mom, you know these dates won't work for us. Daph and Zach would have to miss an entire week of school."

"Yes, but they're only in elementary school. They won't miss very much—I'm sure their teachers would understand. I was an elementary school teacher, you know. I would have understood."

"I refuse to pull the kids out of school for a solid week in February, when they already have a pair of four day weekends that month. That's ludicrous. We pay a small fortune to send the kids to private school and we're not having them miss a month of it so they can hug some perspiring, marijuana-smoking dropout in a Mickey Mouse costume."

"I would hope that you and Elyse could make an exception for a special trip. Didn't your close friends pull their two daughters out of school last winter for two weeks for a special trip?"

"Why, yes, yes they did. However, one of those weeks occurred over the Christmas break. And furthermore, that was one hell of an extraordinary trip. They took their kids to visit their blood relatives in India for the first time. I-N-D-I-A India. Elephants walking around in the streets India. Buddhas all over the place India. They didn't take their kids to visit a reincarnation of a cartoon Snow White cavorting with bunnies and songbirds in the forest. Tell you what—you offer up a trip to Poland and Hungary to retrace my maternal and paternal ancestral roots, and we'll pull the kids out of school for half a month."

"You won't talk it over with Elyse and reconsider?"

"No. Not a chance."

The conversation drifted to the riveting but neutral topic of the weather for a few minutes. We were circling the drain, though; it was time to end the phone call.

"All right, Mom. I have to get running now."

"Okay, Harley. I know how busy you are. You work so hard."

"I'll talk to you in a few days, right after I resurface from the coal mine."

"Very well. I'll keep the Disney cruise reservation for now, just in case. There's no penalty fee assessed for holding onto the stateroom reservations."

"Jesus Christ, Mom!" I yelled. "What else do I have to say to you? What else can I possibly say to you? I told you in no uncertain terms that there is absolutely no way I will bring the kids on a Disney cruise on those dates. Cancel the goddamn reservation! Cancel it three times over. Cancel it in English, Spanish, and Japanese. I'm not going on that cruise, and the kids are not going either." I felt badly for yelling at her, but holy hell! Was I not clear a moment ago?

She finally relented. But the saga continued.

A few days passed pleasantly in silence. But the next conversation with the South Florida contingent snuck up on me. I knew it would happen, but that didn't mean I was prepared for it. Sydelle was either oblivious to my vulnerability or, more likely, preying upon it. She knew that I was programmed to please her. She must have had a microchip implanted in my brain during my tonsillectomy when I was five. My stubbornness was no match for the persuasiveness of her guilt trips.

"I was just thinking, Harley." That always spelled trouble.

"You were, huh?"

"Yes. I was thinking that we could still go on a cruise this winter, but without the children."

"What? I thought the whole idea was to bring the kids along. What am I supposed to do on a Disney cruise without the kids? Hang out with Pee Wee Herman? A cruise without the kids would be like eating a burger without the beef."

"Of course we want to see the children. Who wouldn't want to see those two little darlings? But we think it's important for Bern to go on a cruise once in his life. He's never been on one, and he would love it."

"You do understand that if I go on this cruise, you won't see the kids for about six or seven months. I'm not going on a cruise in February and also bringing the kids to Florida during the same winter. Are you and Dad really going to let more than half a year pass before you see Daph and Zach?"

"We would make an exception this one time. It would be difficult, but we would make the sacrifice so that Bern could go on a cruise just once in his lifetime."

I wondered if similar thoughts ran through Gandhi's mind during his self-imposed hunger strikes.

The details of this new cruise were as nebulous as the Bermuda triangle. The ship was simply going to circle around the Gulf of Mexico for a few days from Fort Lauderdale. It reminded me of kids operating remote-controlled boats in ponds on lazy Sunday afternoons.

"Where are the ports of call?" I asked.

"I'm not sure if there are any," came the reply.

"What?" I assumed that I misheard Syd's answer or that she misunderstood my question. "How can that be, Mom?"

"I don't know, Harley. The cruise itinerary published online didn't mention any ports of call in the description."

"So you're telling me that we're going on a cruise to nowhere?" This was either funny, pathetic, or both.

"Yes, but I'll check the next time I call the cruise line."

"Fabulous."

A cruise to nowhere made me nervous, for in the event of a norovirus outbreak or similar gastrointestinal pestilence, even a fort composed of 100 percent pure ciprofloxacin antibiotics would leave me vulnerable. There was no course in communicable cruise ship bowel disease in medical school. I also couldn't recall any tertiary care hospitals located in the middle of the Gulf of Mexico. But Mom assured me that the innumerable wonders of cruising rendered my concerns baseless.

~

As it turned out, there *may* have been a single port of call—Cozumel. It was never definitively substantiated. If Cozumel panned out, I figured that in the event of a catastrophe, I could row myself to safety in an emergency lifeboat or get a ride from a booze cruise full of college students on spring break. I'd stow a couple of bottles of tequila in my luggage for insurance, should this contingency plan be invoked.

Against my better judgment, I consented to the Cruise to Nowhere with Mom, Dad, and Uncle Bern. Elyse encouraged me to go, eager to hear the new stories that would undoubtedly emerge from a little time at sea with my family. I fell on my sword for the benefit of Elyse and the kids. They could stay home in Minneapolis, while I fulfilled the commitment to spend time with Sydelle, Gerry, and Bern.

As winter approached, I started to mentally prepare myself. Syd and Gerry, on the other hand, were logistically preparing themselves. Real decisions had to be made. Real decisions with real consequences. It wasn't as simple as deciding between the pairs of shorts and polo shirts in their closets. Food was the hot topic up for debate, even though all meals were included throughout the cruise. With the price of a ticket came the option to nosh nearly twenty-four hours a day at no additional charge. The quandary surrounded the need to make a dinner reservation at one of the "specialty" restaurants on the ship, of which there were two—an Italian place and a steakhouse. Syd analyzed the pros and cons of each restaurant the way a hedge fund manager uses his or her financial acumen to predict emerging trends in the stock market.

"Your father and I were thinking that the Italian restaurant would be more authentic than the steakhouse."

This was a hilarious statement even though Mom was not at all trying to be funny. I was ill-prepared for it, momentarily choking on the martini I was sipping at the time. It almost came back out through my nostrils. Full as the glass was, the motion of my coughing caused a portion to spill over the side and drip onto my pants and the armchair in which I was sitting. Seated on the nearby couch, Daph and Zach laughed as they saw my lips silently form the syllables of a familiar four-letter expletive.

"I fully agree. When you're working on an oil rig in the Gulf of Mexico, it's much easier to get authentic, handmade pasta and marinara sauce inspired by some Sicilian great-grandmother's recipes than it is to find nice fresh slabs of grass-fed beef."

Mom sidestepped my sarcasm. "So you would be excited to eat in the Italian restaurant for dinner?"

"Whatever you, Dad, and Bern prefer will be perfectly fine with me."

"You don't have any preferences?"

"No. Do whatever you like. Don't even tell me. Surprise me once we're on the ship."

Three days later, Mom called to tell me that she nailed down a reservation at the Italian restaurant.

"Thanks for the surprise, Mom."

The dinner plans were safely in the books, but there was still no reprieve. It was time to move on to the entertainment phase of the cruise. I would have been more than happy to cap off the evenings sipping port on the cruise with no ports of call underneath the star-filled, pitch-black sky. Any desired companionship could easily be found at the blackjack or craps tables in the ship's casino. Bern would probably be happy to join me, provided that he remembered to bring some cash this time around. Sydelle and Gerry, however, had other ideas simmering. They wanted to see a show. They were afraid of suffering from withdrawal seizures if a week passed without them seeing a troupe of far-off-Broadway talent outfitted in gaudy costumes and overdone makeup.

The real ironic twist sprung up when Mom and Dad reserved four tickets to the onboard ice skating show. Put yourself in my shoes for a moment. Every morning my commute to work between November and April is an ice skating show. People ice skate and play pickup pond hockey on the frozen lakes in our neighborhood from December through March. Elyse and I volunteer to lace up the kids' ice skates during their school's winter physical education program. So if I choose to "get away from it all" for a few days on a cruise in the middle of winter, would I be hankering to see an ice skating show?

I told Mom and Dad that I would be delighted to see the ice skating extravaganza. After the phone call, I told Elyse that we should buy tickets to a professional beach volleyball tournament the next time we traveled to the Arctic Circle. Remembering the Cirque du Soleil fiasco from the Vegas trip, the question at hand was whether or not Dad and Bern could physically stay awake throughout the ice skating performance.

Honestly assessing the situation, I agreed to the cruise for reasons identical to those that lured me to Las Vegas. It was the right thing to do for my family. It was part of my role as an only child. It would delight Mom and Dad. It would be another chance to hang out with Uncle Bern, and maybe even gamble with him in the ship's casino! To be honest, I agreed to the cruise to feed my curiosity. The Cruise to Nowhere was guaranteed to generate recurring and entirely new genres of *mishegas*. It was already shaping up to rival the Las Vegas trip, judging by the talk of dinner reservations and ice skating shows. Rental car fiascos would not come into play this time. However, Bern could find a fistfight or two wherever perceived anti-Semitism lurked. Mom could sterilize her stateroom with lemon-lime scented antibacterial wipes and ward off the theoretical threat of scurvy that existed in her mind at the same time. Dad could gorge himself on the midnight buffets and offend a whole new staff of service industry employees. This was just a small sample of the defined *mishegas* destined to unfold. Similar to the ocean vistas aboard the ship, the true breadth of *mishegas* was boundless.

EPILOGUE

Uncle Bern passed away suddenly and unexpectedly three weeks before the Cruise to Nowhere was set to depart.

With Bern's passing, there was no way that I was going on the cruise with my parents. The fresh memories of Bern's death would have cast an omnipresent pall over the ship. Sydelle and Gerry agreed to cancel the trip; they, too, could not bear the thought of taking the trip without Bern.

I spoke to Bern a few days before his passing, on one of our Sunday phone calls. He told me had a head cold—some sneezing, a stuffy nose, a bit of a cough, and a low-grade fever. He mitigated the symptoms with his usual panoply of home remedies—coffee, sandwiches, and black tea infused with a double dose of brandy. Three days later, he was on life support in the ICU of a local hospital close to his New York apartment.

With his condition rapidly deteriorating each day, I arranged to fly out to New York so that I could be at his bedside. Over the phone, I asked his ICU nurse to put some coffee into the cocktail of meds coursing through his veins to keep his blood pressure up. She laughed. I added seriously that she should put an actual cup of regular black coffee on the table next to his bed as a good luck charm. It was the closest I could come to fulfilling my promise to have his IV line flushed with coffee in the event of his hospitalization.

Bern couldn't hold on, though. Five days after I first learned of his "head cold," he passed away from multisystem organ failure. I suspect it was a case of influenza that rapidly progressed to a fatal pneumonia. The true cause remains unknown. Extrapolating from the way he chose to live, I always suspected he would go down hard and stay down, once his time finally came.

One of the resident physicians supervising his ICU care called me moments after he passed away. I distinctly remember the sound of her voice and the exact place I was standing when the hospital's phone number appeared on the screen of my cell phone—at the TSA security checkpoint in Minneapolis-St. Paul airport on my way to New York. Bern died alone in the sterile environment of the ICU, without me beside him.

Bern taught me to love the Yankees and absolutely no one else in professional baseball. He taught me to love the Giants and absolutely no one else in pro football. If the Yanks and the Giants played simultaneously in the fall months, I knew beyond a shadow of a doubt that the Yanks always took precedent. I knew how to play baseball, football, basketball, blackjack, poker, gin rummy, checkers, and chess because of Bern. He cultivated my appreciation for coffee, beer, liquor, pastrami, corned beef, bagels, and black forest cake. As Elyse pointed out in a singular moment of clarity as I was grieving, Bern was in many ways responsible for making me the man that I am. And yet he died alone. It was a heartbreaking realization, one that I'm still trying to cope with.

As I stood in the airport in Minneapolis, I realized boarding the plane to New York wouldn't make his sudden death any more palatable. I canceled my flight, knowing that Sydelle and Gerry were en route to Queens from Geriatricville later that same day. Since Mom was Bern's next of kin, it made sense for my parents to head out to New York to begin making the necessary funeral arrangements. I walked out of the gated area and headed directly to the nearest coffee shop to buy the largest cup of coffee I could get my hands on. I raised the cup into the air, silently toasting Bern's life as the tears welled up in my eyes.

The funeral occurred the following week in a military cemetery in eastern Long Island. I flew into LaGuardia the evening before. Mom and Dad offered to swing by in their Hyundai rental car and pick me up at the Delta terminal. Against my better judgment, I accepted. After my flight landed, I walked out of the terminal and into the cold January night to look for Sydelle, Gerry, and the rented Hyundai.

Gerry was an absolute emotional wreck. He was more nervous than a colony of ants whose hill was just obliterated by a merciless eight-year-old kid stomping about with a magnifying glass in hand. Throw Bern's unexpected death into the mix and Dad's already short fuse was whittled down to a stump.

Once they arrived at the airport, Gerry had no trouble finding the Delta terminal, but he couldn't physically maneuver his car into the terminal to pick me up. He kept circling the outer perimeter of LaGuardia unable to locate the elusive turnoff to the curbside access lanes to collect arriving passengers. I thought of the Apollo 13 mission that was resigned to orbit the earth until Houston mission control devised a viable reentry plan.

Fed up and depleted of his last shred of patience, Dad temporarily left the airport and drove to some random nearby hotel to ask for directions. Google Maps wasn't an option, as neither he nor Sydelle owned a smartphone. But don't ask me why he didn't use the GPS device mounted to the dashboard of his rental car. He must have encountered a direct descendant of Mother Teresa at the front desk of the airport hotel who took pity on his soul, for my father came out triumphantly with the directions he sought.

Mom did her best to describe their location via her cell phone, while I paced the pedestrian walkway in a futile search for their parked car. From the landmarks she referenced, it sounded like she was either in the middle of an Iowa cornfield or in the subterranean catacombs of an ancient church. All of a sudden, I heard two different male voices rhythmically shouting out my name from opposite directions. It was like being a spectator at Wimbledon, craning back and forth to track a prolonged rally from the baseline. One voice belonged to my father; the other voice belonged to a stranger. Sydelle had been off of her post-menopausal hormone replacement therapy for years now, so I knew that the mystery voice was not the result of a medication dose miscalculation. I stopped dead in my tracks, right in the middle of the crosswalk, to gain some perspective on the situation amid the blustering gusts of wind whipping against my face. Before the traffic light turned green, the answer presented itself.

I saw my father frantically scouring the sidewalk to my right. From the intensity of his search, you'd think he was on the verge of finding the Holy Grail. To my left was a uniformed, badge-carrying, handgun-wielding member of the NYPD. Apparently, Dad had abandoned his double-parked rental car with the engine running to look for me on foot. In the post-9/11 era, this maneuver remained heavily frowned upon by airport security personnel, especially in New York City. Fulfilling his civic duty, the cop approached Dad with the intent of getting his ass back behind the wheel. But Dad miraculously turned the tables on the police officer, just as James Bond perennially escaped the clutches of certain death under the most improbable of circumstances. Dad somehow convinced the officer to allow his Hyundai to remain indefinitely double-parked near the terminal's pedestrian crosswalk. Even more impressively, though, Dad enlisted the cop to search for me. Never in my life did I think there would come a time when the NYPD would actively search for me. I could only conclude that the officer must have been a newly minted graduate of the local police academy. The curriculum in twenty-first century police academies may very well have been state-of-the-art, but no academic exercise could have possibly prepared this officer to deal with my father. Gerry had no precedent.

My eyes danced back and forth between the yodeling duet of voices calling my name. My father was oblivious to my replies of "Dad" and "Gerry." I almost had to tackle him before he recognized my presence. The cop appeared shortly thereafter, satisfied that the double-parked Hyundai posed more of a threat to his own sanity than to national security. As he withdrew, I thanked the officer for exercising restraint, for Gerry could have easily been detained or arrested for loitering, public indecency, interference with official police business, and obstruction of justice. Luckily for former Mayor Rudy Giuliani, he unwittingly quit while he was ahead. Giuliani was able to get the hot dog vendors off of the Manhattan street corners, but he would never have been able to get Dad out of LaGuardia without me installed in the backseat that day.

It was late in the evening and we were all hungry. With the added stress of the funeral to come, we were emotionally distraught. I guided Dad out of LaGuardia without a hitch, using the techniques I learned from French Canadian sled dog guides. The feat was accomplished by following the white arrows clearly printed on a couple of gigantic, unmistakable signs. Dad thought the escape from LaGuardia was a minor miracle, the result of the combined use of the latest satellite technology, a Creole talisman, and the guiding light of Polaris. We took the Grand Central Parkway toward the hotel, stopping at a local diner en route. We hadn't discussed eating at any particular restaurant, but the diner automatically sucked our car in with the force of the Death Star's 768 tractor-beam generators. Once in range, escape was unfathomable for both the Millennium Falcon and our rented Hyundai.

In no mood for lighthearted conversation or friendly banter, I buried my face in a sloppy platter of chicken parmigiana as soon as the food came out from the kitchen. I craved comfort food and the dish hit the spot. Mom and Dad each ordered the chicken potpie based upon the confident recommendation of the perspiring, obese waiter with a conspicuous comb-over and curly black chest hair that freely billowed out of his unbuttoned shirt.

So out came the chicken potpies, and out followed the comments about the gargantuan portion sizes. Not even a cataclysmic event like Bern's death could change this genetically ingrained and culturally reinforced reflex to comment on meal portion sizes.

"Oh, God, Sydelle! Who can eat all this?"

"My God is right, Gerry! Certainly not me. We should have ordered one and shared it."

"Send yours back, Sydelle! Send it! Send it back!"

"Don't be ridiculous, Gerry! I can't send it back now. There's nothing wrong with the food. I can't return a dish just because I ordered too much. It's not the chef's fault."

"The kitchen doesn't have to know that, Sydelle! Use your imagination. Make up some excuse, Sydelle!"

"That's enough, Gerry! Stop hocking me. I'd like to enjoy my dinner in peace for once."

"Send it back. Don't send it back. I don't care, Sydelle. Do what you want." Gerry sounded exasperated.

Rather than interfere, I stared back down at my plate of chicken parmigiana. Thinking about Bern, I quickly lost my appetite. The bill couldn't have arrived fast enough for me. Coffee and dessert were out of the question. Dad pawed a fistful of pastel-colored mints from the bowl alongside the cash register on the way out, brushing aside the partially submerged spoon that provided the illusion of cleanliness. These are the same mints that you're not supposed to eat because they're allegedly laced with the urine residue of the patrons who decided that they didn't need to wash their hands after using the restroom. We passed two drugstores in the two minutes it took to drive to the hotel, so I knew that I had an ample supply of antibiotics close by in case Gerry suffered the repercussions of consuming tainted mints.

I locked and dead-bolted my hotel room door as soon as I crossed the threshold. Elyse called, so we chatted for the few minutes it took to change my clothes, crawl into the less-than-comfortable bed, and turn the TV on to some syndicated sitcom. I felt a little better, having shared the evening's frustrations with Elyse. She remained in Minneapolis with Daph and Zach; we agreed that the kids were too young to go to the funeral. They had a theoretical understanding of death, but had never before faced the reality of losing a loved one. As the older sibling, Daphne took the news of Bern's passing harder than Zach. Seeing this, Elyse thought it would be better to stay home in Minneapolis to console her, rather than accompany me to the funeral in New York.

Four minutes later, I heard a violent knock on my door accompanied by my father's voice begging me to open up. It sounded like the cops about to bust up the core of a crystal methamphetamine lab. I quickly calculated that jumping out of the fourth-story window was not a safe option. Mom and Dad knew that I wasn't out for a night on the town. With no conceivable means of escape, I had to answer the godforsaken door.

Looking through the peephole, I saw both my mother and father standing outside.

"Harley! Your mother needs your help, Harley! Let's go, Harley!"

"What?" I asked, opening the door.

"You won't believe this one, Harley. I can't get out of my coat." Mom was right; I didn't believe it.

"What?" I asked again in disbelief.

"The zipper on my coat got caught on the material. I can't unzip my coat."

Both of my kids had developed the skills needed to take off a coat as prerequisites for entry into their pre-kindergarten classes. This task was usually tackled somewhere after potty training and before mastering the use of a fork.

"Are you kidding me? Please tell me you're kidding me. Please!"

"Well, you're a surgeon, Harley. We thought this would be right up your alley. Who better to ask but a surgeon?" said Sydelle with a proud smirk.

Considering that Syd had abruptly lost her only brother, she appeared to be handling Bern's death particularly well. Since landing in New York, I hadn't seen her shed a single tear, but she had to be hurting on the inside. Of that fact I was sure. But she walled off the shock of her loss enough to act normally. Or at least normal by her standards, with the zipper trouble a prime case in point. Her emotional strength was impressive; it balanced out her physical frailty.

"Are you seriously kidding me?" Bern was unexpectedly dead, and the funeral scheduled for the following morning. It was late at night, I had just flown halfway across the country, and Syd was asking me to solve her wardrobe malfunction.

"Will you just help your mother? It's late already!" To no one's surprise, Gerry was impatient. Janet Jackson weathered the storm of her infamous Super Bowl halftime show wardrobe malfunction all on her own. My mother apparently could not.

"What the hell would you have done if I wasn't here? Call nine-one-one to get the Jaws of Life to extract you from the coat's clutches?"

"Knock off the wisecracks! Help your mother, will you? Help her!"

I shook my head at Gerry to clearly communicate my displeasure and then approached Sydelle. I yanked the entrapped cherry red cloth to the side with my right hand, tugged once on the zipper with my left hand, and liberated her from her material prison.

Mom was delighted, extolling my talents all the way back to her room next door. I was her conquering hero. I was her Caesar with an olive wreath in his hair as he rode triumphantly in his golden chariot through the streets of Rome after adding substantial territories to the Holy Roman Empire. Rather than acknowledging the adulation of the masses, I locked the door, engaged the deadbolt, and went to sleep.

After the funeral, we headed back to the city to clean out Bern's apartment. The apartment was in an abysmal state. Bern, a prototypical bachelor, was never known for his tidiness. The dismal scene was made far worse with the grim knowledge that we had to sort through all of Bern's personal effects, throwing out the majority of what had taken a lifetime to accrue and donating the remainder to local charities. It felt like a total violation of Bern's privacy. Mom worked quietly and efficiently, solemn as the task was. She spoke only when Dad peppered her with questions about the fate of various items he was sorting.

There was this inevitable air of finality to being inside the apartment he called home for his entire adult life, knowing that once we left, we would never be back. As we sorted through his belongings, I memorized the decorations on the tabletops, the position of the furniture, and the way the afternoon sunlight cast long shadows on the walls. I had so many happy childhood memories with Bern in this apartment—studying his coin collection at the dining room table, watching football on TV in the living room, the sound of his coffee pot as it finished brewing in the kitchen. Knowing that memories are fated to fade over time, this was my last chance to cement some of my childhood with Bern in my mind. When we were finished, I fought the urge to look back at his front door as we waited for the elevator to approach. Instead, my last memory of Bern's apartment was the sound of the deadbolt clicking into place as Dad locked the front door.

As we drove to the local Goodwill and UPS stores, Gerry was a veritable mess. He ran at least two red lights in the middle of downtown Flushing. These were not yellow lights that turned red a split second before our car crossed the intersection. These were lights that had been solidly and unmistakably red for a good ten seconds.

Dad only devoted one hand to the control of the steering wheel; the other hand was glued to the horn. No driver on the road was immune to the Hyundai's blare. Pedestrians in the crosswalks dutifully obeying the white "walk" sign heard it. Drivers stopped ahead of us in traffic who didn't hit their gas pedals within four milliseconds of the traffic light turning to green heard it. Cars traveling too closely behind us heard it, too. Who besides my father would honk at a car coasting along behind his own vehicle?

The NYPD missed multiple opportunities to cite Dad for speeding, illegal lane changes, illegal turns, and several other moving violations during the trip. I was grateful to emerge unscathed and miss the opportunity to visit one of the city's emergency rooms. Surprisingly, Gerry only left New York with one parking ticket.

At my suggestion, we ate at Peter Luger in Great Neck that evening. It's widely reputed to be one of the best steakhouses in New York; it seemed a fitting place to pay homage to Bern. I knew I made the right choice when Dad agreed without voicing a single protest. We toasted to Bern over a nice bottle of red wine and shared a porterhouse steak for four. Despite the sadness of the day, Gerry had no trouble polishing off a double portion of steak.

The trouble occurred the following morning at LaGuardia airport. Our flights home to Minneapolis and Fort Lauderdale left within a couple of hours of each other, so the three of us drove to LaGuardia together. The LaGuardia Airport TSA ran Dad's ass up a flagpole.

As we were cleaning out Bern's apartment the day before, we each kept a few items with which to keep the memory of his life alive. I claimed a coffee mug, the remnants of my grandmother's china, and a German anniversary clock that Bern brought back home at the end of his tour of duty in the Korean War. As an afterthought, I shoved a couple of his tools—a few screwdrivers, to be exact—into my baggage. To be clear, this was my checked bag. A checked bag. Checked.

Dad also decided to save a few of Bern's tools—needle-nose pliers, a couple of screwdrivers, and a box cutter. The noteworthy difference was that our hero Gerry packed these items into his carry-on bag. A carry-on bag. Carry-on.

Ahead in the line by about a dozen people, I cleared airport security first and waited for Mom and Dad to catch up. Syd lagged behind, ever so slowly loading her personal items into the bins and onto the conveyor belt. Gerry chastised her for holding up the line. At first blush, it was business as usual at the TSA checkpoint. Travelers loaded and unloaded the crap they couldn't live without onto the conveyer belts. The occasional clueless passenger peppered a TSA agent with naïve questions about liquids. People religiously glanced at their mobile devices to check if the sky had started to fall, having been forced to part with their phones for the sixty-eight seconds the devices spent on the conveyer belt.

The uniformed TSA agents with their shiny faux gold badges methodically repeated the mandatory instructions. "Take your shoes off. Take your heavy jackets and coats off. Take your belts off. Laptops must be removed from carry-on bags and placed into separate plastic bins. All liquids, gels, and aerosols must be out of carry-on bags. Take everything out of your pockets. Keys, wallets, and phones should be out of your pockets. Nothing should be left in your pockets. Take your shoes off." There must be a drug that helps these poor souls tolerate the monotony and make it to the end of a shift in a state of relative consciousness. If not, there should be.

From this vantage point, I had a prime view of what happens when the utter tedium of life as a TSA agent gets disrupted. Three TSA agents suddenly descended upon Dad—one from the south, one from the east, and one from the west. Isolating him from Sydelle, they ushered him away into a sterile corner while a second set of three white-gloved agents scoured through his carry-on bag in another isolated corner of the terminal. The more the TSA interrogated him about his intentions with the contraband, the more confused Dad became. They were getting nowhere fast. Then, in an act of collaboration seldom seen within the ranks of a US governmental agency, the two sets of TSA agents actually conferred with one another. After a vigorous and rigorous pat down that thankfully stopped short of a body cavity search, the TSA agents showed Gerry the confiscated tools, box cutter and all.

The lightbulb went on in Gerry's head. He explained how the tools came to be packed in his carry-on bag, providing a dizzying array of superfluous details that rendered the TSA agents as confused and stunned as Gerry had been only moments ago. The TSA agents probably regarded the fact that the box cutter was found among a box of old clothes in the trunk of Bern's 1990 silver Toyota Corolla as less than essential. What the TSA agents were sure of after this exchange was that my father did not pose a threat to the security of the United States of America. Dad was released as Bern's tools were confiscated behind some locked door in the bowels of the TSA's domain.

Released from the clutches of the TSA agents, Dad feigned outrage with the way he was treated as he met up with me.

Marching straight toward me while pointing with an outstretched arm back in the direction of his captors, he yelled, "Look how they treated me, Harley! Just like a common criminal! Did you see how they manhandled me?"

"I saw the whole thing, Dad. It was the highlight of my morning. I shouted out for an encore performance as they were finishing up with you."

"Why would you say such a thing? They didn't have to be so rude and rough with me, did they?"

"The TSA agents simply followed protocol, Dad. Think about the situation from their perspective. The TSA reacted to an obviously agitated male lunatic trying to slip a box cutter and a set of screwdrivers onto a jumbo jet departing out of New York City in the post-9/11 era. I'm happy that they found the box cutter. It gives me a shred of faith in the TSA, which I previously thought was nothing more than an elaborate ruse, an expensive illusion of safety developed to make us all waste more time in line and increase the international transmission of foot fungus. Until the TSA figured out that you were an emotional catastrophe from your brother-in-law's death and funeral, they were right to assume the worst. What else should they have done?"

"They could have excused me this one time, Harley, given the circumstances."

"Excused you? That's ludicrous! Are you out of your mind? Let's play this out. The TSA agents return the box cutter and screwdrivers to you as they express their heartfelt condolences on the recent loss of your brother-in-law. They send you on your merry way with a warning, a warm handshake, and a pat on the back as a show of support to you during this tumultuous time in your life. Are you with me so far?"

"Yeah," he begrudgingly replied.

"You're on the plane back to Florida. Let's say you're mid-flight over the Pentagon when you decide you're hungry. As you rifle through your bag in search of an elusive nosh, the box cutter tumbles out and lands in the center aisle of the plane. What happens then? Any combination of passengers sees the box cutter. The passengers alert the flight attendants. The flight attendants alert the pilots. The pilots alert air traffic control and air traffic control diverts the plane to Dulles or Reagan National. As the plane lands, three male passengers with a combined weight of 850 pounds—an ex-Navy seal, a nightclub bouncer with forty-six tattoos, and a behemoth with a penchant for overstuffed burritos and egg nog—sit on your prone ass with your hands cuffed behind your back in the rear of the plane. Once on the ground, the FBI swarms the plane with agents and attack dogs, drags you off in a hogtie with a black hood over your head, and interrogates you in the bowels of some unnamed federal penitentiary that looks to the average passerby like a toilet paper manufacturing plant. Eight hours without water pass until the feds come to understand that you made an honest mistake under emotionally trying circumstances. You're released, but you're also without transportation and without a place to stay for the night. Without a smartphone, your ability to call a taxi, find hotel accommodations for the night, and arrange for another flight back to Florida the next day is fundamentally limited. Plus, you're famished because you missed dinner and never found the nosh in your carry-on bag that precipitated the whole fiasco in the first place. So how do you like them apples, Dad?"

"When you put it like that . . ." he said, dejectedly shrugging his shoulders.

"So that's why your little playful banter with the TSA was the highlight of my morning. You made an honest mistake. Your bag is one box cutter and a few screwdrivers lighter, but you're through security and you'll make your flight on time. I'm convinced that Bern saw the whole affair go down and enjoyed it every bit as much as I did."

With that, we exchanged a round of hugs and went our separate ways in the terminal. I enjoyed the comfortable anonymity that came with being flanked by two perfect strangers on the plane back to Minneapolis.

Though unexpected, Bern's death at the age of eighty-two was hardly surprising. His senior commanding officer in the Korean War, Colonel White, guaranteed eighty solid years of life to every one of his troops who successfully completed basic training. So Bern considered every day that passed after his eightieth birthday to be borrowed time. His lifestyle thoroughly reflected this ideology; the man just let himself enjoy life. He never stood in his own way. Aside from slowing down a little in his last years, he always said that he simply felt great.

In his life, Bern had but two regrets: never earning a college degree and failing to outlive The Gooch. In his death, Elyse thought that Bern symbolically gave me one last gift—an escape from the voyage that was The Cruise to Nowhere.

My Sunday morning phone calls with Bern still haunt me intensely, though. However implausible his stories seemed, whether in part or in full, I never tired of hearing them. His stories were repeated often, but they never got old. I miss those stories terribly. I'd give just about anything to hear them just one more time. On some Sunday mornings, I find myself clutching his old coffee mug while staring blankly out of my kitchen window, seeing nothing and feeling nothing but emptiness. But that's not what Bern would have wanted for me. He would have wanted me to fill the mug up to the brim and then refill it a few more times as I enjoyed the company of my beautiful family. So that's exactly what I do.

~

Mishegas may change but it never goes away. Of that fact I am certain. Metastatic lung cancer changed the *mishegas* in my life. Dad was diagnosed in 2009 and he's been fighting the good fight ever since.

The diagnosis took us all by surprise. It hit me with the force of walking into a brick wall nose first with my eyes closed. It started harmlessly enough with hemorrhoids. The hemorrhoids caused a little bit more rectal bleeding than usual. A blood count revealed mild anemia. A colonoscopy was scheduled, to Dad's delight, to exclude a gastrointestinal source of the anemia. A bone marrow biopsy showed an indolent form of lymphoma. A whole body scan performed to fully stage the lymphoma showed a single spot on his left lung. A needle biopsy showed a malignancy. Removal of a lobe of the left lung along with the associated lymph nodes showed metastatic adenocarcinoma. So that's how a seemingly simple case of rectal bleeding transformed into what will eventually be lethal metastatic lung cancer.

For the most part, it was business as usual for the first five years or so following his diagnosis. Gerry sailed through surgery and breezed through radiation therapy. The intravenous chemotherapy infusions knocked him down for a few months, but he picked himself up admirably and carried on with the help of a fantastic oncologist. As evidence, Dad was a full three years into his cancer diagnosis during the trip to Las Vegas. Did he seem like a man on his deathbed to you? His oncologist should be up for beatification.

But just as I knew that Bern would stay down once he went down, I know that my father's cancer will eventually win. Dad was winning for the first five years following the diagnosis, but the cancer caught up to him during the summer of 2014. He returned from a lovely riverboat cruise with Sydelle down the Danube River, drained of energy and with a progressively worsening cough. Scans confirmed inoperable cancer that was rapidly spreading. The cancer is now clearly winning. It's just a matter of time before the inevitable comes to pass.

While some days are better than others, Dad is too sick to travel these days. So I took Daphne and Zachary to Geriatricville for a visit this past Thanksgiving. What I found was a man who was a mere shell of his former self. Lethargy replaced his former energy. Rising from the family room couch to pour a glass of water in the kitchen required several breaks along the way to catch his breath and arrest a coughing spell. He moaned slightly but audibly nonetheless with each shuffling step he took around the house. He fell asleep everywhere except in his own bed, as lying down flat worsened his cough. His left chest wall looked like an Iraqi minefield. He looked haggard and generally defeated. It was a heart-wrenching sight for me to behold.

Daph and Zach knew that their grandfather was sick, but they otherwise went on with their carefree six- and nine-year-old lives. I, on the other hand, could not. I found myself consciously cutting Dad unparalleled levels of slack, yielding to the *mishegas*. I allowed him to get away with antics

I would have been previously quick to call him out on. He asked me for help pouring the Thanksgiving turkey pan drippings into a series of empty plastic yogurt cups. I happily obliged without saying so much as a single sarcastic phrase, although questions accumulated in my mind. How many other empty yogurt cups were stored in the house? Were all flavors of yogurt equally able to collect the pan drippings? Were the empty yogurt cups purposed exclusively for the pan drippings or did they have other potential uses? What was the ultimate fate of the pan drippings? Could the pan drippings themselves be reused for some other purpose? Did the drippings get thrown into the regular trash, recyclable trash, or tossed over the fence into the neighbor's yard? Were the drippings slowly poured out into the street in the style of the annual Antifreeze Saturdays of years past? I was itching to ask but kept my questions to myself instead. My father wanted me to help with the turkey pan drippings and that's exactly what I did.

As I cleaned up Thanksgiving dinner, I came upon a kitchen drawer housing no fewer than forty-one different bottles of vitamins and herbal remedies. These nutritional supplements proved no more effective in battling Dad's cancer than they were in thwarting one of Syd's nefarious sinus infections or stemming the tide of her mucous. These bottles of pills were a welcome sight because it proved that the *mishegas* was still alive and well in Geriatricville. The *mishegas* was camouflaged right underneath the black cloak of the cancer. But fundamentally it was still there.

The next evening, we went out for dinner at an Italian restaurant. Dad was so physically weak that I had to partially lift him out of the front passenger seat of the car. Thankfully, we weren't seated next to another party of eighteen blind patrons this time. He choked through the whole meal, pleading to Mom while coughing and gasping for air as he tried to catch his breath.

"Please, Sydelle! Help me, Sydelle!"

"Slow down, Gerry. Take small bites of food. Take your time swallowing."

"Help me, Sydelle!"

"We're in no rush, Gerry. Take your time between bites. Take a few sips of water between bites."

"Do something for me, Sydelle! I can't live like this! I can't go on like this!"

I was powerless to help my father; I knew it and I felt it. It's an awful thing to see a loved one truly suffering. In between his desperate pleas for help, flashes of vintage Gerry shone brightly. He shot out his hand to prevent ice from entering his water glass. He complained vehemently about the slow service from the waitress. He switched his seat to escape the cold front caused by the air conditioning vent. And he refused dessert as he simultaneously stuffed a forkful of chocolate cake into his mouth.

Dad's suffering will eventually end. But the *mishegas* in my life won't. Nor should it. *Mishegas* is a paradox. It compels me to love those absurdities that drive me to my wits' end. So let the paradox that is my family *mishegas* continue. I will never choose to have it any other way.

CAREER STATISTICS

As my most highly cherished memories coalesced into the greater themes of this work, others incessantly surfaced whether or not they were directly or even tangentially related to the particular subject at hand. Prized in their own right, these memories were each unexpected treats akin to a wadded up twenty dollar bill found in the depths of your pocket while retrieving your keys.

These pleasant little nuggets of *mishegas* add additional layers of depth to the history of the characters that are Sydelle, Gerry, and Uncle Bern. They are compiled in numerical format for no particular reason. Don't waste time applying the pseudo-science of numerology here. I invite you to enjoy them as one enjoys the outtakes or extra scenes at the end of a movie.

Sydelle by the numbers:

1   Number of times she successfully returned Bern's broken, left, second finger into its proper anatomical alignment by stepping on it with her full body weight.

Number of engagements to be married Syd broke off to date the guy that wound up being Gerry.

2   Number of pounds of sweat the average guest loses while visiting her house in Geriatricville in August for coffee and dessert.

6   Average number of doctor appointments scheduled in a typical month.

12   Average number of calories burned while enjoying long walks around the block in an attempt to shed the caloric load of an early-bird dinner special.

20   Number of primary teeth unnecessarily filled by a corrupt pediatric dentist who wound up doing a substantial amount of hard time in an upstate New York penitentiary. Nonetheless, Syd's gums rose from the ashes to triumphantly erupt a pair of adult central incisors large enough to gnaw down a small tree trunk.

37   Sydelle's subjective baseline body temperature (in degrees Fahrenheit). She is resigned to wear two more layers of clothing than everyone else independent of the season or geographic location to counteract this internal permafrost.

48   Average number of minutes devoted to The Weather Channel on TV daily. Sydelle scrutinizes the anticipated movement of a cold front as a professional golfer studies the slope of the putting green on the eighteenth hole of the final round of a major championship.

78   Average temperature of the house in Geriatricville, including the summer season. Nonetheless, she sleeps with an electric blanket on her bed from August to June.

89   Number of greeting cards mailed out in a given calendar year. She keeps both the greeting card industry and the US Postal Service afloat with personal acknowledgments of every friend and family member's birthday, anniversary, birth, death, and major religious holiday celebration. Arbor Day may even be thrown into the mix on occasion.

126   Minimum minutes needed to get her act sufficiently together to be out of the house before 10:00 a.m. Getting out of the house by 9:00 a.m. is a rare possibility, provided that she is given enough notice to make preliminary preparations the evening prior.

213   Number of wonderful lifelong friends Syd acquired during her thirty years teaching elementary education in the New York City public school system. She maintains a level of loyalty to these chums that supersedes that exhibited by a clan of meerkats in the Kalahari Desert.

373 Average number of minutes spent at the beauty parlor dyeing her hair each year. Mom dyes her hair red to maintain a vibrant, youthful look. Her idea of red, though, is the same as my idea of tangerine.

Gerry by the numbers:

0 Number of memories retained from childhood. A sole black-and-white photo from his bar mitzvah proves that my father was, in fact, a child at some point.

Number of hobbies maintained, unless stockpiling bottles of ketchup, apple juice, and ginger ale in the garage qualifies as a hobby.

½ Critical threshold for tank/reservoir levels. Applies to entities like barbeque propane tanks, car gasoline tanks, and coffee machine water chambers. Gerry must always keep the tank/reservoir more than half full. This has nothing to do with an optimist's "glass half full" mentality. He believes that permanent engine damage will inevitably result if the car's gas tank dips below half full.

2 Number of first names my father possesses. Gerry, which of course is short for Gerald, is a standard, solid name for a Jewish guy born in the Pelham Parkway section of the Bronx in the mid-1930s. His middle name is Jerome. In and of itself, there's nothing at all wrong with the name Jerome. The interest lies with the juxtaposition of the two names; if you shorten both names you're left with Gerry Jerry. Gerry Jerry can be further shortened to Gerry squared. What parent does this to his or her child? There's an abundance of Minnesotans with Scandinavian roots, reflected in first name-surname combinations like Paul Paulson, John Johnson and Pete Petersen. But no one puts first name—middle name combinations together like Anne Anna, William Bill, and Steven Stephen. Gerry Jerry is unique in this respect.

3   Number of random articles clipped from the newspaper each week. Once clipped, a red felt-tip pen is used to underline those parts deemed especially important. The articles are then either presented to Mom for her review or mailed to me to read in my free time.

5   Number of possible car models that can be considered for purchase. Only the Corolla and Camry from Toyota, the Civic and Accord from Honda, and the Sonata from Hyundai are viable options. The final choice is governed by the annual Consumer Reports write-up in conjunction with any dealership-sponsored promotional offer Gerry may stumble across. (There exists an exception to every rule. For Sydelle and Gerry, that exception came to pass in 1988, the Year of the Dragon and the Year of the Mazda 323 sedan in my household. I hated that car; sitting in the backseat felt like sitting on top of a block of Styrofoam coated with itchy polyester. Breaking from protocol this one time led to calamitous results. Within two years, the car was totaled while parked outside of one of his client's homes. Gerry interpreted the crash as a sign from the heavens; he returned to the fold with a beige 1990 Toyota Corolla soon thereafter.)

18   Age at which Gerry was drafted into the navy during the Korean War. He was assigned laundry room detail during his stint aboard ship. Since his honorable discharge from the service, he's kept his military-issued can opener on his keychain. Ironically, I have never seen him do a single load of laundry during my lifetime.

35   Age at which he convinced Sydelle he was marriage material.

1,000 Minimum number of miles Gerry requires to "break in" a new car. Babies are breastfed for the first year or so of life as their digestive tracts develop. A new pair of shoes has to be worn in order to stretch out, soften, and mold to your foot. Similarly, a new car must be properly "broken in" over its first one thousand miles. This means traveling at least five miles under the speed limit and applying the brakes as gently as possible. After this critical threshold passes, it's permissible to drive faster, though never exceeding the posted speed limit.

Uncle Bern by the numbers:

+/- 1   Number of middle names Bern had. He was born without a middle name printed on his birth certificate, but the middle initial "P" appeared between his first and last names sporadically over the course of his life on a medley of official and unofficial documents. No one ever knew what the "P" stood for. The "P" was harmless in the first sixty-five years or so of Bern's life. But in his later years, the world of identity theft rendered it a recurring hemorrhoid. What did a florist in Los Gatos, California have in common with an Associate Professor of Law at the University of Chicago and a restaurateur in southern New Jersey? All three owed massive amounts of money to the feds and all three tried to convince the feds that they and my uncle were one and the same person.

4   Number of years Bern spent in high school. Based on his academic performance, this number should have been six. However, Bern used school solely as a vehicle to organize pickup games of stickball after classes were dismissed. He even came to a mutual understanding with his English teacher, who he particularly disdained: Bern happily took an extra lunch period in the cafeteria while the class was in session, in return for a guaranteed passing "D" grade. "Understandings" like these also explained how Bern was able to complete all four years of high school needing only one notebook that conveniently fit into his jacket pocket.

8   Total number of meals consumed in an average day (generally divided into two large and six small meals). Through it all, he maintained a stable weight of about 165 pounds.

11   Age at which his lifelong addiction with coffee started.

19   Personal record for number of cups of coffee consumed during one particularly grueling overnight shift as a lithographer manning a printing press in lower Manhattan while a deadline lurked and his bosses hovered.

21   Age at which Bern was drafted into the US Army during the Korean War. He spent his tour of duty in Germany after nearly being assigned to an infantry unit in Korea. Bern served as an army medic, where he learned crucial skills such as how to apply a butterfly bandage to an open wound and how to convince his fellow troops that syphilis could not be contracted via contact with a toilet seat. Renowned for his prowess making industrial-sized vats of coffee and hoarding snacks from the canteen, he was called to the front of his entire assembled battalion to formally respond to General Matthew Ridgway's inquiry regarding the quality of the food served to the troops.

52   Age at which Bern retired from the printing industry to focus on playing poker, watching televised sporting events, and drinking beer.

82   Age at which Uncle Bern passed away. He unexpectedly passed away while I was writing this memoir, making his inclusion in the anecdotes particularly special and poignant for me.

162   Number of games his beloved New York Yankees played each year (excluding the playoffs, of course), which equated to the number of days he had automatic plans with his cronies.

ABOUT THE AUTHOR

Harley Dresner grew up in Plainview, New York. A midsize town in the middle of Long Island, Plainview's culture and his nuclear family's specific subculture provided the foundation for many of the anecdotes included in

Mishegas. After graduating with a Bachelor of Science degree from Cornell University, Harley earned his Doctor of Medicine degree from the Albert Einstein College of Medicine in New York City. He also left Albert Einstein with a marriage license, meeting Elyse during orientation and marrying her four years later. After medical school,  Harley completed surgical residency in Otolaryngology and fellowship training in Facial Plastic and Reconstructive Surgery at the University of Minnesota.

Currently, he resides in Minneapolis with Elyse and his two children, Daphne and Zachary. He is an Assistant Professor of Facial Plastic Surgery and Co-Director of the fellowship in Facial Plastic and Reconstructive Surgery at the University of Minnesota in Minneapolis, Minnesota. Serving as one of the physicians for the Minnesota Wild professional hockey team and sitting on multiple national committees within the American Academy of Facial Plastic and Reconstructive Surgery compliment his clinical practice of medicine.

To date, Harley has authored eight peer-reviewed journal articles and four book chapters in the medical literature. Mishegas represents his first foray into the realm of popular nonfiction. It has certainly proved to be the most enjoyable literary effort of his life.